Transforming Spirit of Indian Women Writers

Transforming Spirit of Indian Women Writers

Anita Balakrishnan

AUTHORSPRESS

Worldwide Circulation through Authorspress Global Network
First Published 2012
by
Authorspress

Editorial
Q-2A Hauz Khas Enclave
New Delhi-110 016

Marketing
E-35/103, Jawahar Park
Laxmi Nagar, Delhi-110 092

e-mails: authorspress@rediffmail.com; authorspress@hotmail.com
Website: www.authorspressbooks.com

Transforming Spirit of Indian Women Writers
ISBN 978-81-7273-640-8

Printed in India at Tarun Offset, Delhi.

Preface

The fictional discourse of Indian women writers has traditionally focused on the tensions and constraints experienced within familial and domestic spaces. In the last two decades of the twentieth century, the liberalization of the Indian economy, coupled with the rise to prominence of Indian English authors globally, has served as an impetus to writers to explore new genres and themes. In this scenario, the literary output of Indian women writers has been vast and varied. While several critics have commented on the subversive elements present beneath the apparently conventional surface of Indian English novels by women writers, critiques of contemporary women's writing have been rare. The papers collected in this book are an attempt to redress this situation.

The papers in this anthology range from reinterpretations of mythic paradigms in contemporary fiction to investigations of these novels as ethnography. There are studies on the impact of communal tensions on contemporary novels by women writers, the interrogation of British/colonial representations of India, the culture of violence against women prevalent in twenty-first century India, perspectives on the alienation experienced by the single, young female protagonist as a consequence of life in a globalized India, the power struggles of patriarchal authority as they operate in society, insights into the father-son relationship from a woman writer's perspective, the formation of regional identities, the contrary compulsions of motherhood and personal creativity, the autoethnographic features in Dalit writing, and the crossing of cultural borders by women from diverse cultural backgrounds in India, as they seek to express their sexuality, an aspect of female identity that is problematic in almost all cultures.

The inspiration for this book came from the reluctance expressed by several research scholars at the doctoral and masters' level to pursue research into contemporary Indian English fiction due to the paucity of secondary sources. It is hoped that this anthology will be a useful guide to fresh scholars who have been hesitant to undertake research into these emerging writers due to the inaccessibility of critical insights. The sixteen original papers collected here contain many ideas of interest to discerning readers, and provide useful guidelines for future research.

While every effort was made to present a wide range of papers on a number of contemporary writers, there are some genres that could not be included. These range from popular fiction and travelogues to some Diasporic writers such as Shauna Singh Baldwin, Indu Sundaresan and Samira Ali. It is hoped that future work will include these areas.

This book is the result of years of interaction with students at various levels, and the original ideas they sometimes come up with during classroom discussions. It was the inspiring leadership and mentoring of my former senior colleague, Professor Eugenie Pinto, that was the stimulus of this project. I also owe a huge debt of gratitude to my colleagues, both current and past, at Queen Mary's College, Chennai and at Quaid-e-Millath College for Women, Chennai, for their encouragement and good cheer. I wish to thank my colleagues, Dr S. Chitra and Mrs. Amutha Charu Sheela, for their unstinting help at every stage of this project. I also wish to acknowledge the assistance provided by Mr. Mahesh Mithreeven in the formatting and assembly of this book.

Mr. Sudarshan Kcherry of Authorspress has been a most encouraging and helpful publisher. I can state with conviction that this book would not have come to fruition without his support.

But most of all, it is to my family that I owe the biggest thanks. My husband, for his patience and level-headed advice, my daughters, Shalini and Kritanjali, whose refusal to be impressed kept me grounded, and my mother, Rajalaxmi Venugopal, for her energy and drive which was a great example to emulate.

Anita Balakrishnan

Our Contributors

Amutha Charu Sheela is Assistant Professor of English at Sri Venkateshwara College of Engineering, Sriperumpudhur. Her research focuses on the impact of communalism and religious fundamentalism on contemporary Indian English fiction.

Debalina Banerjee is Assistant Professor of English, Vidyasagar Evening College, University of Calcutta, Kolkata.

N. Chandra is a Research Scholar in the Department of English, Pondicherry University.

Kaustav Chakraborty is Assistant Professor of English at Southfield College, Darjeeling. He has published several books and journal articles.

S. Chitra is Associate Professor of English at Bharathi Women's College, Chennai. Her areas of interest include partition literature, translation studies and ecocriticism.

C. N. Eswari is Assistant Professor and Head of the Department of English at Guru Nanak College, Chennai. Her research focuses on the writers of the Indian diaspora.

N. Kalvikkarasi is Assistant Professor of English at DRBCCC Hindu College, Chennai.

P. Karkuzhali is a Research Scholar in the Department of English, Pondicherry University.

L. Kavitha Nair is Assistant Professor of English at VIT University, Chennai. She is interested in the interface between myth and literature.

V.Padma is currently Assistant Professor in English, Stella Maris College, Chennai. She has published a book, *Fiction As Window*, as well as articles on Indian literature.

M. Parimala is a Research Scholar in the Department of English, Pondicherry University.

R. Priya is Assistant Professor of English at Queen Mary's College, Chennai.

P. Rathna is Assistant Professor of English, Senior Grade, at B.S.Abdur Rahman University, Chennai.

R. Revathi is Assistant Professor of English at Bharathi Women's College, Chennai.

Aparna Sundaram is Assistant Professor of English at D.G. Vaishnav College, Chennai. Her research interests are feminism, feminist literature, gender studies and related areas.

Vennila Ramanathan is Associate Professor of English at Bharathi Women's College, Chennai. She is interested in postcolonial literatures and contemporary fiction.

Contents

1

Introduction

These are challenging times for women in Indian society. The putative progress of the postcolonial Indian state has had a negligible impact on the lives of its female subjects. It is a theoretical truism that women have been, and continue to be, repositories of tradition. During the colonial period Indian nationalists did not create a new woman; their concerns were directed against the colonizers, "in the entire phase of the national struggle, the crucial need was to protect, preserve, and strengthen the inner core of the national culture, its spiritual essence" (Chatterjee 243). It was here that women and the family began to be seen as protectors of values and nurturers of tradition. Paradoxically, women came to be the preservers of the very traditions that were responsible for their marginalization.

There exists in India a vibrant women's movement which has spread to various parts of the country. It has been observed that there is no single, monolithic women's movement in India, rather a number of fragmented campaigns that address region-specific issues. Feminist activists see this as one of the strengths of the movement since it is able to adapt easily in the face of social changes and the inevitable backlash such change engenders. One of the most significant, transformative legislations that have altered societal perceptions of women has been the 33 per cent reservation for women in local, village level elections. Despite such advances, any real change in societal attitudes towards women in Indian society remains elusive.

The eventful decade of the 1980s revealed the equivocal nature of women's emancipation. The sati of eighteen-year-old

Roop Kanwar, numerous dowry deaths and the much publicized Shah Bano case, revealed the operation of fundamentalist forces in society. In the following decade, the Indian economic environment underwent a period of unprecedented change and expansion, with its concomitant impact on society. The widespread materialism it unleashed had a double pronged impact on women's lives: while greater employment opportunities became available, rampant consumerism resulted in more numerous instances of domestic harassment. The myth of the great Indian middle class has been exploded by a number of critics, who refuse to allow the superficial prosperity to obscure deeper social inequities. As P. Sainath observes, "the fastest growing sector in India Shining is not IT or software, textiles or automobiles. It is inequality".

This raises the question of the impact of this volatile political, economic and socio-cultural climate on the identity of women in India. Critics as diverse as Gayathri Spivak and Aijaz Ahmed have warned against the neutralizing effect of capitalism on the reformist agenda of postcolonial and feminist analysis, and emphasize the need to restore the political nature of these interventions. Rajeswari Sunder Rajan outlines the nature of this project:

> Culture ... viewed as the product of the beliefs and conceptual models of society ...,as well as the everyday practices, the contingent realities, and the complex process by which these are structured, is the constituted realm of the subject. As a result, culture appears as the chief matter and consequence of dominant ideological investment, powerfully coercive in shaping the subject; but since it is also heterogeneous, changing and open to interpretation, it can become a site of contestation and consequently of the reinscription, of subjectivities. (9)

The function of representation in this process enables intervention, change and strategic reinterpretation. As Rajan argues further, the construction of women in terms of recognizable roles, images and labels occurs in discourse in response to specific social forces even when it is offered in terms of a universal rhetoric of women (123).

The international success of writers from India, particularly since the publication of Salman Rushdie's *Midnight's Children* in 1981, was a shot in the arm for the Indian novel in English. This trend gained further momentum when Arundhati Roy won the Booker Prize for *The God of Small Things* in 1997. Several Indian women writers made their debut in the 1990s, creating a body of work that revealed aspects of the life of women in Indian society. There also emerged at this time a number of diasporic writers, whose novels reveal a distinctly different treatment of women's lives within the Indian family as well as in society. Lisa Lau terms this 'Re-orientalism', whereby diasporic writers appropriate the role of speaking for and representing the 'other', the people of the Indian subcontinent. She identifies three problems with the techniques employed by some diasporic authors which have worsened the negative impact of re-orientalism; the preoccupation with producing a recognizably Indian setting and narrative, the problem of totalisation and generalizations about India and Indians and the deliberate blurring of the boundaries between fiction and autobiography to facilitate insidious 'truth claims'.

Lisa Lau further examines the representation of Indian identity by diasporic and non-diasporic or stay-at-home writers. She concludes that diasporic writers, by and large, tend to cast as representative of the whole community, values and practices which pertain only to certain privileged groups within the collectivity. The 'Indian culture' depicted in novels by diasporic writers often resorts to stereotypes, oversimplifications and a sensationalizing of practices such as bride viewing and arranged marriages. Those writers who remain within India, in contrast, engage actively with the socio-cultural and historical formations and depict their impact on the complications and nuances of identities. Their contemporaneity is not merely a matter of chronology, their work is impacted by the history of their times and because it deals with specifics, it is diverse.

Indian women writers, traditionally, tended to set their novels within the domestic sphere and explore women's experiences in the context of the family. This subject matter was considered superficial in comparison to the more 'literary' themes in novels by male writers. Since the 1990s, women writers have moved away from the domestic novel, engaging with 'serious' issues such as nationalism, communal tensions and religious fundamentalism. In doing so, these writers attempt to construct a female subjectivity that is not ruthlessly forged by patriarchy.

The analysis of fiction by writers from varied locations, albeit within the same time frame, reveals the effects of regional cultures, language, and history on their work. While women's narratives were earlier largely confined to the home as part of the culture of oral storytelling, their adoption of the written narrative marks their entry into the public sphere. This accomplishes an adroit move into the mainstream by these women who thereafter begin to recast stereotypical representations of women in novels by men. This nascent self-assertion and empowerment could in a utopian future scenario lead to a change in the oppressive social structures.

In a social milieu where women are still the targets of egregious violence, the discourses of sati, female infanticide and foeticide, dowry harassment, bride burning and honour killings gain credence. Ania Loomba, in her analysis of critical writings on sati, probes the impact of colonial, Western and Indian feminist writings on the issue. She draws on Rajeswari Sunder Rajan and Lata Mani's important works in order to analyze their function within the nationalist and anti-colonial movements. She traces the difficulty of figuring the burning widow without portraying her as an archetypal victim as Western feminists have, nor as a free agent as is often done in nationalist writings. This extreme positioning of the burning widow led to her being viewed as a woman who is marked off from all other women by her will; thus her desires are revered by the community even as theirs are consistently erased. This leads to the widow becoming a sign of normative femininity. In a diverse body of work she becomes a signifier of either the devoted and chaste, or the oppressed and victimized Indian woman. Ironically, an attempt to control sati legislation during the colonial era, reified it as legal if it met certain criteria, primarily if it could be proved that it was a voluntary act. This legal sanction for sati had far-reaching implications, which resurfaced even during the postcolonial era sati of Roop Kanwar in 1987. The British intervention granted scriptural sanction to the practice due to the opinions of Hindu pundits who were called to testify at trials. This gave a religious backing to the practice which had been variable and uneven. Critical responses to this widow immolation ranged from Ashis Nandy who invokes an ideal of a mythical sati that represents Indian tradition to contemporary feminists who refuse to accept that sati could ever be a voluntary act.

As Loomba points out, this act of volition on the part of the widow, ironically, serves as a recognition of her subjectivity and agency which leads to her annihilation (249). Lata Mani argues that the entire colonial debate was concerned with redefining tradition and modernity. She also states that women "became sites on which various versions of scripture/tradition/law are elaborated and contested"(115). Hence, she argues, nowhere is the sati herself a subject of the debate and nowhere is her subjectivity represented. Significantly, Loomba concludes that feminist writings on sati move towards a collective subjectivity of Indian women who suffer from the consequences of the ideology of sati (254). The debates on sati reflect the connections between social determinations and individual subjectivity. It demonstrates how the contexts of utterance and intervention still determine which of the two will be stressed, however it also reveals a space where a fruitful dialogue may emerge.

Is the Indian woman then always marked by the discourses that deny her access to power and agency? Recent ethnographic research has revealed that this is not necessarily the case as studies on social change in various gendered arenas in India reveal. These analyses point out unprecedented ways in which women deal with patriarchal kinship structures, class-based domination, and state policies to challenge predominant ideologies. This research centres on the connections and relationships of action and social structures, women's lives and the cultural domain. It also attempts to analyze the growing reality confronting women in relation to their social roles and the code of conduct expected of them. These ethnographers explore the alternatives to ingrained patriarchal structures, and consider whether women's search for different sources of empowerment constitutes a form of resistance. They also probe the nature of resistance and ask if conscious intent on the part of the person resisting is required or any transformative practice can be identified as resistance. The Gramscian idea of an interplay of power relations based on domination and subordination leaves the subordinate with the option of either collaborating or resisting. Seen in these terms, resistance can be equated to agency.

Sociologist Sirpa Tenhunen, in her study on the integration of women's work within domestic structures among the housewives of Calcutta, asserts that women's actions that do not directly contest the gender code can also lead to a new awareness, challenging the status quo in ways that are considered respectable. She finds that working at home allows women the opportunity to be proper wives and daughters, at the same time freeing them to take stock of their potential. Lina Fruzetti and Sirpa Tenhunen, in their introduction to the volume, state that social structures and codes of conduct are not permanent entities, they are susceptible to change and challenge. They point out the existence of a clear dichotomy among the women observed; those who openly question cultural gender-based aberrations and provide alternatives for them and other women who choose to operate within the parameters of their code of conduct without directly challenging culture.

Fruzetti and Tenhunen's research asserts that agency exists, but also demonstrates that women's innovations are profoundly paradoxical in their effects. Women are shown celebrating the very social structures and forces that constrain them — even when challenging their cultural code of conduct. Even housework, which is often seen as an example of women's containment within the patriarchal structure of the family, may be interpreted as a kind of agency. These women's agency is their ability to enact what they know best, leading to a total fulfilment of their social roles.

The reasons for such conformity are not hard to find. While western women are motivated towards self-actualization by the prevailing ethos of individualism in the West, Indian women carry the burden of preserving traditional social roles. As Vrinda Nabar observes in *Caste as Woman,* tradition carries a potent and almost ineradicable charge in Indian society. It is Nabar's contention that the failure of Indian feminists to provide a text that would arouse public attention has ensured that more than half of India's population remains undefined, except in androcentric terms. She also points out the near impossibility of a comprehensive female representation, as attempts are generally conditioned by the urban middle class background of the authors.

Elaborating on the influence exerted by tradition on Indian social existence, Nabar emphasizes the need for feminism to discredit some of the legacies of this tradition, thereby historicizing the subject. Though many religious communities exist in India, they have a fair amount of overlap in their attitudes towards the appropriate roles women ought to play in society and the strictures regarding women's dress and behaviour. The term 'Indian woman' conjures up an image that is remarkably syncretic, cutting across religious boundaries, and which women variously conform to or rebel against. It is notable that despite the narratives of communalism and religious fundamentalism gaining credence as the crucibles within which gender, caste and class function in twenty-first century India, there is much conformity in strictures relating to women's roles in society.

The hold of religion and mythology on the Indian subconscious can never be attenuated. While it would be rare to see the Virgin Mary held up as an exemplar of feminine virtues and values in the West today, it is not uncommon to see the values and mores exemplified by the mythological figures Sita and Savithri used as yardsticks to judge women in present-day Indian society. Arvind Rajagopal's perceptive analysis of the television broadcast of ancient epics such as the *Ramayana* and the *Mahabharata* and their reception in Indian society reveals that State television's hegemonic influence as an ideological apparatus is perceived most spectacularly in its representations of women and religion. Rajeswari Sunder Rajan notes that "the conceptual and political space occupied by women in the television medium is identical to that if religion, and hence representations of women and religion frequently coincide. The representations of the central female figures in the television serials of the epics the *Ramayana* and the *Mahabharata* become symbols of 'our' 'national' culture"(127). Sunder Rajan further argues that:

> State-sponsored television, with its dual obligations in its representation of women and religion — on the one hand, to acknowledging the state's commitment to equal rights(in the case of women) and to secularism (in the case of religion), and, on the other hand, to developing a new idiom of 'nationalism', equated with a valorization of the traditional(which is preserved, precisely, in and by women and religion) redefines the two terms flexibly. The traditional is represented as the timeless, and hence inclusive of the modern, while the modern is viewed merely as a transitional phase which disguises the permanent 'essence' of timeless tradition. Thus female figures from history, myth and religion in many television programmes are invested with status and autonomy and serve as the mouthpiece of liberated sentiments.(128)

Such representational strategies are also seen in state-sponsored short films of historical figures such as Laxmibai, Rani of Jhansi, and Mrignayini, the sixteenth-century commoner queen of Pomar as well. These selective readings of historical female figures assert the presence of empowered women of learning, achievement and courage in the past, serve to obscure the oppression and marginalization of 'ordinary' women, and undermine the need for an organized women's movement working towards women's equality.

Such representational strategies serve to reinforce the centrality of the dharma-shastras in shaping female identities and prescribing acceptable behaviour which have in post-epic times continued to shape popular notions about the role of women. These images also throw light upon the nature of Indian traditions and codes which have evolved over a period of time, and reveal the need for feminist interventions to discredit some of the more repressive effects of this tradition.

Contemporary Indian society often displays an outlook that is "sentimental, emotionalistic and melodramatic", as Nabar argues, rather than pragmatic and utilitarian as is seen in the West (22).Unlike in the West where the after effects of the wars led to the evolution of the ideology of individualism through philosophies such as existentialism and movements such as modernism that emphasized man's essential alienation from society, in India Hinduism and other religious ideologies worked together to ensure that individualism has a minimal role to play in the social order. The search for the self is never individualistic in India; meta-characteristics such as caste, class, family, community, religious and linguistic identities almost always impinge upon any such quest. In such a scenario any reformist movement that displays an allegiance to an individualistic ideology would be doomed from its very inception. These social factors reveal the constraints within which Indian women's movements must operate. Perhaps these factors go a long way in explaining the shape of the women's movement in India as an issue-based set of activist groups rather than an ideologically motivated, militant movement.

The Indian collective unconscious, as argued earlier, is based on principles of faith and dogma that serve as the context within which attitudes and perceptions relating women need to change. The stronghold exerted by religion and mythic stereotypes has to be negotiated to shape any agenda for reform. The aggression and militancy seen in Western feminist movements would have disastrous consequences in the Indian scenario, particularly since women are always associated with male- defined roles such as daughter/wife/mother. Furthermore, Indian women face discrimination across a spectrum of classes and castes, leading to problems of forging a unified alliance. Western women may bemoan the limited choices available to them, but for a large majority of Indian women there is a complete absence of viable choices. What may be required is a thoroughgoing overhaul of social attitudes relating to the codes of behaviour and tradition-mandated roles for women, to enable an emancipated feminist praxis to emerge.

It may be to India's burgeoning middle class that one needs to turn to bring about such a complete overhaul of orthodoxies.

As the effects of economic liberalization spread, the middle class has experienced hitherto unseen levels of prosperity. But the persistence of older hierarchies that find new sites of expression undermines any minor changes that may be seen. As Vrinda Nabar asserts:

> ...it is the middle class in India which controls the weapons of change. It is here that the sensibility-shift must be seen as desirable, and the fallacies of Indian womanhood understood. The middle-class world view may be interpreted as broadly 'Indian'. It is one which is defined in terms of family and community. Commitment and responsibility to both are an essential part of this view, and both in turn are visualized in the context of tradition. It is a tradition which is broadly negative in its approach to women, but its fundamental priorities differ so widely from the Western approach that they need ultimately to be tackled in context. It is also a tradition whose hold appeared to cut across class-barriers. (49)

The female half of society is relegated to a position similar to that of the lower castes in Indian society, bearing the brunt of discriminatory practices. Curiously, the margin-centre dialectic was subsumed within this construction, and women-related strictures regarding age of marriage etc. that were initially applicable only to brahmins became the norm, blurring caste differences.

Those engaged in fighting the entrenched orthodoxies and subverting existing hierarchies attest to the near impossibility of their task. Feminist scholar Devaki Jain suggests the more nuanced approach of Gandhi, where practice often gives content to theory. While progressive ideologies such as those posited by Periyar or E.V. Ramasawamy Naicker, who initiated a movement to build the self-esteem of the downtrodden, have been misrepresented in practice, Gandhi's principles still retain their value. Despite the ambivalence evident in Gandhi's principles, their practical and moral values persist largely because of they were grounded in practice.

The Gandhian approach to revolution was especially appropriate to women's experience as it was pragmatic and eschewed the iconoclasm of the western activists. Devaki Jain argues that many women leaders of the national movement have described how Gandhi's call to satyagraha led to a similar liberation in their own personal life from oppressive social mores. Those women who lived in his ashrams were able to leave the constrictions of their domestic lives behind and participate in a wider social milieu. Gandhi was a pathbreaker in asserting the need for women's rights. He believed that no woman should suffer from any legal disability not suffered by man. He sought to liberate women from their roles as household drudges, child bearers and caregivers. He decried as shameful the denial of equal pay for women. All these ideas reveal Gandhi to be far ahead of his time in the matter of women's rights. Devaki Jain observes that Gandhi met Indian tradition halfway, as he directed it away from establishment 'structures' and towards a dynamics of change. According to Jain, "It was this method that facilitated the emergence of women from orthodox tradition" (194). However 'middle path' this approach may seem it succeeded in providing options and vehicles for change. As Ashis Nandy notes, perhaps Gandhi's greatest contribution to the redefinition of women's identity lies in is his according a new dignity to women by making a new equation between womanliness and political potency.

In his essay "Woman versus Womanliness in India" Ashis Nandy focuses on the strong association of woman and motherhood as the defining feature of Indian social life. Nandy traces the valorization of the feminine principle in nature in a predominantly agricultural society such as India. This led to the primacy and potency of the image of the annihilating, aggressive mother. As he states, "the ultimate authority in the Indian mind has always been feminine"(36). This structure of authority finds expression in traditional family and socialization systems as the mother is the only true authority to which the child is exposed. This creates ambivalence toward the mother due to her intermittent presence which deprives the child of the sense of wholeness he experiences in her company. For the Indian mother, it is her motherhood that the traditional family respects; her role as a wife and to a lesser extent as daughter is debased. Nandy asserts that the mother-son relationship is the ultimate paradigm of human relationships in India. He argues that this has led to the downgrading of the emancipation of women and their struggle for equality. For these issues to gain primacy, a culture in which conjugality is central to male-female relationships is needed. Nandy states, "one seeks emancipation from and equality with one's husband and peers, not with one's son. If the conjugal relationship itself remains relatively peripheral, the issues of emancipation and equality must remain so too" (41). Nandy's views emphasize a reinvention of traditional roles accorded to women, a perspective that is in consonance with several other scholars, yet his valorization of the conjugal relationship breaks new ground.

Representation is a term that is often associated with multiple and equivocal connotations. Gayathri Spivak suggests that there are two principal ways of representing "by proxy and portrait", that is by political representation or portrayal (108). Feminist postcolonial studies have grown partly due to the absence of the perspectives of women from marginalized cultures or communities in historical accounts or in literature. This lack of representation occurs in the political, economic and legal spheres. Lacking power, those who are marginalized from the dominant discourse are condemned to be "spoken for" by those who command the authority and means to speak. The Foucauldian nexus between knowledge and power is clearly perceived in this context. Spivak's formulation of the two forms of representation exposes some of the problems that arise as a result. To represent politically, she argues is inevitably also "to represent yourself and your constituency in the portrait sense"(108). Identity is thus not a predetermined quality but one that must be adopted. Along with several other postcolonial and feminist critics, she alerts us to the ways in which the subject position is constructed within the discourse rather that pre-existing the discourse. Representation is therefore always partial because it must imaginatively construct its constituency as a "fiction", and because it can inadvertently usurp the space of those who cannot represent themselves.

Many critics agree that the roles, images and valorized identities of women are structured by specific social pressures, though they are offered as universal categories. As Kumkum Sangari and Sudesh Vaid in their introduction to *Recasting Women*, a collection of essays that traces the reconstitution of patriarchy in colonial India, state "womanhood is often part of an asserted or desired, not an actual, cultural continuity"(17). Rajeswari Sunder Rajan observes that if we accept that femaleness is constructed that forms of such construction are to be found in the socially dominant ideologies of patriarchy, colonialism and capitalism, and that the agents of desire and the politics of control are the motivating factors in such construction then the task of the feminist critic is a radical critique of male discourse. Rajan asserts, "What is required here is an alertness to the political process by which such representation becomes naturalized and ultimately coercive in structuring women's self-representation"(123). These theoretical insights inform the construction of the 'new Indian woman' in the media and in official discourse in India today, a structuring that serves to reconcile the conflicts between tradition and modernity in Indian society in the identity so constructed, as well as to obscure the actual conflicts that women in India experience

The 'new Indian woman', according to Rajeswari Sunder Rajan, is primarily derived from the urban, educated, middle class woman. Rajan further elaborates that "She is new in the senses of both having evolved and arrived in response to the times, as well as being intrinsically 'modern' and 'liberated'" (124). Such images emphasize the modernity of these women, which is encoded in her being distanced from communal markings, from the markings of caste, region, religion and language. This coding however is careful not to portray her as 'westernized'. The primary sites of such constructions are commercial advertisements in the media, both in print and on television. This media-created image draws on the existence of educated, urban, middle class career woman, a small but significant group that exists in cities in India. With the growing purchasing power of the burgeoning Indian middle class, the 'new woman' is constructed as an inspirational figure – the target consumer of advertisements for food, cleaning products, clothes, contraceptives, cosmetics and household appliances. The image of this woman in advertisements is of an attractive, educated, assertive and socially aware individual. This last quality is apparent from her family which is of the right size, with two children—a boy and a girl. She provides this family with 'healthy' foods and maintains an attractive home, besides earning a substantial income as a working professional. In this context Rajeswari Sunder Rajan observes: "In interpellating the users of these products as 'new' women, the advertisements not only provide an attractive and desired self-image for women in general, but also provide a normative model of citizenship that is, significantly, now gendered female"(124). The attraction of this representation lies in its enhanced version of the lived experiences of all women, and in the persuasive language in which it is couched. Advertising professional and media commentator Santosh Desai, in his analysis of the changing urban middle class, believes that the present-day woman has become supposedly freer on the outside merely influenced by a new set of representations that emphasize a persuasive, media-driven image. He sees in this altered self-image a development that is inimical to women as its emphasis on the exterior comes at the expense of a lack of evolution in her societal roles. Desai considers it ironical that at a time when Indian women are possessed of an unflinching desire to attain success in their chosen professions, media representations all but ignore such aspirations.

The insidious nature of such representation emerges in its manipulations of ideology to undercut the political motive of feminisms while simultaneously appropriating the sign system which revolves around the subjectivity of 'woman'. The 'new Indian woman' is liberated without any of the troubling aggression and militancy associated with feminisms in the Indian mindset. The subtle message being conveyed is that feminists have no leg to stand on as the Indian woman is always already articulate, independent and in control of her destiny. A representation that is the outcome of the collusion of complex, capitalist socioeconomic forces is made to seem the result of 'natural' processes, neatly bypassing the need for female emancipation by making it appear to be the matter of individual achievement and choice.

A close analysis of the images of the 'new Indian woman' in advertisements reveals a clear dichotomy. There is marked difference in the portrayals of older and younger women: the older woman, usually married, uses her education and her earnings for the well being of her family, the young woman's western attire is symbolic of her freedom and rebelliousness towards traditional attitudes. More recent advertisements reveal a greater preoccupation with external appearance, a factor that has also affected the portrayals of the older, married woman. The 'new Indian woman' thus portrayed, however, does not pose a threat to tradition as the young woman's freedom and rebellion occur outside the space of marriage where in due course she will be made to conform. Advertising appropriates the areas chosen by the women's movement – sexuality, work, marriage and family — and presents a glamourized or trivialized version that undermines the political impetus of feminism. Another feature of such portrayals of the 'new Indian woman' is the homogenization of regional identities, thereby constructing a subject who is 'modern' and 'liberated'.

So this raises the question of the modernity of this 'new Indian woman' — how modern is this new woman? There is no doubt that the economic liberalization of the 1990s greatly increased the purchasing power of the middle class Indian, but did it radically alter his worldview? Rowena Robinson seems to think otherwise:

> I am sick of reading about the modernity of the Indian middle class: its commitment to democracy as well as its respect for 'tradition'... Where does this modernity of the middle class Indian lie? I can now tell you. In his pocket...He epitomizes modernity as consumption. Pocket modernity or modernity of the pocket.

Gurcharan Das, noted author and social commentator, in contrast, declares that modernization offers the only opportunity for the majority of Indians to raise themselves to a decent standard of living. He debunks the alarmists who predict the demise of our culture and traditions by quoting Rabindranath Tagore who makes a plea for pluralism, "Whatever we understand and enjoy in human products instantly becomes ours, wherever they might have their origin. I am proud of my humanity when I can acknowledge the poets and artists of other countries as my own. Let me feel with unalloyed gladness that all the great glories of man are my own" (qtd in Das 306). Das believes that the peaceful pursuit of a globalized culture will be the chief preoccupation of this rising middle class. But how does this impact the lives of women. Rajeswari Sunder Rajan believes that the cosmopolitan Indian consumerist culture is only skin-deep; women will continue to bear the burden of maintaining the very traditions that construe them as inferior.

Another factor that has emerged as a stumbling block to this 'new Indian woman', trying to balance a career and family life, is that she is often torn between her dual responsibilities with no assistance or sympathy offered to help her face the challenges on the professional and domestic fronts. Work becomes for these women a double burden, rather that a means to financial independence. This societal antipathy towards the quest of these 'new Indian women' reveals that female autonomy is not a notion that all sections of Indian society are willing to accept. Probing the reasons for the resistance faced by these women, Rowena Robinson contends that, "the middle class Indian flees from modernity of the mind. Freedom terrifies him because it demands individual responsibility. Collective (read caste and family) responsibility offers a security that is difficult to resist. Female modernity challenges his patriarchal authority and opens up the frightening abyss of sexual choice."

It would appear that Indian women are denied any change in their socially sanctioned roles, if this challenges the status quo of masculinity or the family. This is because such change either at the individual or at the collective level would undermine the status of upper and middle class women as embodiments of Indian culture and tradition.

These discourses shape female subjectivities at the turn of the century, impelling contemporary Indian women writers to either interrogate or concede to them. As the articles in this volume reveal, despite the 'new woman' emerging at various junctures in large numbers and living a modern life, the hold of traditional roles and societal expectations remain strong. While university education is seen as a positive attribute in the marriage stakes, it often redefines the position of women in the family. Though marriage continues to be portrayed as the ultimate goal of the Indian woman, in many cases the woman is no longer financially dependent on her husband, and even if she does not work outside the home her potential to be financially independent subtly alters the dynamics of power within the family. Besides this, several novels have been written that probe the delicate identity negotiations between a single, career woman protagonist and her family. Contemporary women writers in their work affirm the existence of the 'new Indian woman', who despite having to maintain the status quo of masculinity, constantly seeks greater levels of personal autonomy, challenges the prevailing discourses of communalism and fundamentalism and aspires to change the ossified cultural expectations of the Indian middle class. These women writers writing at the turn of the century show that their portrayal of female protagonists at this crucial juncture in Indian history will enable a fluid, cosmopolitan female identity to emerge.

Despite their diversity of focus, the essays in this volume are united in their exploration of the centrality of gender in the social, cultural and political space of the nation. However, the relationship between gender, on the one hand, and the family, community and the nation on the other, continues to be fraught. In the last two decades of the twentieth century and the first decade of the twenty-first, women have challenged the notion of the masculine citizen subject as normative. In their quest for a more inclusive construction of female subjectivity, women writers acknowledge the power and influence of feminine stereotypes drawn from Hindu mythic sources, but they attempt to reconfigure these in the context of postcolonial "modernity". Kavitha Nair, in her paper "Reinterpretations of Mythic Stereotypes" analyzes contemporary re-presentations of Draupadi, the central female figure in the epic *Mahabharata,* as depicted in two contemporary novels Pratibha Ray's *Yajnaseni* and *The Palace of Illusions* by Chitra Banerji Divakaruni. It is Kavitha Nair's contention that through their reinterpretation of this multifaceted character,

Ray and Divakaruni effect an empowering transformation in Draupadi. This transformation has powerful implications for contemporary women in that it transforms an archetype that is usually associated with powerlessness to one that has far-reaching consequences for Indian female subjectivity. Such revisionist mythmaking is also the focus of the next article where Kaustav Chakraborty examines Githa Hariharan's *The Thousand Faces of Night* as a postmodern, feminist revisionist mythic narrative. He sees the novel as incorporating both mythopoeia and mythography. It is his contention that while comprehending the text readers move from 'reading myth' to mythic reading that is from the interpretation of Indian myths to the remaking of myths from a feminist perspective. He concludes that Githa Hariharan resorts to subtle postmodern strategies to expose the misrepresentation of women in patriarchal mythical culture thereby generating accurate representations for the present.

V. Padma's article analyzes Qurratulain Hyder's *River of Fire* as one of the most significant novels to emerge in both its Urdu version in 1959 and the author's own English translation that was published in 1998. The novel is considered to be a landmark in Urdu literature as it was published in the aftermath of the Partition and its ambitious project of rewriting nearly 4,000 years of India's cultural and political history was considered quite subversive at the time. By the time the English version was published, it was commonplace for English fiction from India to interrogate British/colonial representations. Although the subversive voice was ever present in historical novels, critics tended to valorize the postcolonial questionings of colonial history. In contrast, *River of Fire* posits an India where the very notion of a 'pure' nation is suspect. Indian culture is seen to have always been dynamic, never stagnant, to have always been in contact with other alien cultures. Padma reads *River of Fire* as an exemplary text that offers a vision of India as a nation characterized by plurality and cultural dialogue.

Several critics have observed that women writers of the Indian diaspora have to negotiate the dual tensions of the cultural expectations of their host country as well as the traditions of their natal culture in the process of identity construction. C.N. Eswari in her analysis of diasporic author Indira Ganesan's novel *The Journey* emphasizes the subversion of any essentialist notion of identity in the diaspora. In Eswari's reading, Indira Ganesan through her characters in *The Journey* conveys the message that life is a constant transcending of barriers and divisions, which underscores the concept of transculturalism.

S. Chitra's paper focuses on the elision of regional identities in the construction of the grand narratives of the nation. She focuses on Anthony D. Smith's assertion of the necessity of reconstruction of the ethnic pasts of these communities for their political mobilization. It is her contention that Kavery Nambisan's novel *The Scent of Pepper* functions as an ethnographic text in recuperating such hidden ethnic identities and highlights the functioning of women in these societies, besides gendering the ethnic/regional identity. P.Rathna's article considers Dalit writer Bama's life writing *Sangati: Events* as an autoethnographic text. Rathna invokes a concept of autoethnography that calls into question both the realist conventions and objective observer positions of standard ethnography and the notion of a coherent self posited by conventional autobiography. Citing Deborah Reed Danahay, Rathna notes that the term can signify in two ways either as the ethnography of one's own group or to autobiographical writing that has ethnographic interest. She asserts that Bama exudes the necessary passion and courage to re-examine and relive her emotional past in order to attain self-awareness and identity. *Sangati* reveals the equanimity achieved by her retarded by the "ethno" factors of caste and patriarchy but transcended by the "auto" factors of self-introspection and explication. Through this process she achieves not just personal redemption but enlightens the other marginalized as well.

Aparna Sundaram's article focuses on the culture of violence against women prevalent in twenty-first century India. Though the nineties ushered in an era of change that redefined the ethos of the country and altered the status of women considerably, traditional beliefs and practices continue to hinder their status as equal citizens of India. Aparna considers primarily the crimes of female foeticide and infanticide, honour killings and rapes and sexual assaults perpetrated during times of social conflict. Aparna concludes that through the violence-marred lives of the female protagonists in their novels *Witness the Night* and *Fugitive Histories*, the respective authors Kishwar Desai and Githa Hariharan raise pertinent questions regarding the state of women's lives in twenty-first century India. Amutha Charu Sheela's paper examines the impact of the Partition on the socio-cultural fabric of India through an analysis of Githa Hariharan's novels *In Times of Siege* and *Fugitive Histories*. The spectral presence of Partition haunts Hindu-Muslim relations to this day. The destruction of Babri Masjid at Ayodhya in 1992 triggered widespread violence against Muslim's throughout India. In 2002 India witnessed some of the worst communal clashes ever seen in recent times, with the Gujarat state government being accused of sponsoring the terrorism against Muslims. It is against this fractious backdrop that *In Times of Siege* and *Fugitive Histories* were written.. Gita Hariharan's fictional discourse s resists and questions almost every aspect of social order. Her stories deal with inequalities, power struggles and women asserting their identity. This paper examines various aspects of the author's fictional discourse such as recasting history, the question of secularism, identity and violence, prospects for peace and other narratological models.

Karkuzhali's article on Anjum Hasan's *Neti, Neti—Not This, Not This* offers a fresh perspective on the alienation experienced by the single, young female protagonist as a consequence of life in a globalized India. While fiction by Indian women writers generally focuses on their travails in the context of home and family, Hasan's novel breaks new ground in looking at a liberated young woman and her life in the epicentre of globalization in India, Bangalore. Anjum Hasan's *Neti, Neti—Not This, Not This* discloses the dilemmas of a young Indian woman in her search for identity. Her confrontations with constant road accidents, glitzy shopping malls, late night parties and mindless consumerism make her feel insecure in a globalized cosmopolitan city. She wishes to go back to Shillong, her hometown, for a week to escape from the oppressive environment, but unfortunately all her attempts to recreate her lost identity and happiness prove to be a failure as Shillong becomes a microcosm of Bangalore. Vennila Ramanathan's paper on Anita Nair's *Ladies Coupe* also looks at the problems face by a single woman in society, but the central character of the novel, Akhila is very far from being liberated. Vennila employs Drucilla Cornell's feminist framework which asserts that women are denied power largely because they lack the courage to communicate. It is while travelling in a ladies coupe with a group of women that Akhila learns the therapeutic power of communication and action. Drucilla Cornell points out that it is a mistake to contrast representation against the act of communicative practice. According to Cornell representation is inseparable from action. Nair's heroine represents other silenced people like herself and plunges into ameliorative action though it may not be possible for all women. Vennila argues that all the problems that issue forth from patriarchal domination upon women can be redressed if women cease to be inarticulate.

G Kalvikkarasi focuses on Githa Harharan's short stories from the collection *The Art of Dying,* in her analysis of the power struggles of patriarchal authority as they operate in society. The characters portrayed in the seven short stories selected for analysis, both male and female, challenge the social taboos that inhibit them from living well. By flouting these ossified conventions the characters transform their lives, standing testimony to the Art of Living. Feminist critics have readily acknowledged that it is not men but patriarchy that is responsible for the uneven power structures that operate in society. R. Revathi's article on Anita Nair's novel *The Better Man* offers interesting insights as it looks at the father-son relationship from a woman writer's perspective. Revathi constructs a comparative analytical grid using both Greek and Indian myths to situate her reading of the novel. The oppressed son becomes a better man after he divests himself of the yoke of inadequacy cast upon him by his father. The imaginative ability of the author in being able to probe the consciousness of a son makes this reading unusual.

M. Parimala considers the formation of regional identities by examining the operation of the tensions that govern them. The twenty-first century has brought with many concomitant changes in India, in the cultural, political, religious, economic and social domains as a result of modernization and globalization. These global phenomena have caused homogenization and integration resulting in the merging of regional and national boundaries. Parimala attempts to analyze the transformation of religious and regional identities of the orthodox brahmin communities in India,in the context of modernization, with her focus on two novels–Anita Nair's *Ladies Coupe* and Malathi Rao's *Disorderly Women.* The paper analyses the two women characters, Akhila from *Ladies Coupe* and Kamala from *Disorderly Women*, to evince the extrication of these women from their entanglement in conventional roles. The narrative of these novels depicts how these two women characters from the traditional orthodox brahmin family dismantle and subvert the firmly established conservative values, ethics and customs to harmonize their lives with the changing values of modern Indian society. R. Priya, in her article explores of the contrary compulsions of motherhood and personal creativity in the life of Aditi, the protagonist in Tulsi Badrinath's novel *Meeting Lives.* The Mother, in Indian tradition, is the embodiment of Shakti – the Prowess. She saves her children and acts as their custodian. In any construction of an ideal mother, she has to have many-sided virtues apart from the conviction that her children are to be glorified as well as protected. She gets defined and glorified by her capacity to protect, provide, endure and sacrifice for her child. Torn between her desire to be a good Hindu mother and the attainment of bliss through the creativity of dance, Aditi discovers an alternative creative freedom through her writing.

N. Chandra in her article looks at the crossing of cultural borders by women from diverse cultural backgrounds in India. These transgressions take place as they seek to express their sexuality, an aspect of female identity that is problematic in almost all cultures. Chandra contends that while women writers have previously shown their concern over the economic and societal imbalances that have impacted the lives if women, they have now brought the issue of sexuality to the forefront. The article analyzes the women protagonists of Bharati Mukherjee's *Desirable Daughters*, Salma's *The Hour Past Midnight* and Shashi Deshpande's *In the Country of Deceit*. The manner in which the women protagonists transgress the cultural codes relating to women's bodies and the social reactions to this reveal the patriarchal power structures that operate in that particular society. Debalina Banerjee considers emergence of lesbianism as a theme in Manju Kapur's *A Married Woman*. Second-wave feminist activism began focusing on the need for the sexual autonomy of the female body. Radical feminists have even argued that feminism is the theory, and lesbianism is the practice. Debalina Banerjee in her paper contends that while Manju Kapur introduces lesbianism into her narrative it serves merely as a symptom of the deterioration of the heterosexual marital relationship of the protagonist, Astha. According to Debalina Banerjee, in failing to develop her lesbian plot, Kapur seems to be conforming to Otto Weininger's delineation of a social order that constructs an 'ideal' sexual antithesis as opposed to a potentially chaotic 'bisexual' order.

The multifarious perspectives on contemporary fiction by Indian women would seem to belie the notion that women's writing from India is mired in the vicissitudes of mythic stereotypes and the iron grip of tradition–mandated roles. While the marginalization of women is still a potent factor in the representations of women by women, there are beginning to appear narrative encodings that suggest the greater empowerment of women. Of particular interest is the exploration of altered masculinities which signifies the possible emergence of an independent female fictional persona. The appearance of the single, career woman as protagonist is also a significant pointer in the right direction, as well as the rebellion of married women, however tentative. For Indian women who were to a large extent circumscribed by traditional roles, any gesture of rebellion that precipitates a move away from the home and family may be seen as a move towards autonomy. Perhaps the growing reading population, a positive after-effect of economic liberalization, will spur the creative potential of women writers to create enabling,culturally-sensitive, transformational female identities.

WORKS CITED

Chatterjee, Partha. "The Nationalist Resolution of the Women's Question." K. Sangari and S. Vaid. Eds. *Recasting Women: Essays in Cultural History*. New Delhi: Kali for Women,1990.

Das, Gurcharan. *India Unbound: From Independence to the Global Information Age*. New Delhi: Penguin India, 2002.

Desai, Santosh. *Mother Pious Lady: Making Sense of Everyday India*. New Delhi: Harper Collins, 2010.

Fruzetti L. and S.Tenhunen. *Culture, Power and Agency: Gender in Indian Ethnography*. Kolkata:Stree, 2006.

Jain, Devaki. "Feminism and Feminist Expression: A Dialogue." Kamala Ganesh and Usha Thakkar eds. *Culture and the Making of Identity in Contemporary India*. New Delhi, Sage Publications, 2005.

Lau, Lisa. "Re-Orientalism: The Perception and Development of Orientalism by Orientals." *Modern Asian Studies*. 43 (2009).

Loomba, Ania. "Dead Women Tell No Tales: Issues of Female Subjectivity, Subaltern Agency And Tradition in Colonial and Postcolonial Writings on Widow Immolation in India." Reina Lewis and Sara Mills eds. *Feminist Postcolonial Theory*. Edinburgh: Edinburgh U P. 2003.

Mani, Lata. "Contentious Traditions: The Debate on Sati in Colonial India." K. Sangari and S. Vaid eds. *Recasting Women*. New Delhi: Kali for Women, 1990.

Nabar, Vrinda. *Caste as Woman*. New Delhi: Penguin India, 1995.

Nandy, Ashis. *At the Edge of Psychology: Essays on Politics and Culture*. New Delhi: Oxford U P, 1993.

Rajagopal, Arvind. "Uses of the Past: The Televisual Broadcast of an Ancient Epic and its Reception in Indian Society." Ph.D.Diss, University of California, Berkeley, 1992.

Robinson, Rowena. "The great Indian middle class" *The Hindu*. http:/www.hindu.com/the hindu/2001/01/13/stories/13140611.htm. Web.

Rajan, Rajeswari Sunder. *Real and Imagined Women: Gender, culture and postcolonialism*. Routledge: New York and London, 1993.

Sainath, P. "The feel good factory." *Frontline*. Vol.21.5. http:/www.flonnet.com/fl2105/stories/20040312007800400.htm. Web.

Sangari K. and S. Vaid. Eds. *Recasting Women: Essays on Colonial History*. New Delhi: Kali for Women, 1990.

Spivak, Gayathri. *The Post- Colonial Critic: Interviews, Strategies, Dialogues*.Routledge: London and New York, 1990.

2

Reinterpretations of Mythic Stereotypes

— L. Kavitha Nair

The stories of the *Mahabharata* are retold – with selection, addition, and modification – reflecting the *zeitgeist*, exploring the multiple layers of consciousness and narrative embedded in it. This "close link" allows the epic to be claimed by every age for itself, thus, discovering new possibilities and meanings in it.

"We have a text which for centuries has been growing, not only upwards and downwards, but also laterally like the Nyagrodha (banyan) tree" (Dandekar 1990: 90). Essentially an oral epic, which was transmitted by rhapsodists and the bards, the *Mahabharata* travelled from generation to generation, from place to place and from bard to bard, before Vyasa gave it its present written form. In all these forms, storytelling is of immense importance as it is the essence of the epic form. Every genre and sub-genre of literature has made use of this great epic to make sense of the world around, rendering every word of Vyasa's *Mahabharata* contemporary. This has been a result of a reorientation of the cultural past to inspire the present and shape the future, making the study of mythic stereotypes relevant.

The Indian understanding of womanhood has been largely drawn from the two great epics of this country, namely the *Ramayana* and the *Mahabharata*. Just as the *Ramayana* has "Many Ramayanas", to use Paula Richman's term, similarly the numerous interpretations of the *Mahabharata* can be called

"Many Mahabharatas". Both these texts are replete with women characters who represent almost every facet of womanhood and who go through experience and face issues that are relevant even today. These mythic women have, thus, been subject to change. The different layers of human consciousness that the characters are loaded with in the epics make it possible for every age to discover a new layer. It is only in the recent times that an engagement with the dynamic, assertive, and active self in the portrayal of women characters in the epics has been taken up. It is in this context that a study of contemporary re-presentations of Draupadi becomes significant. Draupadi is a floating character, who lives multiple lives in the different versions in which she figures. Each version in which she appears brings out a new dimension of her multifacetedness and her "infinite variety". This points to the multivalence in Draupadi's character and suggests that a complete exploration of her character is virtually impossible.

This paper focuses on two contemporary novels: *Yajnaseni: The Story of Draupadi* by Pratibha Ray, and *The Palace of Illusions* by Chitra Banerjee Divakaruni. The remarkable differences between the novels in their portrayal of Draupadi are reflected in the distinct narrative techniques employed by them. The 'subject to change' here, is traced by a study of the novels in the light of concepts associated with the Indian narrative tradition, identified by K. Ayyappa Paniker, in *Indian Narratology*. The narrative techniques employed by the women writers Ray and Divakaruni explore the dilemmas in decision making that women face, and through the most inspiring of the mythical characters, Draupadi, the two novelists bring out the manner in which the change, that present-day women desire, has been ushered in.

Pratibha Ray's novel *Yajnaseni: The Story of Draupadi* was written in the last quarter of the twentieth century (1984), when the role of women within the Indian society was beginning to be re-assessed. Fired by the re-orientation in understanding brought about by India's Freedom Movement, the Women's Movement within the country and the emergence of Women

Studies within the academia, a radical re-visioning of women's position within the society took place. Pratibha Ray's novel captures the early impulses of this movement, when, though a traditional understanding of women was still operative, attempts were beginning to be made to understand the importance of articulating women's inner concerns and passions. As Nandini Sahu observes in her article "The Position of Women in Oriya Literature", Ray "depicted through her bold and reformist women characters the declining values and transformative adjustment between tradition and modernity, between desire and decision, with natural psychological stress associated with it". Perhaps, this is the reason why Ray chooses to keep Draupadi largely within the framework of Vyasa's text but then seeks to give her a depth and a dimension that would speak to the twentieth-century context and audience.

Pratibha Ray's *Yajnaseni*, like S.L. Bhyrappa's *Parva*, is an attempt at fictionalizing the epic from Draupadi's point of view. The plot of the *Mahabharata* is derived from a seemingly simple tale of fraternal struggle which results in the Great War. However, in the hands of Ray, this story of the Great War ("Maha Bharata") becomes the story of Draupadi, especially the story of her inner life which comes to the fore only occasionally in Vyasa's story. Vyasa's *Mahabharata* leaves us with numerous unanswered questions, which different authors have attempted to answer in their own individual way, according to the times they live in. Ray, too, seizes these moments from Vyasa's text and extends them imaginatively, thus presenting a Draupadi whose inner life is rich and complex, and, even more importantly, a Draupadi who speaks to the contemporary reader in an authentic voice. In this exceptional fictional work, Ray makes Draupadi, the authoritative, all-knowing narrator. She voices the silences which Vyasa had left for posterity to uncover, discover and recover. As Warrier observes in her article, "If it were not for her, the story of the Kuru dynasty would have taken quite a different turn".

Pratibha Ray attempts to look at Draupadi not just as a mythical character, but as a flesh and blood woman, who lived an extraordinary life in which she is forced to make difficult choices, choices filled with ethical and moral dilemmas, at every point of time. K. Kunjunni Raja observes:

> In great literature as well as in real life, the problems that confront people in different situations are not based on the conflict between right and wrong, between *dharma* and *adharma*, but on the conflict between different and often opposing duties; between one's duty to one's kith and kin and that to society, between truth and non-violence, between what is immediately feasible and proper and what is ultimately correct. When there are opposing pulls from strong moral values, such as truth and non-violence, the problem is to determine the relative strength of these, and to decide what to do in the context.
>
> (qtd in Matilal 49)

It is such choices made by Draupadi that guide the future course of events throughout the epic. Furthermore, whether willingly or unwillingly, she often causes events of historical significance to happen. Therefore, Ray's Draupadi, or rather Yajnaseni – by narrating the story of her life to Krishna at the very moment of her death and by attempting to justify the choices she made at important junctures in her life – seeks to relive it and interpret it, as much to herself as to others.

As the title suggests, what Ray is presenting in her work is the story of Draupadi rather than the story of the *Mahabharata*. In her work, the heroine, Yajnaseni, is more interested in narrating her story rather than what was happening around her. It is her reactions to and feelings about every incident that goes to make the *Mahabharata* that she wants to focus on. She becomes the centre with reference to which every incident in the novel is interpreted. The novel tries to give us a glimpse into the mind of Yajnaseni, by tracing her emotional journey from being a much-admired and loved princess in the palace of Drupada, through becoming the wife of five men, the descendents of one of the most powerful race in the Bharatavarsha, to realizing her own spiritual position as the friend, "sakhi", of Krishna.

All the other great characters of Vyasa's *Mahabharata* appear in the background so that the life of Yajnaseni becomes the only focus. Nevertheless, this is a life that has been extraordinary – no other character in the vast ocean of the Indian tradition goes through such vicissitudes as she does. Her birth out of a sacrificial fire, her marriage to five men at once, her being disrobed in a public hall by her own kinsmen, her exile with her husbands – any one of these events in itself would qualify a life to be termed extraordinary but, in the case of Ray's Yajnaseni, each one of these becomes just another incident in a hugely eventful and dramatic life: "Peculiar scenes thronged this predicament-filled act of my life-drama" (332).

Ray does a fine selection of events which highlights the conflicts that Yajnaseni's mind must have gone through: "...and then my life, the life of one born of this spark created by the friction of wood and fire – how could that be complete without conflicts" (47). Her marriage to the five Pandava brothers raises much controversy, even today. In fact, Ray makes Yajnaseni herself voice this anticipated ridicule, while pondering over her marriage to the five Pandavas:

> This would not add to the fame of woman as a species.
>
> For all future time Draupadi would remain condemned in the history of the world as a woman of despicable and stained character. So much so that in the Kaliyuga people would call fallen women having many men as "Draupadis of this era", making me the butt of scorn. What would they understand of the situation in which Panchali became the wife of five men? (59-60).

In *Yajnaseni,* Prathiba Ray reacts strongly and passionately to this stigma attached to the name and character of Draupadi. In an interview with Sue Dickman in *The Book Review*, Ray states the reason for writing a novel on Draupadi. She says: "What made me write on Draupadi and Ahalya? You may ask why I did not write on Sita. Because these characters are eclipsed and misunderstood. I have always had a weakness towards a group of misunderstood people" (33).

In *Yajnaseni*, Ray brings to light the dark, undisclosed passages of Draupadi's mind, which underwent unimaginable heights of suffering. Draupadi, in fact, has often been seen as an advocate of Women's rights. Susan Bassnet and Harish Trivedi observe in *Postcolonial Translation* that the two great Indian epics are "worked and reworked by countless writers in Sanskrit as well as in all Indian languages with various shifts of emphasis and ideology through which gaps in the original were inventively filled in, silences were rendered poignantly articulate" (9). Through the first person narrative technique which enables us to hear Draupadi's voice, Ray examines her psyche and is able to excellently communicate her interpretation, understanding and perspective of the events of the epic, filling in the gaps imaginatively.

Traditionally only two roles of Draupadi's have been foregrounded – one, that of a faithful wife, and the other that of a daughter-in-law, while all her other roles have been pushed to the background. Chaturvedi Badrinath observes that Draupadi is, "known widely but frozen in popular culture and writing into two or three standard clichéd images" (177). Pratibha Ray's Draupadi is not merely an obedient daughter, sister, wife of the five great Pandavas, daughter-in-law and affectionate mother, but also a good friend, a great constructive social thinker, spokesperson for women and a queen. In Vyasa's version, her voice seems to be rather muted. Ray, on the other hand, gives her all the space, air and freedom of speech. Though her predicament remains the same in Ray's novel, she has a larger role and reveals the multidimensionality of Draupadi that makes her a floating character who escapes rigid categorization.

Vyasa's *Mahabharata* records history from the perspective of all the action in which the Pandavas participate, while Ray's *Yajnaseni* records history from the perspective of Draupadi's inner life.

The emotional inner life of Draupadi is what contributes to the richness of her character and so Ray enters imaginatively into Draupadi's mind and creates, to use Susan Langer's idea, a "virtual space" (77), which she then goes on to explore. In the novel, Draupadi raises certain important questions about her own life. Finding herself facing the predicament of serving five husbands and remaining faithful to each one of them, she is shattered when she slips and falls during the last journey of her life and her five husband's do not turn back. It is this incident that impels Draupadi to look back at her own life and search for the meaning of all the trials and tribulations that she has undergone:

> What agonies did I not suffer for preserving dharma? I had thought that on the strength of my adherence to dharma and fidelity as a wife I would be able to accompany my husbands to heaven. Yet, I had but touched the golden dust of Himalaya's foothills when my feet slipped and I fell! Five husbands – but not one turned back even to look. Rather, Dharmaraj Yudhishthir, lord of righteousness, said to Bhim, "Do not turn back to look! Come forward!"
>
> Those very words of his shattered my heart. I mused: how false is this bond between husband and wife! Affection, love, sacrifice and surrender! If man suffers the consequences of his own deeds, then offering myself at the feet of five husbands for the sake of preserving Yudhishthir's dharma, why did I have to bear the burden of the whole world's mockery, sneers, innuendos, abuse, scorn and slander? (2-3).

These lines evoke sympathy for the agony and pain that Draupadi has gone through. Pratibha Ray wishes Draupadi to be relieved of this pain. Draupadi herself says that all the tales (the retellings) till now about her, have only made her "food for mockery and jest amid the perverted sexuality of Kaliyuga's debauched men and women" (3). Until and unless the real tale is told "how will these people appreciate that five-husbanded Draupadi had to burn inch by inch in the cause of chastity?" (3). She wants to narrate the story of her life herself to seek justice:

> ...I shall speak the truth. The story of my life, is nothing other than the life-story of any human being on this mortal world. Read the indelible words of this letter. Seeing each

> hair-raising incident of my life the people of Kaliyuga will be able to decide whether the insults Draupadi suffered have ever been borne by any woman of any time. God forbid that in future anyone should ever suffer such abuse (4).

As Ray unfurls every hidden leaf of her life, Draupadi comes across as a person with clarity of thought and purpose. She wants the world to see the real story – the truth. Through the complex, emotional landscape of the story, *Yajnaseni: The Story of Draupadi*, Ray shows the life and evolution of a woman. Though Ray does voice her concerns and fears, she is not able to translate them into action. Her dilemmas are never ending. Ray beautifully sums up the predicament of Krishnaa, "The dilemma lies stretching endlessly, the night somehow always ends" (77).

In Ray's novel, Draupadi has traces of a feminist consciousness which fiercely questions the assumptions of patriarchy, a facet also hinted at by Vyasa. The extraordinariness of her life is suggested in the manner in which she handles the traumatic experiences she encounters. She is portrayed as aspiring to be an empowered woman who does not accept the belittling constructions of women. Draupadi strikes us as our contemporary when one reflects on the issues raised by her.

After Arjun wins her in the svayamvar, she is taken to the potter's hut. There is a poignant description of the first night spent at the hut of her future husbands. Since her marriage to the five Pandavas is yet to be solemnized, she finds herself facing a delicate situation of having to share the single room available with her future husbands and her mother-in-law. She says, "Only one room. My five husbands lay down on beds of grass and went to sleep one after another. Mother-in-law went to sleep at the upper portion of the bed, touching her sons' heads. My bed was at my husband's feet. Making a cushion of my body of five elements, all ten feet would be placed on it. This would be my appropriate dharma as a woman" (65). She is in a lot of pain having to abide by the decision of marrying the five brothers, and is unable to digest the fact of becoming a question for posterity. When she hears Maharishi Narad talking about her situation in a very derogatory manner, Yajnaseni rises in revolt, though only in her thoughts. "She stood up in revolt against the laws of the abode of gods, according to which one man might accept as many women as he wished, but if one woman married more than one husband she would be branded a sinner" (92). She defends her position strongly by saying that, "If the standards of virtue and sin had been identical for women and men, the female race would not have been oppressed by social tyranny" (97).

In the novel, Yajnaseni often becomes a spokesperson for women. She is seen reflecting upon the predicament of women in general, questioning patriarchy, the system which has established unjust and partisan laws to subjugate women. This woman of such strong and learned views is wronged in the ugliest manner in the Kuru Sabha in front of all the great men of Aryavarta. Yajnaseni, who is wrapped in a single piece of cloth – as she is menstruating – is dragged to the court and stripped even of that one protection of her dignity. She comes down heavily upon the so-called establishers of dharma. She says:

> Since the beginning of time till today never has such a hellish, horrible thing happened, nor will it ever happen till the end of eternity. When Ravan was abducting chaste Sita, trees and plants, animals and birds – everyone shed tears...To rescue Sita, an army of bears and monkeys laid down their lives (241).

Her questions are unsparing. She says, "Alas! At one time comparing Dharmaraj Yudhishthir's personality to that of Ram I used to feel immensely glorified. For protecting the honor of chaste Sita how much sorrow and pain did Ram not undergo.... While my husband having staked me and having handed me over to others is sitting there. A mute spectator, he is watching me being insulted" (241).

Almost similar is her rage at King Virata's sabha while being insulted by Keechaka. The terrible fact is that, once again, no one comes forward to stop this outrage on her womanhood. This lawless, gross injustice and tyranny demeans the entire male sex, including her five husbands. She says that her husbands were just mute spectators to the scene which is the most pathetic and heinous scene a woman has ever been in.

Fierce as she is in defending her position, it is intriguing that Ray's Yajnaseni should choose Sita as her role model. She constantly compares herself to Sita, always using the epithet *sati* before the name of Sita. Considering that Sita is a woman of an entirely different mould, Draupadi's invocation of Sita at every point of her life seems to be rather incongruous. However, by and large, Ray's *Yajnaseni* can be deemed a feminist text because Yajnaseni attacks the paradigm of patriarchy with such vehemence that the other characters in the novel are shocked by her rage.

Later in the novel, Draupadi becomes an ambassador not only of women but also of a changed society in general. She calls for an open, lifelong war against the rituals and rules created in a society built around the "distinctions between rich-poor, high-low, brahmins-chandals, male-female and such others, the profound inequities that had been set based upon considerations of virtue and sin – against all of these a lifelong war would have to be waged" (92-93). However, Yajnaseni is much more than that. Her role is that of an all-encompassing pacifist and messenger of world peace, which is something only a person "permeated with Krishna, bliss, love" (397) can provide. She does not wish to attain *moksha* but to be re-born on the sacred earth of Bharata so as to turn it into a "pathfinder of the whole world in friendship and peace" (398).

Draupadi's nationalist concern in *Yajnaseni*, is her way of resolving the emotional conflicts within herself. She moves from being shackled by personal emotions to going beyond them by concerning herself with national issues. In *The Palace of Illusions*, she journeys even further into the spiritual realm.

The Palace of Illusions by Chitra Banerjee Divakaruni is a retelling of the story of the *Mahabharata* from a different perspective, written in the first quarter of the twenty-first century. She chooses the voice of the iconic Panchali, also known as Draupadi, to unravel Panchali's intensely emotional story. It is Draupadi – 'queen of queens envied even by goddesses' (39) – who is celebrated as the central character here, the only heroine, with no other leading male character reaching her heights. Divakaruni narrates 'her' version of the story of Vyasa's *Mahabharata*. Every version seems to have a different view and outlook on the happenings in that epic of epics. Every version, depending upon its focus, takes a different retelling. As Krishna says in the novel, "Truth, like a diamond, has many facets" (55). The web of each story, which is spun in every version, is the result of the imagination of the writer and of the times he/she is in.

Divakaruni is, in fact, not just re-visioning Draupadi's story but is rather making a re-assessment of the whole *Mahabharata*. The multiple, conflicting narratives play an important role in the novel and since Divakaruni's Draupadi herself is pre-occupied with the power of narratives, a study of narratology in the light of K. Ayyappa Paniker's narrative paradigm will provide an insight into the construction of the novel and the evolving character.

In *Indian Narratology,* K. Ayyappa Paniker identifies ten narrative devices, which, according to him, have been employed in the Indian Narrative tradition: Interiorization, Serialization, Fantasization, Cyclicalisation, Allegorisation, Anonymisation, Elasticisation of time, Spatialisation, Stylisation, and Improvisation. Chitra Banerjee Divakaruni's novel can be placed in this narrative tradition and, therefore, a study of some of the narrative devices employed by her provides an interesting insights into her characters.

Of the devices listed, *interiorisation* is well employed by Chitra Divakaruni. Using Vyasa's narration of the Draupadi-story as a frame, Divakaruni narrates it in her own way to bring out the complexities that lie embedded in the story. Ayyappa Paniker defines interiorisation as:

> ...the process by which, a contrast or even a contradiction is effected between the surface features of a text and its internal essence.... A text is often a multiplicity of layer upon layer of signification, and it may even be that the simpler a text looks the chances of the inner text being contradictory to it are much greater.... Surface simplicity is often a clever device to interiorise a deeper and more complex end (4-5).

Vyasa's *Mahabharata* then provides the surface features for Divakaruni to explore the internal essence of Draupadi. The narrative in the novel can be seen in terms of frames within a frame. The outermost frame is that of Vyasa's *Mahabharata* within which is the narrative frame of Divakaruni. However, Divakaruni, as mentioned earlier, surrenders her authorial consciousness to Draupadi, who becomes the narrator of her own story, thus introducing the most important narrative frame. From being in the periphery in Vyasa's story, as far as her emotional life is concerned, Draupadi moves to holding the central position in Divakaruni's novel because "it was my turn to play storyteller" (13). Within this narrative framework of Draupadi's, other narrators such as Dhai Ma, Dhri, Sahadeva, are allowed space. Draupadi is the most qualified to be the narrator, since she is fully alive to the layeredness of a story. This is evident when she comments on the unreliability of stories by calling them "agitated imaginings" (15). Because of her awareness that no story can give a complete understanding, she questions the epistemological process itself. A story can never be contained within a final form and can never lay claim to complete expression of Truth. Draupadi realizes that a story, more often than not, is constructed from rumors, lies upon which our own "agitated imaginings" act. She captures the essence of the act of narration when she reaches this understanding. As a result, she is able to fuse text and counter-text in a single narration, thus exploring and, ultimately, optimizing the potential of the story. A perception of the limitedness and falsification of the linguistic constructions of her own life leads to the perception that Reality is also constructed. She understands the similarity between the constructedness of Reality and the construction of her 'self'.

In this context, Vyasa's role as narrator within the frame of Draupadi's novel becomes significant. In the conversation between Vyasa and Draupadi about her destiny, Draupadi wants to know whether he can change the course of her destiny: "I've heard that great seers have the power to change the future they foretell. Please – can't you shape mine so that I don't harm those dearest to me?" (40). At this point she is still caught up in her personal likes and dislikes and her concern is for those dearest to her. Vyasa's response to her is that the Great Design cannot be tampered with. However, Draupadi in the course of the novel will show that, even if the great design cannot be altered, what can be altered is one's perception of and response to it. Therefore, when Vyasa asks her to leave because he is writing her story, her response is one of passive resignation. It is significant that, at this juncture, she has a partial glimpse of the elephant-headed god, Ganesha, the scribe of her story. From now on, she will not only endeavor to change the course of history but also to have an enlightened perception of the Great Design. The Great Design is not only the karmic chain of her own lives but is also the multiple lives that the *Mahabharata* has had over centuries of retelling.

Serialization, another narrative device identified by Ayyappa Paniker, refers to "the structure of the Indian narrative, which seems to prefer an apparently never ending series of episodes to a unified, single-strand, streamlined course of events centering around a single hero or heroine and whatever happens to the central character" (6-7). In Divakaruni's novel serialization can be seen in the many embedded narratives of Dhai Ma, Dhri, Sahadeva and the implied narrative of Vyasa, all of which are brought together into an organic unity by Draupadi's narrative. The principle strand in the narrative is Draupadi's story, which leads sometimes to other strands which are only seemingly digressive. Each one of these strands can be transformed into the main strand of another telling. This narratorial consciousness in Draupadi makes her an ideal reader as well as a consummate narrator of tales. Such a narratorial consciousness, which intiates and sustains a dynamic equilibrium among varying narratives, is captured effectively by Paniker through an architectural image:

> The long narrative in India is reminiscent of the Indian Temple or palace architecture, there are many entrances, many substructures, which give to the whole structure a spatial extension: ...The episodic looseness of the Indian narrative allows for variations in tone and style in the middle of the work: even gaps are provided for as part of the system... (7).

When read in this light, the fascination that palaces have for Draupadi is the fascination that the art of storytelling has for her. For instance, in the context of narrating the conflict between king Drupad and Drona, Draupadi uses the metaphor of opening and closing door and windows. Both Dhri and Draupadi attempt to tell the story of this conflict. Unhappy with Draupadi's representation of Drupad, Dhri wrests the narration from her: "You're looking at the story through the wrong window," he said. "You've got to close it and open a different one. Here, I'll do it" (15). Though Draupadi knows that she has opened the right window, she allows him to narrate the story up to a point and then takes over unobtrusively, giving Dhri still a sense of controlling the narration. Through assays of bias, Draupadi, through indirections finds directions out: "Having shaped our father's motivations the way he wished them to be, he was willing to let me tell the rest" (17).

Yet another use of serialization is revealed in Dhai Ma's narration of the story of Draupadi's birth and the prophecy. For a moment, almost playfully she deflates Draupadi's inflated ego:

> "They said, *Behold, we give you this girl, a gift beyond what you asked for. Take good care of her for she will change the course of history.*"

> " '*Change the course of history*'! Did they really say that?"
>
> Dhai Ma shrugged. "That's what the priests claimed. Who can tell for sure? You know how sounds boom and echo in the hall...And then we had the best feast this kingdom has ever seen." (5).

Draupadi's obsession with her destiny is playfully undermined by Dhai Ma who deliberately shifts the focus to the feast that followed her 'history altering birth'. However, Draupadi knows that "each story will come in its own time" (3).

Stylisation and *Improvisation*, two closely interlocked narrative devices identified by Paniker, are also employed in the novel. "Stylisation is a factor that imposes limitations on the writer or story teller, while Improvisation is a liberating factor...Stylisation is discipline, improvisation is freedom" (2003:16). Stylisation as a narrative device makes the work conform to the expectations of the readers by staying within the confines of the traditional mould. On the contrary, improvisation breaks free of the mould and through surprise leads them on to wonder.

Stylisation provides the bare skeletal framework for *The Palace of Illusions*, while improvisation infuses it with flesh, blood and spirit. Draupadi's concern with narration her and engagement with multiple narrations is a significant instance of improvisation. Her discussion with Vyasa about the story of her own life, her emotional responses to her five husbands, the introspective mode that she gets into during her humiliation at the Kuru Sabha, and the easy relationship she shares with Bheeshma – all these are instances of improvisation which liberate Draupadi from the shackles of stylized narration. The final triumph of the impulse of improvisation is achieved when, in the end, Draupadi as Pure Consciousness ascends to heaven. It is through the creation of her own character that Draupadi, perhaps, attains artistic liberation.

The use of multiple narrative devices, a characteristic of Indian narrative mode, lends multivalence to a text. As Ayyappa Paniker observes:

> Like a collapsible bag, the text of the Indian narrative expands or contracts, as the case may be, to accommodate improvised materials. The stylised narrative is the minimal text, but improvisation helps to make it suit different contexts and situations.... This is yet another reason for the fluidity for the narrative in India (17).

It is in Chitra Banerjee Divakaruni's *The Palace of Illusions* that Draupadi breathes free, casting away all her previous restrictive constructions. Here, she reinvents herself by becoming the author of her own life's story. Evincing a keen interest in different modes of narration, she studies every construction of her life's story to contest and then cancel out that construction. *The Palace of Illusions* begins thus:

> Through the long, lonely years of my childhood, when my father's palace seemed to tighten its grip around me until I couldn't breathe, I would go to my nurse and ask for a story (1).

In the very first sentence of the novel, Draupadi indicates that she feels almost stifled by what her father's palace stood for. Her father, King Drupad's palace represents all the previous versions of the Draupadi story which belittle her by misrepresenting her life. Enraged by such faulty constructions, Draupadi wants to tell not only her story but also that of others in the *Mahabharata*. This she wants to do to get away from the claustrophobia caused by demeaning narratives. Draupadi says that whenever she suffocates she would go to her nurse and "ask for a story". A story for her, and that too a story which is a re-vision of the earlier rendering, is like a whiff of fresh wind which will invigorate her. Her interest in listening to stories brings out her innate desire for fresh renderings because only multiple renderings will bring out the truth which, "like a diamond, has many facets" (55). Draupadi in *Yajnaseni* sees life as utterly meaningless, whereas Draupadi in *The Palace of Illusions* sees life as "a riot of color and sound" (7) because she is in control of the script of her life's story and so is in control of life itself. Making Draupadi script her own destiny within the parameters of her story in Vyasa's *Mahabharata*, Divakaruni adopts improvisation as a narrative strategy since improvisation is "... a means of going beyond the limitations imposed by the code of stylisation. It helps provide elements of surprise..." (K.Ayyappa Paniker 17).

Divakaruni surprises her readers by presenting a Draupadi who will effectively see through all faulty constructions through an alternative reading of her story. Reborn in *The Palace of Illusions*, leaving behind all her earlier constructions, particularly the one in *Yajnaseni*. Draupadi proves that "a story gains power with retelling" (20). The changes that Draupadi in *Yajnaseni* wanted to bring about in her life become a reality in *The Palace of Illusions*. The combination of vision, strength, boldness and determination, which Ray's Yajnaseni woefully lacks, is found in abundance in Divakaruni's Draupadi. By preferring improvisation to stylisation, Divakaruni suggests that Draupadi has a new lease of life or a new birth in which she climbs "upwards to full spiritual knowledge of our true immortal Selves or, in other words, to Adeptship..." (Geoffrey Hodson 45). This can be seen as an instance of transmigration.

Transmigration refers to the belief that in every birth the soul continues mental dispositions and Vasanas from all its previous births. So, picking up from where she stopped in *Yajnaseni*, Draupadi, in *The Palace of Illusions*, transcends limitations as well as weaknesses to surge forward and realize the limitless possibilities of the spirit. She becomes one with the universe having no "other" to fall in love with, to hate or to wreak vengeance upon. She sees the unity of all life which is the summum bonum of all life.

M. L. Varadpande in *Mahabharata in Performance* observes, "The expansion and the growth of the *Mahabharata* acquired new dimension when a corpus of literature based on the Mahabharata episodes started appearing independently of the epic" (15). Both Ray and Divakaruni draw upon selected incidents of the encyclopedic *Mahabharata* in their novels. They deal with incidents in which Draupadi plays a significant part or incidents which have a bearing on Draupadi's life and character. Thus, in a sense, the two novels can claim an existence independent of the epic, though they owe their origins to it. They use different narrative strategies in their works. Ray's novel is epistolary.

The story of the novel unfolds through a letter written by Draupadi to Krishna. In this letter Draupadi expresses her personality which comprises her feelings, thoughts, emotions and attitudes. It is a deeply personal account which enables Draupadi to articulate the unsung aspects of her life and to give vent to her frustration, anger, disappointments and sadness. That she writes this letter to Krishna shows that she shares her personal life only with her confidante Krishna. Through this letter she can only express her desires and dreams which remain unfulfilled throughout her life. It becomes one long letter of lamentation. The process of letter writing does not impel her to concrete and constructive action. Thus, Ray's Draupadi gets a chance, hitherto denied her, to express her emotional self and to raise questions about her existence. On the contrary, Draupadi in *The Palace of Illusions*, right from the beginning, is for concrete and constructive action. The story is not told to any single character. It locates its audience in a space extended beyond the frame of the novel. Choosing to tell the story of her life and of those related to her, Draupadi becomes aware that a "story is a slippery thing" (15) and that a single telling cannot render all the facets that lie embedded in the story. With this awareness, Draupadi makes allowances for other versions of the same story. But at the same time she does not tolerate misrepresentation of facts and uses her authorial consciousness to correct the slants. At a point in the novel, there is a shift in her perception – she is not interested in her own story anymore, but is trying to comprehend the nature of reality itself. This pursuit leads her to the realization that realities are constructed through language and that language itself is also a slippery thing. In the end Draupadi transcends these concerns and meditates on Reality and the means of comprehending It. This journey takes her beyond language and experience to become a witness in the realm of Pure Existence.

It is interesting to note the bold difference in the characterization of defiant Draupadi in the two novels, which can be exemplified by quoting a single line from each of the novels. The two lines reflect the attitude of the author in their interpretations, in different times. Pratibha Ray's Draupadi in *Yajnaseni: The Story of Draupadi* says:

> I became the subtle thread for keeping the five flowers bound together, whom no one would see; whose pain and anguish no one would know; word of whose torment would reach none (68).

By contrast, Chitra Banerjee Divakaruni's Draupadi in *The Palace of Illusions* says:

> If they were pearls, I was the gold wire on which they were strung. Alone, they would have scattered, each to his dusty corner (151).

This is the change that has been ushered in by Chitra Banerjee Divakaruni through her subject – Draupadi. Thus, every representation of Draupadi in various tellings of her story is like a block that goes to make up the final, but still evolving, structure – the archetypal Draupadi.

Works Cited

Banerjee Divakaruni, Chitra. *The Palace of Illusions*. London: Picador, 2008.

Badrinath, Chaturvedi. *The Women of the Mahabharata: The Question of Truth*. New Delhi: Orient Longman, (2008).

Bassnet, Susan and Harish Trivedi. *Post-Colonial Transformation*. London: Routledge, (1999).

Bhyrappa, S.L. *Parva*. trans. Ragavendra Rao, K. New Delhi: Sahitya Akademi, (1990).

Dandekar, R. N. ed. *The Mahabharata Revisited*. New Delhi: Sahitya Akademi, (1990).

Hodson, Geoffrey. *Through the Gateway of Death*. Chennai: The Theosophical Publishing House, (2000).

Langer, Susan K. *Feeling and Form*. New York: Scribners, (1953).

Matilal, Bimal Krishna. ed. *Moral Dilemmas in the Mahabharata*. Delhi: Motilal Banarsidass, (1989).

Paniker, Ayyappa K. *Indian Narratology*. New Delhi: Indira Gandhi National Centre for the Arts, Sterling Publishers Private Limited, (2003).

Ray, Pratibha.*Yajnaseni*. Trans. Pradip Bhattacharya. New Delhi: Rupa Books, (1995).

Sahu, Nandini. *The Position of Women in Oriya Literature*. http://www.boloji.com/women/099.htm.

Warrier, Anu. http://www.lokvani.com/lokvani/article.php?article_id=569.

Varadpande, M. L. *Mahabharata in Performance*. New Delhi: Clarion Books, (1990).

3

From 'Reading Myth' to 'Mythic Reading': Githa Hariharan's 'Re-vision' of Myths in *The Thousand Faces of Night.*

— Kaustav Chakraborty

> ...myths are both necessary and relevant to human lives, they come out of some human need.... We are looking for a fresh knowledge of ourselves in them, trying to discover what is relevant to our lives today. We don't reject the ideals, but we know we can't approximate to these pictures of ideal womanhood. And we will not bear any guilt that we cannot do so. More important than knowing what we are not is to know what we are, what is possible for us?
>
> (Shashi Deshpande "Stereotypes, Images and Realities")

> ...but as mythologies do not offer anything more positive, it has to be seen as a variation on demythologization, propounding its own myth as mythlessness
>
> (Laurence Coupe *Myth*)

One of the major components of postmodernism is the decannonization of all existing master codes, conventions, institutions and authorities. Both Feminism and Postmodernism have worked to make us understand the dominant modes of representation at work in our society. Cultural production is carried on within a social context and an ideology. If the personal is political, then the traditional separation between private and public history must be rethought. In other words, feminists have reconsidered both the context of historic narrative and the politics of representation. The critical stances of Feminists and Postmodernists are similar because both underline and undermine received notions of the represented subject. Feminism has refocused attention on the politics of representation and knowledge and also on power. Decolonization as a metaphor acquires multiple dimensions in postcolonial/ postmodern/ feminist writings. It means the need to liberate the self from all traditional structures. The dominant theme of contemporary women's fiction is 'Re-vision', i.e., the reconstruction of a new history and a private space as a way of grappling with patriarchy. "Re-vision is the act of looking back with fresh eyes, of entering an old text from a new critical direction," observes Marcia Landy, "For women, Re-vision is more than a chapter critical history; it is an act of survival." (18)

Re-vision, however, does not simply mean, "looking back" nor is it a mere "act of survival". Rather if refers to a re-visionist remaking of the past and re-invention of a new tradition so much so that it becomes an act of creation, transcreation. Regarding the 'Re-vision' of past Linda Hutcheon comments:

> The unevenly hung canvas backdrop calls attention to itself as *backdrop*, pointing to the entire photograph's existence as *Construction* - not as reflection - of woman as subject and also as object. By recalling the texts of the past - of literature or even of history - postmodern novels similarly use parody to question whether there can ever be such a thing as a final, definitive 'inscription' of selfhood or subjectivity in fiction. (8)

Mythology seems an inhospitable terrain for a woman writer In myths one finds not only deities of pure thought and spirituality who are superior to Mother Nature but also the sexually wicked Venus, Circe, Pandora, Medea, Eve etc. In *Managing Monsters: Six Myths of our Time* Marina Warner offers a history of myth in terms of its rereading, its rewriting, its re-creating. She is deeply conscious of the ambiguous power of stories: their capacity to enchant can be both life-affirming and destructive. Our obligation is to be both receptive and vigilant. Realising that myth is always going to be open to change, we must participate in the operation: "I believe the process of understanding and clarification ... can give rise to newly told stories, can sew and weave and knit different patterns into the social fabric and that this is a continuous enterprise for everyone to take part in" (Warner, xiv). What for Fredric Jameson is a source of regret, namely, the loss of a sense of originality and authenticity, is for her a sign of constant renewal, of cultural life. She states this clearly as follows: "Every telling of a myth is a part of that myth; there is no Ur-version, no authentic prototype, no true account". (Warner, 8). Again:

> Myths offer a lens which can be used to see human identity in its social and cultural context - they can lock us up in stock reactions, bigotry and fear, but they're not immutable, and by unpicking them, the stories can lead to others. Myths convey values and expectations which are always evolving, in the process of being formed, but - and this is fortunate - never set so hard they cannot be changed again. (Warner 14)

That is a fair summary of the principle that we call, radical typology. We must trust, we are told, in the very power of myth to change and, in the process, to change us. 'Intertextuality' is not the problem but the solution, if positively understood. For, unlike Levi-Strauss and Barthes, she does not believe that myth is something that happens behind our backs, as it were: she insists that we have the capacity, as tellers and retellers, interpreters and reinterpreters, to maintain the interaction of myth and history.

In order to achieve these goals, Indian feminist writers have exerted their energies to deconstruct the past, reconstruct a more meaningful present. They have unraveled the thick tapestries of male hegemony and analyzed the reasons for the persistent reproduction of conscious and unconscious presumptions about women and they have knitted up a woman's tradition. They have also made a study of sexual difference of what is 'male' and what is 'female'. In such a venture, the postmodernist inquiry with its exploration of the pluralistic implications of a universal culture becomes meaningful. Women writers have come to resort to more subtle (feminine) strategies of (re)naming and (re)affirming their identities. They have sought to expose the mechanisms of their misrepresentation by restoring their past, generating accurate representations for the present and by projecting their equivocal future. According to the postmodernists, the ambition of antiquity to legitimize myth by reference to metaphysical foundations must be interrogated and nullified. But so must the ambition of modernity, to discredit myth by reference to scientific foundations. Richard Kearney has summarized Gianni Vattimo's alternative, his postmodernist mythopoeia, which involves,

> retaining myth as a secular interplay of multifaceted meanings; an interplay which dramatizes our cultural memories and traditions as historical interpretations rather than idolizing them as timeless dogmas. The postmodern 'overcoming' of myth which Vattimo counsels...proposes to salvage myth in the transposed form of an ironically distanced or diluted reinterpretation. By not taking itself too seriously (that is, literally), myth can be taken seriously once again. Whence the curious paradox: it is precisely when the modern cult of 'demythization' is itself unmasked as a myth (an Enlightenment myth of absolute Reason) that the mythic imaginary can recover its legitimacy. But this legitimacy resides in the very acknowledgement of the limits of myth—its inherent modesty and faibless*e* as an experience of truth. The weakness of myth is its strength. Its disclaimer to absolute truth is its claim to partial truth—the only kind we, as finite historical interpreters, can ever presume to possess. (Kearney 183-84)

Modest as the scope of myth now is, it may yet overcome the modernist "opposition between rationalism and irrationalism" and thereby open the way to a new kind of thought (Vattimo 43). Kearney relates this suggestion to Ricoeur's 'poetics of the possible', and give regards both to Vattimo and Ricoeur for opening up an 'ethics of possible':

> Postmodernism, understood in Vattimo's sense of a non-foundational and non-functionalist theory of interpretation, solicits an ethical task of remembering that is not a simple repetition of tradition but its joyous recreation. Such remembering emancipates tradition from servile conformism, transposing it into a historical transmission

of overtures to possible modes of being-in-the-world.

(Kearney 185-86)

That is, the very act of remembering and recreating the sacred narratives of the past in secular, aesthetic terms, as has been done by the Postmodern Feminists, would turn into an act of emancipation: not in the Enlightenment sense of rational progress, but in a new spirit of 'ludic imagining'. While Kearney does not elaborate this 'ethics of possible' here, we can infer from the rest of his argument that it is an ethics of 'otherness'. The Postmodern Feminists recalling of the myths first projects an 'other' world. Secondly, the myths reminds us that there is always something else, something 'other', to be said or imagined. Finally the reinterpretation of the myths from Postmodern Feminist standpoint, as a play of past paradigm and future possibility, gives expression to this 'other'. Postmodern Feminism then is an epistemology that justifies knowledge claims only in so far as they arise from a violation of the universalist and the homogenized assumptions about women. It dwells on the politics of 'difference'.

In the fictional world of Githa Hariharan we see a multilayering of postmodern - feminist differences. What her feminist writings bring out is that subjected to a multitude of forces, often contradictory, the women in India not unlike women elsewhere, have begun to move toward self-perception, self-expression and self-determination, slowly indeed and not entirely against tradition, but within the family bindings. The western concepts of equality, individual rights and personal choice would challenge and dismantle the Indian family structure, which is based on sharing and accommodation. Githa Hariharan's fictions dwell on this "difference" of postmodern feminism. Her first Commonwealth award-winning novel *The Thousand Faces of Night* may be read as revisionist myth-making programme in which the novelist attempts to renew the whole community of women through representation of myths.

Myths always need retelling and reinterpreting, and the women's movement, feminist and post-feminist, has made striking contributions to this process. Some of the most important acts of mythic reading inspired by the women's movement in India have been works of fiction. In the novel *The Thousand Faces of Night*, mythopoeia (forging new possibilities of narrative of women) and mythography (interrogating the dominant male narrative) are brilliantly achieved at the same time. While comprehending the text, the readers will move from 'reading myth' to 'mythic reading': that is, from the interpretation of the Indian myths to the readjusting and thereby remaking of myths for feminist missions.

The Thousand Faces of Night could be described as, what Malashri Lal calls "a narrative of split consciousness" (109). She maintains that there is a paradigm of the 'Law of the threshold' in the Indian context that implies a strong sense of the 'inside' and 'out there'. She adds that men have partaken of both the worlds. The law allows 'multiple existences' for men, a single for women and 'a step over the bar is an act of transgression. She observes that "women have long been complicit in such gendered roles" (Lal 109).

After spending a few years in America, Devi comes to India to live with Sita, her widowed mother. While returning home she had to leave behind the memories of Dan, a black American, for a better life in India which her mother promises she surely would find. The main story of her life is written by Devi herself and into this frame a number of other stories are incorporated; the legends of the mythical heroines narrated to Devi by her grandmother; the stories of wives of saints and other pativratas recounted to Devi by her father-in-law and real life experiences of actual women either observed by Devi directly or narrated to her by her housekeeper Mayamma.

> This commonplace story of marital discord and woman's quest for identity outside marriage is turned into a remarkable rendering of the collective struggle of women for self-liberation through the author's play with narrative structures—framing texts within texts, with texts overlapping in curious ways; her carnivalesque accumulation of intertexts ranging from the tales from the *Mahabharatha* to folk stories and her deft interweaving of these with the lives of real women. Hariharan's narrative voices strike a powerful chord in contemporary literature

> returning to the multi-dimensional vibration of voices unfolding within a vast mythic social time space.
>
> (Vijayasree 177)

Devi becomes familiar with God-like heroes and heroines from the stories of her grandmother. In her adolescence Devi had listened to her grandmother's stories, which were drawn from the *Ramayana* and the *Mahabharata*. Their focus was on women's pride, destiny and self-sacrifice. She listened to her narration of Gandhari, Amba, Ambika and Ambalika. They were a prelude to her womanhood, an initiation into subterranean possibilities. Gandhari had blindfolded herself as a subservient wife because her husband was blind. Perhaps the other aspect of Gandhari's blindfold was her protest against an injustice imposed on her (by getting her married to the blind king Dhritarashtra). Her mind rebelled against seeing more and more injustices in the rest of her life. Devi draws a poetic equivalent of Gandhari's blindfoldedness with that of her own parents:

> In their blinkered world they would always be one, one leading the other, one hand always in the grip of other. (29)

Devi's grandmother's narration is a kind of revisionist myth-making in its own right - she does not dwell only on the more prominent figures of the Hindu myths — Sita, Savitri or Anasuya—often celebrated as paragons of female virtue. She retrieves marginal figures like Gandhari, Amba and Ganga. When Devi questions her grandmother about her mother Sita who is seen holding a veena in her hand in a photograph, the latter tells her the story of Gandhari. Gandhari is an example of a woman who turns her anger against herself. Gandhari, the mythical figure in *Mahabharata,* was given in marriage to the Prince of Hastinapur, Dhritarashtra. Though initially she was impressed by the refinement of culture and riches of the people of Hastinapur, later she became very angry on knowing that she was married to a blind man. In her anger she tore off a piece of cloth and tied it tightly over her eyes. "She embraced her destiny - a blind husband -with a self-sacrifice worthy of her royal blood" *(Night* 29). Devi's mother Sita resembles

Gandhari. She skilfully plays veena and is also well trained as a daughter-in-law. One day the same music invites the anger of her father-in-law when he finds all things undone in the prayer room. In her anger Sita pulls away the strings of her veena and never plays it again in her life. She cuts herself off from the link with the past in order to be a perfect housekeeper, a blameless wife. The attainment of these goals too is rather superficial, as over the years of her intense struggle, Sita has distanced herself from her "dreamer" husband and "elusive" daughter. The story told to Devi by her grandmother reads like this:

> Then one day, my husband sat in front of the gods, ready for his morning prayers. He couldn't find a thing he needed. The flowers had not been picked, the floor had not been swept. "Sita", he called, his voice trembling with anger. She did not hear him, but from her room we heard the sound of the veena in rapturous flight.
>
> I put down my knife in the kitchen and hurried to her room. But he got there first, and I heard him roar, "Put that Veena away. Are you a wife, a daughter-in-law?"
>
> Sita hung her head over the Veena for a minute that seemed to stretch for ages, enveloping us in an unbearable silence. Then she reached for the strings of her precious Veena and pulled them out of the wooden base ....
>
> She looked at my husband, her eyes dry and narrowed, and said in a clear, stinging whisper, "Yes, I am a wife, daughter-in-law."
>
> We never saw her touch the Veena again. She became a dutiful daughter-in-law the neighbour praised, and our household never heard the heart rending music again. (30)

Devi finds this self-effacement of her mother meaningless. She expresses her anger in these words:

> Gandhari's anger wrapped tightly round her head in a life long blindfold, burnt in a heart close, very close to mine. (29)

She further confesses:

> The lesson that was more difficult to digest was human anger, that it could seep into every pore of a womanly body and become the very blood stream of her life. (29)

Another figure in the *Mahabharata* who could be regarded as the incarnation of penance is Amba. When Bhishma went to Kashi he heard of a Swayamvara at the king's palace. He went to the palace to get a girl for his stepbrother, Vichitravirya. He abducted all the three beautiful princesses, Amba, Ambika and Ambalika from the swayamvara. Nobody could stop them including the King of Salwa who was about to be garlanded by the elder princess Amba. Devi questioned her grandmother why they did not stop him. Her grandmother answered, "Once he (Bhishma) had laid his manly hands on her shoulders, Devi, she was no longer a girl. A woman fights her battles alone" (*Night* 36). Amba pleaded with Bhishma to let her go but the king of Salwa rejected her saying that it was Bhishma who had a rightful claim over her as he had won them all in the Swayamvara. Amba returned to Bhishma and asked him to marry her but he rejected her because he had taken the vow of celibacy. She took offence and with the desire to take revenge on him went to the forest to perform penance. Shiva, pleased with her penance, touched her garland and promised her that whoever wore it and fought Bhishma in a battle would be able to kill him. She threw the garland around a pillar in King Drupada's court and went to the forest to meet her death. She was born again as Drupada's daughter Shikhandi. She was brought up as a son and later at the Battle of Kurukshetra she wore Amba's garland and went to the battle to see Bhishma's death. Devi parallels Amba's story with Uma's story, who is Devi's cousin and a common girl. Uma gets married into an affluent family. On one occasion, Uma's father-in-law in a drunken condition kisses her on her lips. She comes away from that house to stay with her grandmother till the old woman's death. Uma is unlike Amba since she does not have her fighting spirit.

The mythical stories become so much a part of her life that Devi thinks of herself as the very incarnation of all the avenging deities. If at all she is wronged she would be the mythical Devi-like avenger. The illusory life of Devi comes to an end when she is married off to Mahesh after her return from America. Some of the grandmother's stories have presented an idyllic world; the story of Nala and Damayanti that Devi heard from her grandmother in her childhood proves to be a lie when she is faced with a 'Swayamvara' of another kind. The mythical 'Swayamvara' of Nala and Damayanti measured against the tribulation of a girl displayed/ exhibited as commodity to the prying eyes of the prospective groom and his family, is reduced to a travesty/mendacity. In grandmother's tale, the 'Swayamvara' of Nala and Damayanti, is imbued with a dream-like quality in its perfection, "The morning of the 'Swayamvara' the sun shone more brightly than usual" (18). Damayanti, fragrant and dazzlingly beautiful entered the portals, garland in hand, to choose her mate among the brave men assembled there. Damayanti took certain steps towards Nala, the king of Nishadas and chose him above all else, and they united in love. Grandmother's tales were resplendent with princesses waiting to be joined in love with a noble prince in a happy ending. Such tales conjure an elusive world of flawlessness, where doubts, fears, questionings, the intrusions of the real world are attenuated. The story of the romantic love of Nala and Damayanti, heard in her childhood, resurfaces in Devi's consciousness when she grows up to realise that "the princesse's robe" that her grandmother had so lovingly stitched for her is "frayed round the edge and two sizes too large." Set against the idyllic image evoked by the grandmother's stories, the reality confronted by Devi is a degrading charade of 'Swayamvara', demeaning her self-respect and self-worth.Mahesh has an executive job and enormous riches. When Devi wishes to take up a job, he says that a woman has much work to do at home as he cannot accept her liberty. Mahesh thinks that marriage is only "a necessity, a milestone like any other. It's a gamble" (*Night* 49). Devi feels cheated like Gandhari, slighted like Amba. She seeks solace in the presence of her father-in-law Baba, a retired Sanskrit scholar, who tells her few stories that are supplementary to her grandmother's stories. "Her stories were a prelude to my womanhood, an initiation into its subterranean possibilities. His define the limits. His stories are for a woman... an exacting touchstone for a woman, a wife" (*Night* 51).

Baba tells her the story of Muthuswamy Dikshitar who had two wives. Dikshitar's second wife asked for jewellery to match her beauty. He said that when the goddess Lakshmi was with him, why should he care for unworthy mortals. The same night goddess Ambika, in her glittering jewellery come in her dream. Overwhelmed with the sight of the goddess she forgets her desire for ornaments. The story is intended to show how a woman subdues her wishes for the sake of her husband. Baba's stories are replete with legends and anecdotes about womanly sacrifice and fortitude how the wives of great saints by their self-effacement had spurred them along the path of 'Dharma.'

Jayadeva's wife Padmavati was blessed with the visitations of Lord Krishna who had restored the immortal lines "Dehi Padapallava Mudaram" in the manuscript of Githa Govinda, initially struck off by Jayadeva believing it to be sacrilegious. Purandara Das, a saintly composer, was a wealthy tradesman before he was converted to life of devotion because of a selfless act of his wife. Narayan Tirtha could embrace a life of an ascetic because of his wife's self-denying nature. In Baba's mythology, a virtuous wife dies before her husband, a 'sumangala,' the mark of vermilion illumining her forehead. The wives of Shymashastri, Thyagaraja, are emblematic of this tradition where women are venerated only when they accept self-denial and trap/mould themselves into the roles stipulated for them.

Though Baba himself is no villain—in fact he appears to be a good man by any standards—his stories are instruments of oppressive socialization and 'conditioning' imposed on women. The categories of devoted wife and pure woman have been culturally internalized - the virtue of a woman is tested by the normative behaviour of Sita or Savitri. There has been in epics and myths a systematic devaluation of women under patriarchy. Baba's stories elaborate these role definitions based on gender and the tendency of worshipping or valorizing women when they submit to these gender specific roles. Devi is exposed to the taboos and conventions of a traditional society, especially of a Brahminical order, through her father-in-law's stories: "His (stories) define the limits. His stories are for women who have already reached the goal that will determine the guise her virtue will wear" (*Night* 51).

Devi finds solace in the story of Mayamma, the old housekeeper in Mahesh's house. She narrates the story of her own life, which is a tale of tears and traumatic experiences. She is forced to undergo ten years of penance to get a son but the son grows into a wastrel son. Finally he dies. Mayamma then learns the strategies of survival and as she herself puts it, "I have learnt how to wait, when to bend by back, when to wipe the rebellious eyes dry" *(Night* 126).

Devi's interest in life is renewed with the arrival of Gopal, a classical singer. She decides to move out of the house of Mahesh "seeking a goddess who is not yet made" (*Night* 95). She accompanies Gopal's troop but, as months pass, she no longer enjoys his concerts and becomes restless of this life too. Her initial fascination for Gopal wanes since she discovers that he is a flirt. Her life has come full circle with Devi choosing to come back to her mother to begin her life afresh. As she nears her house, she hears the music of a veena. Sita plays the veena for her self-satisfaction and waits for Devi to return to her. Sita too is reborn as she retrieves her lost self by returning to her music. As Vijayasree points out:

> The mothers of Devi's rebirth are, thus, manifold. Besides her mentors, there are many other women whose lives offer new and useful lessons to Devi. She draws on her biological matrilineage as well as well as spiritual and mythical heritage. The invisible energies of the ancient goddesses—Devi, Kali and Saraswathi among others—as well as genetic inheritance from all women who lived in the past ages and experiential wisdom of her own contemporaries—all these contribute to the eventual psycho-spiritual growth of the protagonist. (181)

Devi ultimately identifies herself with Durga, the goddess who is the destroyer of evil. She says:

> I lived a secret life of my own. I became a woman warrior, a heroic. I was Devi. I rode a tiger, and cut off evil, magical demon's heads. (41)

The ferocious and awe-inspiring image of *Kritya* is also evoked in her psyche. She says:

> I read about a *Kritya*, ferocious woman who haunts and destroys the house in which women are insulted. She burns with anger, she spits fire. She sets the world ablaze like *Kali* shouting in hunger. Each age has its *Kritya*, in the age of *Kali*, I read, each household shutter's a *Kritya*. (69-70)

Devi feels that throughout her life she has "stumbled on stage alone, greedy for a story of 'her' own" (157), and now the time has come when she has "to stay and fight, to make a sense of it all" (139).

In order to break the pressure of cultural politics in the form of the dominance of gender ideology, Githa Hariharan has taken it upon herself to deconstruct the past and thereby reconstruct a more meaningful present. Warner has warned us of the fact that:

> a myth shows something, it's a story spoken to a purpose, it issues a warning, it gives an account which advises and tells often by bringing into play showings of fantastical shape and invention - monsters. Myths define enemies and aliens and in conjuring them up they say who we are and what we want, they tell stories to impose structure and order.
>
> (Warner 19)

Githa Hariharan has resorted to subtle postmodern strategies in order to expose misrepresentation of women in patriarchal mythical culture thereby generating accurate representations for the present. Bhargava terms such texts as 'fencing texts':

> Indian women writer's texts are 'fencing texts' where not only does the narrator want to sit on a fence that demarcates fields of perception, but more importantly from where she likes to fence—to be clad with gauntlets and masks, equivalents of irony and subtexts and flick out at the opponent with fast, deft, disguised strength and precise grace. The fencer should love the choreography of the game (the technique).... Anger is a necessary foil in Indian women's narratives—the middle passage between suffering and healing, between passivity and activity,

> between fear and forgiveness. Rage inspires movements, silence announces death, but anger keeps one alive and thus the question of a 'self' trying to find itself is kept alive in our writings
>
> (Bhargava 77)

In both her novels and short stories, Githa Hariharan erodes the age-old wisdom contained in mythologies. Her anger expresses itself through the mode of satire, irony, 're-vision' interrogation and 'inversion'. Her vision encompasses the whole history of women's role and edifies the emergence of a new woman who is true to her own self. The struggle for self still remains vital for women as an ideal to be achieved— through persistent mythography and mythopoeia.

Works Cited

Bhargava, Rajul. "Infidel Heteroglossia? Postmodern Feminist Configuration in Githa Hariharan's *The Art of Dying*" ed. Rajul Bhargava *Indian Writing in English: The Last Decade* New Delhi: Rawat Publication, 2002.

Hariharan, Githa. *The Thousand Faces of Night*. New Delhi: Penguin Books, 1992.

Hutcheon, Linda. *The Canadian Postmodern: A Study of Contemporary Canadian Fiction.* Toronto University Press, 1988.

Kearney, Richard. *Poetics of Imagining: From Husserl to Lyotard*, London: Harper Collins, 1991.

Lal, Malashri. "Writing the Self: Indian Women Writers in English". *Literature and Ideology*.ed Veene Singh. Rawat Publishers: Jaipur, 1999.

Landy, Marcia. "The Silent Woman", *The Authority of Experience:Essays in Feminist Criticism.* ed. Aflyn Diamond & Lee Edwards. Amherst: University of Massachusetts Press, 1977.

Ricoeur, Paul. 'Myth and History', *Encyclopedia of Religion*, ed M. Eliade, new York and London: Macmillan, 1987.

Vattimo, Gianni. *The Transparent Society*, Cambridge: Polity Press, 1992.

Vijayasree, C. "Revisionist Myth-Making: A Reading of Githa Hariharan's *The Thousand Faces of Night*". *The Postmodern Indian English Novel: Interrogating the 1980's & 1990's* ed. Viney Kripal Bombay: Allied Publishers, 1996.

Warner, Marina. *Managing Monsters: Six Myths of our Time*, London:Vintage, 1994.

4

Of Academics, Travellers and Wars: The *Dastaan* of India—A Reading of Qurratulain Hyder's *River of Fire*

— V. Padma

Qurratulain Hyder's Urdu novel *Aag ka Dariya* was first published in 1959 and immediately became something of a landmark novel in modern Urdu literature. Hailed for its non-linear narrative and its ambitious project of narrating nearly 4,000 years of India's cultural and political history, it was translated by the author herself into English as *River of Fire* in 1998—nearly 40 years after the 'original' was published. The English version did not create as many ripples as did the Urdu one—possibly because it came out at a time when English fiction from India was already involved in the ambitious project of rewriting Indian history and 'correcting' British/colonial representations. Perhaps the fact that the translation came out at a time when non-linear narratives—especially historical narratives—had almost become the norm in what was increasingly and swiftly becoming a formidable body of writing that fused history and fiction also contributed to the relative non-presence of *River of Fire* except in the form of reviews or essays in anthologies.

River of Fire is noteworthy for many reasons – like many Indian novels that were published in the 1980s and 1990s, it 'rewrote' Indian history, but its scope was much vaster than most other texts of the period. The method in which it chose to rewrite Indian history too marks it out as significant as does the image of India that it presents. It is also noteworthy that in a thematic field like historical revisioning which was largely a male-centred one, Hyder's is one of the few female voices. It is from largely these perspectives that this essay will read *River of Fire*.

I

Politically and culturally, the last two decades of the previous century witnessed a somewhat dual movement in India. On the one hand were the various regional and local voices clamouring to be heard while on the other, were the nationalist, homogenizing discourses that sought to subsume these multiple voices into the overarching metanarrative of nationalism. The same movement can be observed in the literature and criticism of the period too. A number of texts, many in English, sought to stress their 'Indianness' by returning to pauranic historiographical narrative modes that so blatantly flouted the norms of the European realist tradition. The non-local, nationalist discourse that this grand narrative structure appeared to valorise was countered by the many petit historical narratives focusing on smaller communities (like the Kammavar community in *The Gopallapuram Chronicles* or the Parsi community in *The Memory of Elephants*). These little narratives, often but not always subversive, posit an India that offers space for dissident voices without denying the need for nationalist discourses. In other words, they offer a space where the two seemingly opposite and mutually exclusive discourses can cohabit.

The English literary scene in India in the 1980s and 1990s was characterized by a spate of novels that are today characterized as 'postcolonial.' Though the term is much criticized today, the period under discussion was one when it was marking its space out in the academic world. Hence, novels written in any former colony willy-nilly became part of the 'postcolonial' tradition. Texts like Rushdie's *Midnight's Children* published in 1981 and dealing with 'stock' postcolonial themes were critically clubbed along with earlier texts like Raja Rao's

Kanthapura that dealt with similar issues and themes. Critics like Gayatri Spivak and Homi Bhabha (although they wrote and published from outside India) and Harish Trivedi, G.N. Devy, Meenakshi Mukherjee etc. further canonized the postcolonial model of reading and writing texts. That writers like Rushdie and Amitav Ghosh also wrote critical work contesting or concurring with the postcolonial model further consolidated the postcolonial critical method. The institution of awards like the Commonwealth Writers' Award further helped in institutionalizing the postcolonial canon of critical and creative works.

Among the thematic concerns of 'postcolonial' literature were the impacts of colonialism on the colonized and the rewriting of colonized history. That both of these were from the perspective of the colonized in a bid to regain lost narrative space is today too passé an idea to need elucidation. Hence, an influential novel like Salman Rushdie's *Midnight's Children* sought to rewrite a little of pre-independence and a chunk of post-independence Indian history from the point of view of an Indian (it is another important thematic matter that this 'Indian' turns out to be an Anglo-Indian brought up in a Muslim household and is married to a Hindu) just as Vikram Chandra's *Red Earth an Pouring Rain* published at least ten years later dealt almost similarly with colonial Indian history (it is again another thematic matter that this 'Indian' is also an Anglo-Indian with magical antecedents).

Postcolonial criticism has focused not merely on 'what' history has been re-written, but also on 'how' this has been done. With increasing awareness that historiography is not the innocent, disinterested discipline it was long taken to be, the metanarrative that is used, consciously or otherwise, to order historical facts has been much critiqued. That the use of such a metanarrative has deep implications for the image of the 'nation' that emerges from these novels is again a common enough critical idea today. Perhaps Rushdie's comment regarding the narrative structure of *Midnight's Children* best captures this; he insists that this plural narrative structure is necessary for capturing the 'too-muchness' that is an integral part of Indian culture.

This also introduces the idea of representation of an 'authentic' India. Often, English texts dealing with Indian history face the charge of homogenizing Indian culture and disregarding local variations and voices. This homogenization is often seen to go hand in hand with the method of narration used. The cyclical, non-linear, jack-in-the-box narrative structure adopted by many English novels of the period has been linked by critics and the writers themselves to Classical Pauranic narratives that similarly fused history, mythology and legend. This narrative structure, though potentially plural and having the capacity to include subversive, contradictory voices is nevertheless associated with a homogenized classical metanarrative that posits India as a space where the colonial encounter ruptured a 'pure' culture. The focus on themes like colonial encounter, the changes in 'Indian culture' due to this encounter, the problems with the English language and European narrative models encouraged by early postcolonial criticism forged an image of India as a nation whose culture before the coming of the British (and in many historical narratives, the Muslims) was pristine. Fiction in these cases was used to recreate such a space. Although the subversive voice was ever-present, critical commentary on many canonical postcolonial texts tended to rather ignore them. Hence, very few critical materials on *Midnight's Children* have focused on Salim Sinai being an Anglo-Indian, a community that virtually came into existence during the British rule and that sometimes by its very existence, questioned the binaries of colonizer-colonised. The same can be said for Vikram Chandra's *Red Earth and Pouring Rain*. Despite the novel very obviously having three broad strands, all dealing with various periods of Indian history in different narrative modes, critical commentary has focused on Sanjay's story, possibly because it deals with the colonial period and also because it is written in the pauranic mode so much a favourite with the postcolonial model.

In contrast to all these, *River of Fire* posits an India where the very notion of a 'pure' India is always suspect. Indian culture is seen to have always been 'on the move,' never stagnant; to have always been in contact with other, alien cultures; to have always been in dialogue with them; it also acknowledges that this dialogue is often violent, drawing unsuspecting victims into itself. Implicitly, it also questions the centrality of the colonial period in modern Indian history, thereby deflating one of the earliest assumptions of the postcolonial critical model. It is in this context that the vast sweep of the novel needs to be read.

II

River of Fire has four broad strands. The first one, set in Magadhan India, portrays the cultural changes that occurred in the country because of the coming of Budhism and Jainism. From here, the novel takes us through Islamic India and British colonial India to the Independence struggle and the Partition of 1947. Some of the motifs that run across the four large historical strands of the novel are introduced right in the first part – characters such as the academic, the traveller and the artist, women in love who wait and love that is at the mercy of historical events. Running across and cutting through these motifs are ordinary lives that are affected to various degrees by historical events over which they have no control. If these motifs cut across 4,000 years of Indian history, so do the names of people to whom these events happen – Gautam Nilambar, Champa, Nirmala, Kamal, Cyril – appear in almost all the stories. The Hindu student and the Hindu women are present right from the first section while Kamal, representing the Islamic community comes in later and Cyril Ashley, a Christian, comes in even later. How long they have lived in India, however, in no way decides their 'Indianness.' Kamal, in the second section, towards the end of his life when he is arrested for 'originally' being a non-native laments:

> He had no quarrel with the Afghans or the Mughals, he merely wished to be left alone . . . This was his country, his children had been born here, his dear wife lay buried here. He had put all his energy into making these fields bloom, spent years beautifying the language these men were speaking. He had written songs and collected stories and he was going to continue living here. No one had any right to call him an outsider or a traitor.
>
> (*River of Fire* 102)

The suspicion with which any 'outsider' – human or idea – is seen is brought out here in all its pathos.

The India that emerges from *River of Fire* is a country that has always been a site of cultural dialogue; if at times, the dialogue becomes a clash and even violent, the fact in no way makes a difference to the fact that the existing 'Indian' culture has been transformed by this new culture. Whether it is the 'traditional' Indian culture meeting Buddhism or Islamic culture or the British one, *River of Fire* foregrounds the fact that the evolution of Indian culture has been a process of an almost dialectic dialogue between what existed and what 'came in' from outside. In the process, both the host and the guest cultures underwent changes. Hence, we have Kamal in the second strand of the novel asserting how 'native' he has become, ("… he had started thinking of himself as a Hindustani. He was no longer a Viklayati." (*River of Fire* 87)); just as Buddhism had become an inextricable part of 'Indian culture' in the first strand.

This is not to claim that *River of Fire* is the only, or even one of the few novels that portrays this dialogue as an integral part of Indian culture. However, it *is* unique in that it is devoid of any sense of nostalgia for a pre-contact, 'pristine' culture. This 'nostalgia' we might remember was a staple of much postcolonial criticism and fiction. What Hyder's novel portrays rather, is the inevitability of such an interaction and dialogue.

In this context, we need to also note the time during which both the Urdu and the English versions of the novel came out. 1959, we may remember was a few years after independence and Partition; it was the time when the two newly independent nations were consolidating their national identity. This 'national identity' was, perhaps inevitably, seen in terms of a 'pure,' singular national-cultural identity. 1998, the time when the translation was published saw India in a similar cultural situation. Cultural nationalism was fast becoming monological and homogenizing. Notwithstanding dissenting and subversive voices, this homogenizing voice was getting louder. The suspicion of outside voices, the large number of reported and unreported ethnic and communal clashes that rocked the nation during this time is evidence of this.

It was amidst this that *River of Fire* voiced a notion of India as a place where a search for a 'pristine,' 'pure' culture was a futile task. For the cultural-political entity called India as we know it today was always and already an amalgam of dissenting and assenting cultures and voices.

Therefore, the repetitive nature of the novel in terms of its themes, motifs and names of its characters is significant – for it helps underscore the timelessness of the plurality and dialogic nature of Indian culture. While a number of critical readings of the *River of Fire* have noted its resemblance to Gabriel Garcia Marquez's *One Hundred Years of Solitude* in terms of its treatment of time and its repetition of names of characters, both these features are inextricably linked to the image of the nation that Hyder's novel projects.

If therefore, Gautam Nilambar, a Hindu student and part of what may be called 'mainstream culture', in the first strand exclaims, "I am not interested in King Nanda, Vishnu Sharma and Chandragupta. Why must they drag me into their conflict?" (*River of Fire* 39), the same sentiments are echoed by Kamal in the passage already quoted. The flow of history is relentless and in a multiple, multicultural country like India, it is all the more so, making the concept of a pristine, pre-contact Indian culture a myth. Both in its Urdu version and in its English translation therefore, the novel offers an almost subversive view of Indian culture – one that accepts, without judging, the many strands that go into its making.

This pluralistic vision of Indian culture is also presented in a way very different from what the English reading public of the 1990s was used to. As already noted, critical commentary had tended to foreground pauranic narratives as perhaps the only possible alternative to the European historiographical model. That this pauranic narrative model had deep affinities with the postmodern narrative form made it all the more significant. This importance given to the pauranic mode has tended also to obscure other narrative modes like the 'everyday historiography' that the *Gopallapuram Chronicles* uses. In this context, *River of Fire* is significant in its use of the Persian *dastaan* mode of historiography narration.

Today largely associated with the romance mode, the *dastaan* as a mode is ornate, oral history. Used in Persia and many central Asian countries, the *dastaan* mode narrated the trials of a single hero in getting independence for his tribe / community. J. B. Paksoy's studies, especially his very useful "The Dastan Genre in Central Asia," itemize the various features of a dastaan – among them the travails of the hero, the help he receives on his way and the fate of his tribe resting on him. Paksoy further brings out the political importance of the *dastaan* mode. He points out that the *dastaan* was the storehouse of the identity of the tribe. While the content of existing *dastaans* was strictly guarded, newer *dastaans* could emerge only under two situations – either when a hero achieved something great enough to have a *dastaan* written about him, or when the identity of the tribe / community was gravely threatened. The dastaan was thus the means of consolidating the identity of the community. The subversive nature of the *dastaans* is nowhere better evident than in the ban imposed on the creation of new dastaans and on anthologizing older ones by the Stalinist regime in the USSR:

> . . . dastans were collected by the authorities in order to be hidden away; reciters were killed . . . . Many paid with their lives. The message of that era was, once again, freedom. ("The Dastan Genre in Central Asia" 6)

It is this use of *dastaan* to consolidate national identity at times of crisis that we need to focus on. In the light of the monological, nationalist discourses threatening to subsume the plurality of India, a new 'dastaan' was needed that would stress the essentially multiple nature of Indian culture. This is a *dastaan* that cannot, by force of its theme, have a single hero—it has to narrate several stories and it has to narrate them across centuries. Hence, *River of Fire* insists that Indian culture is a plural entity and necessarily interweaves various narratives: "There are many ways of telling a *dastaan*," says Talat. "How shall I begin? I don't know which characters are more important. Where did this story start? What was the climax?" (*River of Fire* 184). There is no single 'hero' whose exploits are celebrated in the novel; it is Indian culture itself that faces oppression and opposition, but emerges resilient precisely because of its ability to be inclusive. Hence, the epic sweep of the novel. Hence also our reading that Hyder's novel transforms both the traditional and literary idea of Indian culture as well as the form of the dastaan itself.

What binds this plurality is the idea of history as a relentless force affecting and being affected by nameless and countless people in its way. It is not mere a narrative extravagance that so much space time is spent intermittently in the novel on historical developments in other countries like Spain and the Middle East. History is the binding force; binding and separating lives, bringing lovers together and separating them, taking people tantalizingly towards a new home and leaving them insecure there. The cyclical and repetitive nature of history is merely reinforced by the repetition of character names and the situations they see themselves in.

III

It is this constantly moving and changing history that makes possible the country called 'India.' While postcolonial criticism has looked at the problematics of the 'notion of nation,' and has spent considerable time on what constitutes 'India,' it has tended to see India largely as an imaginative entity brought into being by the Grand Narratives of nationalism and national development. *River of Fire,* while not overtly contesting the idea of the nation as, to use Benedict Anderson's famous coinage, an 'imagined community,' nevertheless brings out the fact the 'nation' is an important construct especially in times of historical and cultural crisis. It is in this context that the image of India as a plural nation where cultures and ideologies are constantly in dialogue with each other becomes significant.

However, for this dialogue to take place, physical mobility of people is an important precondition. People have to move from a place of one idea / culture to another to even become aware of the existence of the other culture. This physical mobility is again something that postcolonial criticism in its treatment of the diaspora has foregrounded. However, while the focus there is on the psychological, emotional and physical problems faced by the diasporic community, *River of Fire* sees this travel across and between cultures as something positive—notwithstanding the problems it creates at an individual level, this movement has brought ideas and news from other countries to India and these have made possible further changes in the cultural fabric of India.

In this context, the figure of the academic becomes important – s/he travels across lands, is open to 'other' ideas and is therefore able to sift the news s/he gets from other places and is also youthful. Gautam Nilambar in the first strand, Rubiya is the second, and all the young people in the last strand are students. Historically, we may remember, students' uprisings have had deep political and cultural impacts— the 1968 agitation in France and in America in the same year are notable. The former – much talked about – wrought important changes in the political and academic culture in Europe while the latter asked for and succeeded in getting Ethnic Studies as an accepted academic discipline in American Universities.

In *River of Fire*, it is the figure of the student who allows for cultural dialogue. The philosophical discussions between Gautam and the absconding prince in the first strand, and that between Kamal and Rubiya in the second introduce important points of contemporary debates such as the impact of Buddhism and Jainism on Indian culture and the importance of education for women, and show how these issues have caused important changes in what we may term 'Indian culture.'

Along with the character of the student is that of the traveller – Kamal in the second strand and Cyril in the third are all travellers to the 'fabled land of Hindostan.' They travel for a number of reasons – to gain knowledge, for business and for adventure – but their travel allows them to enter into dialogue with the existing culture. Kamal, for instance, is asked to translate Sanskrit texts into Persian. Together, students and travelers consolidate the concept of 'India' as a nation. Debates about 'what' India is enter the text right from the first strand—questions like what is 'Bharatvarsha' and 'Hindostan' are questions both Gautam Nilambar and Kamal are forced to face.

It is in the last strand, dealing with the political independence of India and the traumatic Partition that the student and the traveler take on slightly different, not so pleasant overtones. The political insistence on a 'singular' identity of the nation effectively denies the possibility of a cultural dialogue. Homesickness and a question of identity had been following the migrants in the text right from the beginning—be it Kamal or Cyril, but with Raza migrating to Pakistan, more immediate and puzzling questions are introduced. As the train to Lahore passes Agra, the passengers suddenly realize that the Taj Mahal, the monument that had for centuries been part of 'their' heritage is no longer 'theirs,' it belongs to their new rivals – Indians. The migration to Pakistan is partly a result of personal choice and partly forced; but being the result of a 'singular' worldview that denies the validity of any discourse apart from itself, the schism between 'before' migration and 'after' migration becomes very sharp.

In the midst of these, there is yet one thing that seems able to withstand vicissitudes of history – art. The sculpture of Sudarshan Yakshini that Gautam Nilambar created in the first strand emerges again in the last chapter – the testimony to Champak's beauty returns to haunt the twentieth-century Champa and her friends, also providing a link between the two stories separated by nearly 4,000 years. The same link is provided by the painting of Cyril Ashley's 'Bibi.' And, we may add, by the novel *River of Fire* itself. Art, therefore, is not merely an aesthetic reproduction of the material world, it is also a record of events preserved for posterity. The events in themselves may be of little significance – private loves and lives of ordinary people like Gautam Nilambar. But, the novel asserts, it is in these lives and their loves that we can see history working. Larger political events – macrohistory – does have its place (as evidenced by the sudden intrusion of world history into ordinary conversations), but the often ignored little histories or microhistories actually show us the impact of historical events. So, when Gautam and Kamal both lament that their lives have been affected by wars and enmities that they are largely indifferent to, they are also articulating the actual space where the impact of history can be seen and felt.

Hence, *River of Fire* appropriates for itself a space where 'history' is seen to be made up of a series of microhistories. In the form it uses – an appropriation of the dastaan – the novel also insists on its role as consolidating national identity at a time when this identity was being threatened. By fusing different stories from across centuries, the novel also presents an image of India and Indian culture as a space that is continually being created by a dialogue between the existing culture and the incoming one. The large number of stories making up the novel are related also to the number of forms that exist in the novel—the third person narrative works alongside letters, travelogues and memoirs – again reinforcing the importance of plurality in defining 'Indian' culture. Finally, it also isolates two things that connect these disparate strands – the omnipresence of war and its impact on unsuspecting ordinary people and the role that art can play both in providing a subversive perspective as well as in preserving microhistories in various modes like painting, sculpture and novel.

River of Fire then, both in its English translation as well as in its original Urdu version, can be seen to operate as a text that offers a vision of India as a nation characterized by plurality and cultural dialogue. In the process, it also insists that to try to define India in any monological way may be a complete falsification of Indian culture.

Works Cited

Hyder, Quratullain. *River of Fire* 1959. Trans Qurtullain Hyder. New Delhi: Kali for Women, 1998.

Padma, V. *Fiction as Window: Critiquing the Indian Literary Cultural Ethos since the 1980s*. Hyderabad: Orient Blackswan, 2009.

Paksoy, H. B. "The Dastan Genre in Central Asia." 1 January 2011. <http://www.ku.edu>

Rushdie, Salman. *Midnight's Children*. 1981. London: Picador, 1982.

_______. "Exclusive Interview." *Salman Rushdie: The Essential Guide: Midnight's Children, Shame, Satanic Verses*. London: Vintage, 2003.

5

Celebrating Transculturalism: A Study of Indira Ganesan's *The Journey*

— C.N. Eswari

Though fiction has now become a dominant genre of Indian writing in English it had its beginnings only in the 1930s, just a decade before Indian independence. The novelistic genre always had a tradition of constructing and consolidating the idea of the nation and hence, it was no coincidence that the novel in English attained importance in India during the 1930s. Since then it has been slowly but steadily gaining momentum resulting in the literary explosion of the 1980s.

The 1980s witnessed resurgence in Indian writing in English— a resurgence in terms of creativity, productivity and experimentation. Several literary and extra literary factors were responsible for shaping the works of this new generation of writers. International cultural trends like postcolonialism and postmodernism influenced the writers of the subcontinent. They drew inspiration from the technical complexities of the postmodern novel and experimented with new and subversive techniques. This new Indian sensibility received an impetus from Salman Rushdie's experimental work, *Midnight's Children* (1981).

In the wake of Rushdie's fame, a whole flood of quality fiction was produced by Indian writers. Some of the notable writers are Amitav Ghosh, Allan Sealy, Shashi Tharoor, Rohinton Mistry, Boman Desai, Firdaus Kanga, Upamanyu

Chatterjee, Farukh Dhondy, Amit Chaudri, Vikram Seth and others. The women writers have matched the men in both quality and quantity, and chief among them are Shashi Deshpande, Bharati Mukherjee, Namita Gokhale, Githa Hariharan, Sunetra Gupta, Kaveri Bhatt, Meena Alexander, Gita Mehta and others. Most of these writers are diasporic writers. They have the added advantage of viewing their native land from a distance, which gives their work a clearer perspective. Though they are part of a rich national heritage, they have exhibited great comfort and facility in trans-cultural and trans-linguistic literary productions.

The problem of identity is what besets many of these writers, for uprooted and unsettled they experience instability. The problem is further accentuated in the case of the diasporic women by the double marginalization they face due to race and gender. The multicultural societies of the West have a tendency to stick ethnicity on people, thereby fixing them in their nations of origin and hindering the process of assimilation. Within the diasporic society there exists a particular patriarchal cult, which tends to fixate women to home, whereas mobility and the notions of progress are accorded to the men. As far as the conditions of migration and diaspora are concerned, the women are often called upon to preserve their national identity through the restoration of their tradition in their new home. The women feel the need to challenge such biased objectifications that thrust a fixed and preconceived identity on them. The Indian diasporic women writers have turned this challenge into an important aesthetic concern and construct in their narratives. They find in their writing process, a space in which to articulate the debilitating nature of patriarchy and racism, and to examine alternative modes of self-representation. This paper aims to show how the problem is pursued and resolved narratively by embracing a 'transcultural' identity — an identity established not by reconciling one culture to another or by subordinating one to another but by recognizing the validity of both. For this purpose Indira Ganesan's *The Journey* is taken up for analysis.

Indira Ganesan was born at Srirangam in India and moved to St. Louis, Missouri, at the age of five. She returned to India for one year of college and then went back to New York, to complete her Bachelor of Arts in English. She graduated with honours from Vassar College and received her MFA from the Iowa Writers' Workshop. At present, she teaches at Southampton College of Long Island University and Lesley University. She is also fiction editor of *Many Mountains Moving*, a literary magazine. She is the author of two novels, *The Journey* (1990) and *Inheritance* (1998).

Before proceeding with an analysis of *The Journey* as a work celebrating transculturalism it is imperative to know why transculturalism has become an important tool in demolishing the hegemonic practises of the Western metropolises. As *The Journey* is set in the US it will be studied in the context of the American society.

To establish dominance over other nations, the European colonizers devised binary oppositions between the centre/margin and the civilized/primitive races, thus creating a hierarchal cultural difference between the West and the other. Even after the collapse of the imperial rule, the difference is carried on by the neo-colonial tendencies of the American superpower. Western metropolises promote multiculturalism to emphasize this difference between the dominant and the marginalized cultures. All these factors have precipitated the necessity for a negotiation between different cultures and creation of a world order based on transnationalism and transculturalism.

America has traditionally been referred to as a 'melting pot', welcoming people from many different countries, races and religions, all hoping to find freedom, new opportunities and a better way of life. The term 'melting pot' refers to the idea that societies formed by immigrant cultures, religions and ethnic groups, would produce new hybrid social and cultural forms. The concept has been criticized as unrealistic and racist because it focused on the Western heritage and excluded non-European immigrants. Ideally, it should have encouraged the learning about other cultures, in order to enhance understanding, mixing and mutual enrichment resulting in one common culture. Instead, the ethnic minorities were forced to accept the dominant culture.

A direct consequence of such racial visibility and forced marginality was the Civil Rights Movement of the 1960s. With it a new ethnic awareness surfaced and this came as a shock to many social theorists, who believed in the 'melting pot' concept. Their expectations were belied as the new, mysterious ethnic force manifested itself everywhere – Native Americans, Latinos Americans and Asian Americans quickly followed the lead of African Americans in asserting pride in their different cultural heritages. This new emerging trend challenged the traditional concept of a unified American society and it gave way to the image of America as a land of cultural pluralism, in which differences are powerful and enduring — the 'melting pot' theory had to be replaced with that of the 'salad bowl'. The US became a multicultural society, whereas the 'melting pot' dealt with differences by promoting uniformity, multiculturalism aimed to contain them, by the inverse strategy of promoting self-centredness and structured ethnic identities.

This tendency of multicultural nations to view their ethnic minorities as essentialist entities has come in for attack from different writers. Rushdie (1991) criticizes essentialism as "the respectable child of old-fashioned exoticism. It demands that sources, form, style, language and symbol all derive from a supposedly homogeneous and unbroken tradition"(67). Echoing Rushdie, Jasbir Jain (1998), in her introduction to the book, *Writers of the Indian Diaspora: Theory and Practice*, critiques multiculturalism for turning "ethnic communities into museums of exoticism"(13). Chandra Mohanty Talpade (1991) makes a similar accusation against Western feminists. She criticises them for perpetrating the ongoing hegemonic practice of giving specificity of location and cultural belonging to the postcolonial woman, to label her as the 'other'. From this it follows that categorization of ethnic groups has become an important mode in metropolitan societies for reinforcing hegemonies, thereby denying ethnic minorities their rights to integrate into the host cultures.

The critical mood of dissatisfaction with cultural essentialism springs from the conviction that the metropolitan centres are responsible for the preservation of cultural essentialism and ethnic purity. Correspondingly, this critique is accompanied by an urgent appeal to transcend the banalities of nativism. Said (1994) draws attention to the stifling effects of nativism and advocates a cosmopolitan view. He writes, "Nationality, nationalism, nativism: the progression is, I believe, more and more constraining .... In any case nativism is not the only alternative. There is the possibility of a more generous and pluralistic vision of the world" (277).

According to Homi Bhabha "hybridity" is central to the diasporic identity and in *Location of Culture*, he (1994) deals at length with the creation of a cultural identity that evolves in the ambivalent and contradictory space which he calls the "Third Space of enunciation"(37). For Bhabha, 'hybridity' is more than a simple descriptive concept denoting the effects of hybridization of different cultures in a colonial context; it is an effective strategy of negotiation in an ambivalent situation. Avtar Brah (1997), in her *Cartographies of Diaspora: Contesting Identities*, calls "diaspora space" the intersection of borders where all subjects and identities become "juxtaposed, contested, proclaimed or disavowed; where the permitted and the prohibited perpetually interrogate, and where the accepted and transgressive imperceptibly mingle..." (208-209).

The notion of 'in-betweeness' conjured up in relation to diasporic lives is further elaborated in the refusal to think of cultures as pure or holistic. The purity of cultural identity too becomes untenable for it emerges precisely in the "Third Space" under the continual influence and exchange of cultures. Thus the concept of diaspora forecloses the diverse forms of purity encompassed within essentialist theories. By demolishing traditional modes of identity as being stable, single or pure, diasporas have succeeded in introducing new, dynamic ways of thinking about identity as being transcultural.

Indira Ganesan's *The Journey* is a poignant account of a young girl's search for self within two different and contradictory cultures. Renu, an introvert nineteen-year-old adolescent, experiences psychological trauma while trying to balance her traditional upbringing with the progressive life that America offers. Her problem is further accentuated by the death of her cousin, Rajesh, who though thousands of miles away, was her only link with her roots. The crisis within her is resolved when she succeeds in de-linking herself from the past. She returns to the US as a regenerated individual, ready to face the challenges of the New World.

Ganesan sets the novel on an imaginary island called Pi. Renu is born and brought up in a conservative household in Pi till her parents, who are scientists migrate to the US. The father, wishing to bring up his two daughters, Renu and Meenakshi, according to the American ideals prohibits the entry of any trace of Pi into their Long Island home. After his death their mother, Rukmani, reverts to the traditional way of living and advice regarding the upbringing of the two girls pours in from Pi in the form of long and detailed letters. Rukmani's judgement on what is culturally acceptable grows out of a simple and definite sense of morality and she inculcates in her daughters the values she believes in, advising that Island girls had to preserve themselves for the sanctity of marriage. Adhering to such strict codes of conduct amidst the progressive American social life creates ambivalence in the two girls and at times, in childish desperation, they attempt to swap parents. While on shopping trips, the girls would get lost in the crowd with the hope that they would be claimed by some American parent.

As they advance in years, Meenakshi, with total disregard for her mother's wishes adopts an American identity. She calls herself Manx, a name which she invents to ward off traditional restrictions imposed on her. As Meenakshi she has to acknowledge her otherness, the rules that make her different from her American friends but as Manx she is able to assimilate into the mainstream culture. Even after her return to Pi she continues to lead her Westernized life impervious to the family's reaction to her short hair, boyish appearance and nonchalant attitude. At fifteen, she does not exhibit Renu's shy hesitation towards the other sex and strikes an uninhibited friendship with a forty year old itinerant American called Freddie. During their travel across the island she shocks and embarrasses Renu by sleeping with him, which makes Renu wonder if she and Manx are really sisters. Thus, Manx escapes the dilemma of living between cultures by creating her own identity.

If Manx succeeds in assimilating into the American culture, Renu hovers on the margin, implicitly obeying her mother's codes. Unable to actively participate in American social life she withdraws from it, assuming an air of indifference to the world around her. Her lack of involvement is evident in her attitude towards her education. While her classmates planned for their future with enthusiasm she hopes for graduation to end soon so that she would be out of the university and spared the embarrassment of having to invent excuses to keep away from boys and dates. Neither is she able to accept with complacence Pi's tradition of treating men and women as aliens to each other and devising separate lines for them in temples, buses and cinema houses. She becomes, as Om P. Juneja (1995) describes, a "... product of two or more social worlds, and is poised in psychological uncertainty of these worlds".

For Renu, who can neither acculturate into an alien culture like Manx, nor have her mother's undisputed faith in native traditions, Rajesh becomes her only source of comfort. Overwhelmed by the complex realities of life she often drifts into an illusory world where she and Rajesh are the only inhabitants. She thinks of him as her twin because Rukmani and her sister Chitra had conceived and delivered them both at the same time. Hence, his untimely death in a train accident leaves her totally shattered, a rootless individual, "an errant satellite in need of a motherly body, something large to use as a fixed point, something to guide her path"(30). Through Renu Ganesan illustrates that the tenacious clinging to the past is what deters a diasporic individual from assimilating into the host culture. The dissonances in Renu's life get resolved during her journey across Pi.

Here it would be interesting to note that Ganesan recreates Pi as a typical postcolonial nation in the Bay of Bengal, off the Indian coast, which has experienced the debilitating effects of imperial rule. In 1726, some Dutch explorers stumble on the island and believing it to be uninhabited claim it for Holland. Later, when it is learnt that it is prosperous and advanced in civilization, the French and the English stake claim and the island is placed under European rule till its independence in 1947. The Island is renamed Prospero's Island by the colonial rulers and since then it is known by its shortened name, Pi. It may be noted that just as Prospero established his hegemony over Caliban, whom he considered as an inferior race, the Europeans subjugate the islanders in the guise of a civilizing mission. When they depart they leave behind a depleted economy and a less perceptible but more far—ranging effects such as the loss of identity.

Adda, Renu's uncle illustrates the identity crisis suffered by the islanders. He, like the innumerable other postcolonials, carries within him the colonial baggage, and it is his acculturation to Western ideas that prompt him to invalidate his own cultural traditions and dismiss the quest for reality as irrational. This becomes evident in the story of Vishnu's Dream that he narrates to Renu. According to Hindu mythology Vishnu contains the entire universe within him in slumber. The world is believed to be his dream. One day, a sage who was walking about in the world chanced to slip out of Vishnu's mouth, which hung slightly open in sleep. The sage found himself in a strange ocean, a world existing outside of his own existence. To be within Vishnu he was part of a dream, but to be outside was not to exist at all (26).

The plight of Adda is akin to that of the sage. Caught between the two worlds, that of the colonizers' and his own, he loses sight of reality and suffers from a schism and tension that manifest themselves in the way in which he conducts his life. Compelled by a desire to adopt Western ideas he undertakes a tour of Europe in the 1930s and incurs the displeasure of his family by bringing back a Spanish bride. Though charmed by her fair skin and physical appearance he is indifferent to her inner struggle in adjusting to an alien culture. This drives her to the extreme step of finding asylum in a convent where she meets with a tragic end. Oblivious of her sufferings he involves himself actively in the Island's struggle for freedom from the British by joining the "Free Island Party" launched by his friend and revolutionary leader, Amir.

When India is granted independence Pi too is freed from British domination. Adda, who had lent his support to Amir's revolutionary party during Pi's struggle for freedom betrays his friend by aligning himself with the moderates who accept India as the new power centre. Amir and his supporters continue to struggle for Pi's autonomy while Adda leaves for India to represent Pi in the newly elected Government. Thus, Adda loses his wife Alphonsa and is estranged from Amir because of the chasm in his thoughts and feelings created by his loss of identity. Similarly, he proves to be an irresponsible son to his father and an unsympathetic brother to his sisters. Having internalized the values of science propagated by the colonizers he fails to understand the problems of his siblings, who are bound by tradition. His fragmented vision of life makes him a failure and earns for him the epithet 'the family rake'.

Adda's Spanish wife Alphonsa, embodies the experiences and sufferings of an immigrant who fails to establish roots in the host culture. Alphonsa, overcomes her husband's neglect and the hostility of the family by finding solace in an illicit relationship with Amir. She is forced to enter the convent in order to hide her pregnancy and there she commits suicide after delivering a male child. Underlying Alphonsa's tragedy is her inability to empathize with the host culture.

Renu too is haunted by a dilemma that results from an inability to reconcile two contradictory cultures but fortunately for her, she is able to harmonize the ambivalences that trouble her. Freddie, the American immigrant in Pi, inspires Renu to come to terms with her bi-cultural identity. A dropout from Columbia University, Freddie, disillusioned with the "plastic expectations" (93) of America, travels to India and then to Pi "to meld into the East and pick up salvation and grace on the way" (94). He renounces his family name and calls himself Freddie Flat, a name he had invented to give himself an identity independent of his roots. During the course of his search for meaning, to give shape to his life he figures that it is not possible to seek meaning directly and that it would approach him one day. He also realizes that life, unlike the sciences, does not have any given absolute from which to operate. He arrives at the conclusions that there are different ways of perceiving reality and that an individual is presented with a choice of creating his own absolute.

In his case, what gives meaning to his life is the presence of a beautiful, tea-estate heiress called Mirazi, the Light of the World. No one knew where she lived and she disappeared for months. It is her elusiveness that attracts Freddie and he follows her around. It begins as a fancy and soon ends up in obsession. He would wake up in the morning wondering if he would get a glimpse of her and sometimes it is the only reason he got out of bed. When Freddie learns that she has left for Lahore in Pakistan, he prepares to follow her.

To Renu, Freddie's life becomes a lesson in diasporic living. He does not attach himself to any one reality. Instead, he creates his own absolute to give meaning to his life. Freddie's philosophy of life has a benedictory effect on her personality. She is no longer the diffident girl, overawed by an alien society. She evolves as a regenerate individual, ready to embrace a culture other than her own. Yet, it is achieved not at the expense of invalidating her own native tradition. This becomes evident in her act of referring to her sister, Manx, by her original, traditional name, Meenakshi. The novel ends with Renu, cleansed of all her prejudices preparing to return to her home in America, alone but confident of facing the challenges of the New World. Her transformation is presented thus:

> Imagine Renu like this, cut off from the inside of herself unaware of the world — a teeming, passionate world – around her. Imagine that with each step, she was walking away from her superstitions and fears away from her self—wrought sickness, her desire to live in the past. Imagine stepping away from her inherited weights, demanding flight (173).

In sum, it may be concluded that Indira Ganesan advocates transculturalism in *The Journey*. Rukmani, who clings to her Indian tradition makes life miserable for herself and her daughters in America. On the other hand, Meenakshi by erasing her Indian identity becomes a total misfit within her own community. Adda, carries the colonial baggage even after independence and is isolated from his friends. Alphonsa as an immigrant makes no attempt to understand the host culture and ends up a failure. Only Renu, under the influence of Freddie, is able to reconcile differences and adopt a transcultural identity. She emerges out of her cross-cultural experiences as an empowered individual ready to face the challenges of a hegemonic society. Through the experiences of Renu, Indira Ganesan tacitly conveys the message that the world is a multilayered reality and that life is but a constant transcending of barriers and divisions thus celebrating the concept of transculturalism.

Works Cited

Bhabha, Homi K. *The Location of Culture*. New York: Routledge, 1994.

Brah, Avtar. *Cartographies of Diaspora: Contesting Identities*. New York: Routledge, 1997.

Ganesan, Indira. *The Journey*. Boston, Massachusetts: Beacon Press, 2001.

Jain, Jasbir, Ed. *Writers of the Indian Diaspora: Theory and Practice*. Jaipur and New Delhi: Rawat Publications, 1998.

Juneja, Om P. *Postcolonial Novel: Narratives of Colonial Consciousness*. New Delhi: Creative Books, 1995.

Mohanty, Chandra Talpade. *Under Western Eyes: Feminist Scholarship and Colonial Discourse* in *Third World Feminism and the Politics of*

Feminism. Eds. Chandra Talpade Mohanty, Ann Russo and Lourdes Torres. Bloomington and Indianpolis: Indiana University Press, 1991 pp.51-73.

Rushdie, Salman. *Imaginary Homelands: Essays and Criticism, 1981-1991.* London: Granta, 1991.

Said, Edward. *Culture and Imperialism*. New York: Knopf, 1994.

6

Chronicling the Saga of a Clan: Gendering Regional Experiences in Kavery Nambisan's *The Scent of Pepper*

— S. Chitra

Concepts of nation and region correspond to the hierarchical structuring of the dominant and the subordinate. The former is a grand theory constructing homogeneous socio-cultural identities. The latter demonstrates ethnic components contributing to the heterogeneous the identities of the nation. The confrontation of these notions interrupts dynamic clan functioning as observed in Kavery Nambisan's *The Scent of Pepper* (*SOP*). The narrative highlights the dual pressures of colonialism and anti-colonial nationalism that ruptures ethnic kinship within the Kodava community a dominant group from Coorg district in Karnataka. Among the Kodavas Nambisan traces the fortunes of the Kaleyanda clan, a family of warriors and owners of vast estates. The repercussions of the dual pressures are shouldered by the female protagonist Nanji whose industrious spirit and stoicism sustain the clan and the family.

Kaveri Nambisan, a medical practitioner and fiction writer, hails from Coorg district in Karnataka. She is a surgeon who practices in rural India. Her career in medicine has been a strong influence in her fiction. She studied medicine in St. John's Medical College, Bangalore and then studied surgery in England. She began writing under her maiden name Kaveri Bhatt for children's magazines. She wrote stories for the now defunct children's magazine *Target*. She has published the following novels so far: The Truth about Bharat (almost), *The Scent of Pepper*, *Mango-Coloured Fish*, *The Hills of Angheri*, *On Wings of Butterflies* and *The Story that must not be Told*.

Preserving the ethnic and regional identity under extraordinary historical constraints like colonization and nationalism requires remarkable physical and mental strength. The role of women during such exigencies is outstanding but they are not endorsed and more so trivialized. The text mostly performs the role of an ethnographic discourse attempting to resurrect such erasures. The basis for such elisions lies in the grand theory of nation and nationalism which failed to accommodate heterogeneous identities which emerge from regional ethnicities. While defining the concept of nationalism, Ernest Gellner argues that it ". . . is a theory of political legitimacy, which requires that ethnic boundaries should not cut across political ones, and, in particular, those ethnic boundaries within a given state . . . . should not separate the power-holders from the rest" (1). This statement validates the fact that nationalism politically consolidates the structure of a nation without impingement of regional and ethnic identities.

Nations are often narrated as single entities privileging dominant cultural practices and marginalizing local and regional identities. Homi K. Bhabha in his seminal essay "Dissemination" interrogates this as follows: "We may begin by questioning the progressive metaphor on modern social cohesion—*the many as one* – shared by organic theories of the holism of culture and community, and by theorists who treat gender, class or race as social totalities that are expressive of unitary collective experiences" (142). *The Scent of Pepper* serves as a counter-narrative detotalizing its singular representations. Homi K. Bhabha's critiquing of such singular national discourses serves a pointer and he quotes Fanon to elaborate this. Fanon writes, "Culture abhors simplification." Such pedagogical knowledges and continuist national narratives miss the "zone of occult instability where the people dwell" (qtd in Bhabha 152). The stability that Fanon critiques in mainstream national narratives is interrogated by Julia Kristeva in her celebrated essay "Women's Time". She claims that the borders of the nation constantly face double temporality where identity is constituted by historical sedimentation (the pedagogical) and the loss of identity in the signifying process of cultural identification (the performative). Kristeva insists that the gendered sign can hold together such multiplicities (qtd in Bhabha 153). This feminist and postcolonial critiquing rethink on designating people of a nation as singular identity.

Nambisan's narrative employs both British histories (pedagogical) as well as local myths (performative) to record/establish Kodava identity. The story of Lady Feodora and her husband Alistair Fox's entry into Coorg in 1855 and Clara's reading of *The Rajendranama*, a biography-cum-historical record of Doddaveera Raja, the Haleri king who rule Kodagu from 1788 to 1809 are presented as historical evidences in the text (*SOP* 59-62). But the text is entrenched in a number of local myths, tales, superstitious beliefs which give it the ethnic colour. Nanji the protagonist was proud of her heritage. According to one myth the Kodavas were descendants of the troops of Alexander where the Macedonian soldiers, unable to continue their voyage, chose a peaceful corner and decided to settle in Coorg. The nobility of the Kodavas is also testified by their blood which was said to stay red even six hours after their death (*SOP* 176).

The role of ethnic communities in a given nation is analyzed by Anthony D. Smith, renowned scholar and critic a on nation and nationalism. He writes in the book titled *The* Ethnic origins of Nations about the ethnic communities (ethnies) as "named human populations with shared ancestry myths, histories and cultures, having an association with a specific territory and a sense of solidarity" (qtd in Smith 191). According to John Breuilly these pre-modern ethnic identities are essentially local and apolitical and hence these are established outside institutions. Therefore they are ". . . necessarily fragmentary, discontinuous and elusive" (qtd in Smith 196). These fragmentary identities and their reconstruction are essential to integrate them into the nation, otherwise, Smith opines that it would be difficult to mobilize them for political action. "Better, then, to 'rediscover' and reappropriate an ethnic past or pasts that mean something to the people in question, and so reconstruct anew an existing ethnic identity, even where it appears shadowy and ill documented" (198). The *SOP* functions as an ethnographic text in rediscovering such identities and especially highlights the functioning of women in such societies.

Analysing the role of women in nation and nationalism one can perceive many overlapping principles which determine ethnic identities of women. Symbolism and ideology are two main dimensions along which Floya Anthias and Nira Yuval-Davis locate women within ethnic and national processes. They regard women as central to the creation and reproduction of ethnic and national projects and five major dimensions of their activity and presence. Women, they argue, should be seen as:

a) as biological reproducers of members of ethnic collectivities.

b) as reproducers of the boundaries of ethnic/national groups.

c) as participating centrally in the ideological reproduction of the collectivity and transmitters of its culture.

d) as signifiers of ethnic/national differences – as a focus and symbol in ideological discourses used in the construction, reproduction and transformation of ethnic/ national categories.

e) as participants in national, economic, political and military struggles (qtd in Smith 207)/

Dominant male nationalist symbols and narratives proclaim the need for men to defend both the 'Motherland' and the nation's women who symbolize and express its purity (Smith 207). But an ethnographic text like *SOP* deals with how nationalism impacts the ethnic society like that of the Kodavas when Subbu, the son of Nanji, joins the Indian National Congress much to the chagrin of Nanji and Baliyanna. This creates a void in sustaining the family which totally depends on agriculture and Nanji shoulders the burden.

While rediscovering ethnic pasts and clan identities their gendered aspects are crucial as both of them are subsumed under the lofty creation of nation and nationhood. Feminist critic Patricia Lina Leavy accentuates this fact that "Grand theories have historically been oppressive for women and all minorities because they do not account for the difference in a nuanced way nor they challenge the assumptions on which they rest . . ." (91). Feminist ethnographer Katherine Borland underscores the above point, "As feminists recognized that male bias in existing scholarship systematically ignored trivialized or distorted women's perspectives . . ." (621). Retrieving gendered regional experiences through literary narrative is the focal point of Nambisan's *SOP*. It operates as feminist ethnography which in the academic context regarded the women they researched as cultural authorities within a larger social and scholarly environment (Borland 621). Nanji the protagonist collectively represents the regional/ethnic gendered consciousness of Coorg disinterring subordinate identities.

The Scent of Pepper traces the fortunes of the Kaleyanda clan, a family born of warriors and owners of vast estates in the Coorg district in Karnataka. Kavery Nambisan captures the beauty of the regional locale, its biome, food, coffee plantations, caste hierarchies, culture, rituals, myths, and folk deities and tales. The Rao Bahadur's family of the Kaleyandas over four generations acts as atrope in contextualizing the Kodagu region and their clan.

Rao Bahadur Madaiah and his son Baliyanna, the vet, show unrelenting faith in their clan and lead the 'public' space establishing their identity. While the 'private' space is led by the royal Chambavva and the industrious Nanji sustaining the inner grit of the family which already shows signals of disintegration. The colonial intervention creates newer trajectories for the Kaleyanda men to deviate from their age-old tradition of farming, taking care of animals, maintaining lands, plantations etc. Professional digressions, change of life-styles and the spirit of anti-colonial nationalism that invades Kodagu impacts the life of Subbu, Nanji's son.

A loss of five out of her thirteen children and with none of the remaining ones eager to continue in the Kodagu, Nanji's sole hope lies with Subbu. Born with paralysed legs and then miraculously healed, Subbu exhibits his eccentricity shifting from being a nationalist to enlisting in the British Army. In the aftermath of Baliyanna's death the repercussion of these male absences are borne by Nanji who works hard in the fields. With India attaining freedom Subbu returns to Kodagu and its soil much to the chagrin of his wife and son. The revived hopes of the grand matriarch are belied by Thimmu, her grandson, who squanders wealth chasing the mirage of migrating to the US and starting industries. Nanji's hopes lies with Neelamma, her strong-willed granddaughter. Through the indomitable will of Nanji and the fortunes of the Kodavas, the regional identity is mapped.

The text as an ethnographic discourse preserves subjugated knowledge which mostly exists only in the oral tradition. Though it is primarily a literary discourse it operates on such critical frameworks adopted by academic ethnographers. The recording of specific Kodava cultural practices valorizes the alternative knowledge provided by regional literatures contesting mainstream/dominant narratives. The subordinate knowledge disseminates chiefly through women as the colonial intervention leads to professional and familial digressions even within the Kaleyanda clan. These digressions impact the regional demography and the felt effects of such migration begins in the colonial period. The Kaleyanda patriarch Rao Bahadur Madaiah sends two of his sons to England to pursue higher studies in law and medicine. One can also witness changes in profession within the family unit. Though the Kaleyanda clan is basically a martial race they are rooted in agriculture. But Baliyanna the eldest son of Madaiah, is a veterinary doctor who treats animals, and hence the burden of maintaining the agrarian background falls on Nanji the protagonist who labours in the fields.

The text belongs to the female canon which endorses and legitimizes multiple voices of women. The construction of the female body in the agrarian society becomes the central focus.

According to feminist critic Radha Chakravarty in the 1990s the textualized body came into focus with Judith Butler's theorization of the body as text inscribed by power, created through performance (43). The performance of the Nanji's body in a patriarchal society is not simply a submissive one but charged with performance, that too in the context of male absences and passivity. Baliyanna almost turning into an indolent and slothful drunkard and the male heirs going in search of material pastures almost leaves Nanji in a stagger. The self-willed exploitation of the female protagonist is a pointer in constructing specific regional identities of women. In order to sustain the Kaleyanda clan and its identity despite the passive role of its male members Nanji exemplifies leadership qualities, which are generally associated with patriarchy, through her physical labour and mental strength. Her long hours of labour at home and in the field, maintaining the family accounts, saving jewellery and money validates that she substitutes the male responsibility in an agrarian society that faces deterioration. This endows her with an androgyny that combines both male aggressiveness of work, leadership and female responsibility of home-making.

In this context Sherry Ortner's arguments throw key insights. According to her ". . . There is much ethnographic evidence that women are perceived as particularistic and fragmenting in many societies". These are ". . . but consequence of processes in which female labour and reproduction are privately appropriated for the aims of male household heads – aims often called 'social' but more appropriately labeled as clan or patriarchal family" (qtd in Coontz16). Analogous to this observation Nanji as delineated in the novel bears thirteen children to the Kaleyanda clan. Nambisan writes, "Nanji struggled; cared for the children, handled them in herds, spanked and loved them in a unit" (SOP 111). She not only labours in their fields but also introduces innovative cultivation practices particularly the growing of pepper in the region of Coorg. Hence her 'body' is appropriated for sustaining clan identity which is conventionally male-centric. It is argued that this appropriation is self-willed and through this a gendered regional identity emerges.

In the Indian society, social historian Ashis Nandy contends that in an agricultural society there existed a symbiotic relationship between women and nature. These societies tend to emphasize the feminine principle in nature. Further, the Brahminic tradition attempted to limit the dominance of women in society. But in the pre-Aryan societies dominance of women were retained in many areas. "This undeniably is a matrifocal culture in which femininity is inextricably linked with *prakriti,* or nature, and *prakriti* with *leela,* or activity" (35). Hence the role of women in agrarian societies is powerful whereas it is rendered passive in the hegemonic construction of nationalism's womanhood. The latter construction is primarily based on the Hindu and Brahminical ideologues, and hence it differs from the regional construction.

Nambisan brings this contradiction through the character of the industrious Nanji and her sophisticated daughter-in-law Mallige, where one can witness the shift from 'sowing', to 'sewing' where one can notice the influence of nationalism even in constructing regional identities. Nanji successfully integrates her granddaughter Neelamma into her agrarian/industrious fold while her grandson apes Western culture aiming to migrate to the United States.

Some of the specific features embedded in the narrative to establish women's role in regional/clan functioning are:

(Re)presenting the body of women.

Celebrating work ethics in clan by women.

Reproduction not viewed as an impingement on women's body autonomy.

Household chores such as cooking/cleaning not looked upon as drudgery dumped on women but integral part of cultural clan ethics.

Women rooted more to the soil than men.

Women play the role of cultural transmitters.

The above points precariously edge on arguing the text romanticizing female roles and labour in maintaining clan identities. But inquiring into gender roles through such critiquing tools mars the voices that emerge through the narrative.

The period of the narrative also contributes in shaping gender identities. The narrative is linear beginning with the nineteenth century colonial period and concluding with post-independent India. But it moves back to ancient times to locate the myth of the Kodavas and sometimes as to when the colonizer established coffee plantations in Coorg as also the arrival of the father of the British planter Rupert Fox. Apart from the character of Nanji there are a host of other women characters including the English woman Clara who secretly falls in love with Baliyanna. Nambisan's authenticity in depicting these roles without the influence of feminist theoretical intrusions is witnessed. Its simple aim is to valorize women's role in clan identities that are usually relegated or trivialized. Her protagonist is more close to nature rather than culture, and hence Nanji is distanced from the cultural construction of nation and its women.

It is not surprising to note that Nanji and Baliyanna detest the cultural construction of the grand theory like nation and nationalism. Both of them are critical of the non-violence movement spearheaded by the Mahatma. To Baliyanna the 'Charka' is an effeminate symbol contrasted with the Kaleyanda's martial background. Nambisan writes, "Baliyanna nursed a permanent grudge against the Charkah (the wheel) which threatened to overthrow their ancient tradions of valour" (*SOP* 175). It is not only the Kodava men but also the women are born tough. Elsewhere in the novel Nanji claims, "a Kodavathi is born tough" (*SOP* 104). She also abhorred Gandhi for his crazy belief in equality. "She believed that it was honourable to be born a Kadava" (*SOP* 175). Hence she loathed Gandhiji's ideology of intermingling of castes. She firmly believed that the entry of *Polayas* 'harijans' defile the house. But her warnings were unheeded by her son Subbu who expressed defiance.

Similarly the intervention of non-alcoholism strictly adhered by Subbu during his marriage with Mallige creates a public furore. Any Kodava wedding is incomplete without alcohol.

Subbu's decision to celebrate a dry wedding without alcohol infuriated Nanji and she said, "No alcohol and it ceases to be a Kodava wedding . . . . How can we deprive our relatives and the village elders? And we can't let the bride's party leave without a touch of it, even if it is fermented gooseberry wine" (*SOP* 190). The regional/clan identity delegitimizes the Hindu ideological construct of nationalism spearheaded by Gandhi. A Kodavathi like Nanji insisting on alcohol exhibits the fragmentary identity contesting the overarching construction of Indian womanhood. The narrative challenges the privileging of dominant religious ideologies which shape the conceptualization of the nation and interrogates its gender construction.

Nanji's body displays industriousness and lacks feminine grace. This is illustrated contrasting her with the feminine Mallige her daughter-in-law. Like most ideal women Mallige believes that an ideal home had to be filled with decorative fluff. For Nanji, "'Beauty without usefulness is criminal,' Nanji cried out in frustration. There's work, work, and work waiting to be done'" (*SOP* 199). But Mallige symbolizes the colonial interruption and its idea of education that had already entered the Kodava society and also the nationalist construction of womanhood. The divergent attitudes of Nanji and Mallige are illustrated in the text as follows:

> Mallige took out her sewing basket and book of embroidery and made six heart-shaped, redfrilled cushions and embroidered on them the figures of English girls in flowing skirts, bonnets and ribbons, in a garden of violets and iris. She sewed 'Good Night' pillowcases and 'Good Morning' tablecloths, mirror-work bedcovers, cross stitch tea-cosies, satin-stitched Duchess sets, runners and doilies; she crocheted a lace curtain for the front room and strung it with beads of coloured glass that made maddening music all day and drove Nanji crazy. It delighted visitors, though, who sent their daughters to borrow patterns or learn a new stitch from Mallige. (*SOP* 199)

One can compare this with Nanji's entrance as a daughter-in-law into Rao Bahadur Madaiah's house. She triggers off a frenzy of cleaning and the servants unused to such hard work cannot contemplate what really hit them. After the death of her father-in-law one can see Nanji herself work in the fields

> She went to the field, picked out a sheaf of green paddy and, bending from the waist, began to plant. She loved the feel of the soft mud in her hands and the breeze on her ankles. Nanji came from a family where the women were industrious, without the lazy drinking habits of men. They stepped into the field like cranes, worked alongside the Yeravas, planted, threshed paddy and stacked hay. Kodava women were practical: they wore their sari with the pleats at the back, so when they bent over wet fields, the pleats did not come in the way. (*SOP* 26)

In delineating the character of Nanji, Nambisan projects her as the child of nature rather than that of culture. This leads to the divergent attitudes of Nanji and Mallige. The latter is more influenced by the growing concept of a larger identity called the nation which is culturally constructed. While discussing about the role of women in clan functioning Sherry Ortner opines that women's biology and domestic role make her appear closer to nature. "Nature . . . is in turn seen as lower than culture, so that women are perceived as lower in the social scale and subject to the restrictions that culture puts on both nature and domestic unit" (Qtd in Coontz 14). Mallige's departure from the clan functioning is influenced by the larger unit called the society and nation, and so does Timmy, her son, whereas Mallige's daughter Neelama nurtured by Nanji is expected to willingly perpetuate the clan ethics.

Nambisan eulogizes the natural instinct of her protagonist and fantastically claims that it is Nanji's inquisitive nature that leads her to the discovery that the climate in Kodagu is ideal for growing pepper. From a Mapla she exchanges fish for cuttings of pepper which she has planted near every tree and "within a year the trees were festooned with the frilly apparel of pepper vines" (*SOP* 34). The native knowledge and commonsense of Nanji make her realize the medicinal value of pepper as carminative, digestive and when mixed with honey, effective in soothing sore throats. She always carries a handful of pepper tied to the edge of her sari to help people in crisis.

The magical cure of, Subbu who remained a cripple for nearly nine years through tiger milk ointment given by a Kuruba tribal woman, forms an interesting part of the story. But after the application of the tiger milk ointment Subbu rans a raging fever and he almost stops breathing and remains still. "She (Nanji) untied the knot on her sari, crushed some corns of pepper between her palms and rubbed the powder into his nose. This was the height of his fever and Dr. Seshagiri had said that there was no hope. But Subbu began to kick his legs" (SOP 38).

The analogous functioning of the landscape and the inscape of the ethnic women are observed in their native knowledge and beliefs which are usually assigned a subordinate status in the elitist hegemonic knowledge systems. Nambisan records ethnic faiths and convictions which generally exist in oral tradition. Nanji's firm belief in the goodwill of her ancestors illustrates this. She believes that "When the ancestors were happy with their progeny, the rain fell vertically and nourished the land; if the spirits of the ancestors were displeased the rain slanted at an angle . . . if the ancestors were truly incensed – as when a Kodava married an outsider – the rain fell transverse . . ." (SOP 177). Ancestral worship is an integral customary practice of the Kodavas. Besides they also worship local deities like Lord Iguthappa and also Hindu deities like Lord Shiva.

Baliyanna too firmly believes in the religious practices and beliefs of the Kodavas. The clash of ethnic faiths and colonial elitism is witnessed in the hunting trip of Clara and Baliyanna, when he show her a solitary oblong stone about two feet by one, balanced at the edge of the rockface where pregnant women stand on it and turn thrice praying for the baby in the womb. Clara thinks it is a "foolhardy penance". When they come to the 'forest of death' or the 'kolebana' it seem that they are standing on some strange promontory of earth, at the end of an epoch. "If a man killed another he was brought here and left to the mercy of the tigers. The next day, the villagers collected his remains. Back in the village they performed his last rites and addressed his spirit: 'We did not kill you, we killed the cruelty in you. We want you to be born again in this *nad*'" (SOP 71). Similarly when Clara tries to shoot two mating cobras he forcefully stops her. To Clara they are simply dangerous cobras but to Baliyanna they are mating animals and they should not be killed according to the hunting laws. Such native culture and ethnic beliefs are highlighted throughout the text.

The double resistance of the narrative emerges from its endorsing pluralistic ethnic codes and in the process recuperating the stifled women's voices that had been disseminating subjugated knowledges. In retrieving the specific Kodava cultural practices, the text functions as an ethnographic account defying norms of uniformity in national discourse, thus gendering the regional/ethnic identity.

Works Cited

Atkinson, Paul. *The Ethnographic Imagination: Textual Constructions of Reality.* London & New York: Routledge, 1990.

Bhabha, Homi K. *The Location of Culture.* London: Routledge, 1994.

Borland, Katherine. "The Case of Feminist Ethnography". Ed. Sharlene Nagy Hesse-Biber. *Handbook of Feminist Research Theory and Praxis.* California: Sage, 2007. (621)

Chakravarthy, Radha. *Feminism and Contemporary Women Writers: Rethinking Subjectivity*. New Delhi: Routledge, 2008.

Coontz, Stephanie & Peta Henderson. "Introduction" to *Women's Work, Men's Property: The Origins of Gender and Class.* London: Verso, 1986 (1-43).

Gellner, Ernest. *Nations and Nationalism*. Massachusetts: Blackwell, 2006. Second edition.

Hobsbawm, Eric & Terence Ranger. Eds. *The Invention of Tradition.* Cambridge: CUP, 2009.

Kavery Nambisan. < http://en.wikipedia.org/wiki/kaveri_Nambisan.>

Lash, Scott. "Genealogy and the Body: Foucault/Deleuze/Nietzsche". *Sociology of Postmodernism*. London: Routledge, 1990. 55-78

Leavy, Patricia Lina. "Feminist Postmodernism and Post structuralism". Eds. Sharlene Nagy Hesse-Biber & Patricia Lina Leavy. *Feminist Research Practice – A Primer*. London: Sage, 2007 (83-108).

Nambisan, Kavery. *The Truth about Bharat (Almost).* New Delhi: Penguin, (1991). Reprint 2002.

______ *The Scent of Pepper*. New Delhi: Penguin, 1996.

Nandy, Ashis. *At the Edge of Psychology: Essays in Politics and Culture.* New Delhi: OUP, 1993.

Ramakrishna, P.S. et.al Eds. *Mountain Biodiversity,Land we use Dynamics and Traditional Ecological Knowledge.*Oxford & IBH, New Delhi & Calcutta: 2000.

Smith, Anthony D. *Nationalism and Modernism*. New York : Routledge, 1998.

7

Multi-domain Marginalisation of Dalit Women in Bama's Autoethnography *Sangati: Events*

— **P. Rathna**

> The true privilege of man is not to be the master of his world, but to be liberated from it; his mandate is not to employ other creatures as instruments for his own needs and desires, but to use himself, his own human existence, as a vehicle of self-transcendence.
>
> (Halbfass qtd. in Dallmayr 132)

Casteism is still prevalent in India, in spite of the many-sided efforts to obliterate it completely. It is a bitter pill to swallow that casteism has gone so deep into the society that even the mighty forces of government cannot uproot it. This gross social acrimony, caste hatred and violence result in the increasing percentage of undeveloped or underdeveloped mass, consequently affecting social solidarity and harmony. Such a huge population, permanently living in the lowest echelons of the social order, without any basic amenities, in deplorable conditions, will be detrimental to the development of the country. According to Nagarajan:

> Among caste groups, SCs and STs have their highest proportion in the lowest monthly per capita expenditure brackets. In short, SCs, STs, Muslims and women, especially the poor among them who would constitute over a third of the country's population, continue to be excluded from India's development story for more than six decades after independence. (2)

There is a proportionate increase in the awareness mainly because of the initiatives like introducing Dalit studies in the universities across the nation and across the world. This internationalisation of the Dalit issues through literature quickens the process of social transformation. As stated precisely by Janet Vucinich in her Preface to *Government Brahmana:*

> The social nature of storytelling bridges distances and enables us to see ourselves in a reality and to question that reality. The questioning is a critical stage in both personal and social change. (xvi)

Taking into consideration these factors, the relevance of Dalit life-writings gain more significance in dissolving the borders and empowering the Dalits in India to enjoy the fundamental rights in their democratic country without any discrimination. As there is an exigency to study the literature of the marginalised in order to catalyse the formation of an egalitarian society, the present study endeavours to focus on the multi-domain marginalisation of Dalit women as revealed in Bama's *Sangati: Events*, through the autoethnographic lens.

It is interesting to note that most of the Dalit literature is in the form of autobiographical writings. In fact, the pioneer of Dalit literature, Ambedkar himself has preferred only autobiography as the powerful mode of expression: He avers: "The problem is how best to give an idea of the way the untouchables are treated by the caste Hindus. A general description, or a record of cases of the treatment accorded to them, are the two methods by which this purpose could be achieved. I have felt that the latter would be more effective than the former" (4). To study the life-writings of the marginalised writers as mere autobiographies is to do only fractional justice to their contribution. These life-writings are written with a cause – to expose the malicious impact of oppressive socio-cultural and political factors in the personal lives of the writers and to share with the outside world, their endeavours to achieve freedom by carving an identity for themselves. The writers reveal their struggle against the disparities in the social system and their strong desire to create an egalitarian society, where their subhuman existence could be wiped out and they would attain redemption from their marginalised predicament. The life of the marginalised is so severely impacted by the socio-cultural and political factors that it is impossible to extricate the influence of these factors from their writings. Since the life-writings of the marginalised are their souls' perception of the "ethno" factors that retard the socio-cultural and political empowerment of the respective communities, these narratives are more autoethnographical than mere autobiographical.

According to Ellis and Bochner, the major proponents of autoethnography, it is "an autobiographical genre of writing that displays multiple layers of consciousness, connecting the personal to the cultural" (qtd. in Porter). While autobiography can be simply defined as the life story of a person written by him/herself, ethnography "involves the intensive study of other cultures" ("Ethnography," def. 238), employing "participant observation and qualitative methods" (238). "Participant-observation", according to Clifford "serves as shorthand for a continuous tacking between the 'inside' and 'outside' of events: on the one hand grasping the sense of specific occurrences and gestures empathetically, on the other stepping back to situate these meanings in wider contexts" (266). Both autobiography and ethnography, as literary genres, "share a 'commitment to the actual'" (Russel). Autoethnography, a product of the post-modern philosophy, is considered as a qualitative research method with wide ranging applications in various disciplines such as psychology, sociology, medicine, ethnography, anthropology, management studies and so on. In *Ethnographic I: A Methodological Novel About Autoethnography,* Carolyn Ellis defines it as:

> ... research, writing, story, and method that connect the autobiographical and personal to the cultural, social, and political. Autoethnographic forms feature concrete action, emotion, embodiment, self- consciousness, and introspection portrayed in dialogue, scenes, characterization, and plot. Thus autoethnography claims the conventions of literary writing. (xix).

The term "autoethnography" was originated by Hayano in 1979 (Wall), and thus has been in use for more than thirty years. It introduces a whole new dimension in the pursuit of social and cultural knowledge using subjective methodology. As defined by Ellis, "*Ethno* means people or culture; *graphy* means writing or describing. *Ethnography* then means writing about or describing people and culture, using first hand observation and participation in a setting or situation" (26). According to the anthropologist Deborah Reed Danahay:

> The concept of autoethnography... synthesizes both a post modern ethnography, in which the realist conventions and objective observer position of standard ethnography have been called into question, and a postmodern autobiography, in which the notion of the coherent, individual self has been called into question. The term has a double sense – referring either to the ethnography of one's own group or to autobiographical writing that has ethnographic interest. Thus, either a self (auto) ethnography or an autobiographical (auto) ethnography can be signaled by 'autoethnography.' (qtd. in Russel)

Thus Danahay presents the broad applications and implications of the term.

The life writings of the marginalised are enriched with ethnographical insight in addition to autobiographical elements, which draws them closer to the genre of autoethnography. In the present study, autoethnography is viewed as a portmanteau word, a blend of autobiography and ethnography, combining the study of self and culture. In the researcher's perspective, the autobiographer becomes the ethnographer who plays the dual role of a participant observer (ethno) and the observed (auto), and thus enriching the realness of the study by means of sharing first-hand experience. As the participant is from the same ethnic background, he/she has the advantage of observing at the closest range and gets the feel of the culture at ease without any alienation. Bama, the most celebrated contemporary Tamil Dalit woman writer, has been at the forefront of Dalit literary activism, and has given Dalit aesthetics the visibility it had previously lacked in the literary campus of India. The first two full-length works *Karukku* and *Sangati* are in successful English, German, French, Telugu, and Malayalam translations. Bama's *Sangati: Events* is translated from Tamil by Lakshmi

Holmtröm. Bama's "*Sangati* moves from the story of individual struggle to the perception of a community of *Paraiya* women, a neighborhood group of friends and relations and their joint struggle. In this sense, *Sangati* is perhaps the autobiography of a community" (Holmström xv). Bama portrays the ordeals of the womenfolk which start at a very young age from looking after their siblings, struggling hard to make both ends meet with their drunkard menfolk, accepting discriminating practices in the workplace, enduring sexual violence at home and the work place to subsisting with marginalisation in all domains. Though the critics view Bama's *Sangati* as the "autobiography of a community", based on the assertiveness of self revealed in Bama, this study substantiates it as autoethnography.

In *Sangati: Events*, the life-writing of Bama, not merely the personal accounts of the writer are narrated but the everyday life of the whole community, their ethos and the social, cultural and political factors which destined their marginalisation are elucidated. As the representative of the oppressed community, Bama speaks of their anguish, emotional turmoil, and their anxious attempts to break the shackles of marginalisation in her narrative. The social implication is complemented with the individual representation in this life-writing. Indeed, she has the more serious responsibility of enlightening not only her people but also the outside world about their predicament and victimisation. Autoethnography serves as the best genre to realise this objective.

The social cause gains more significance than the individual representation in Bama. The fact that autobiography and ethnography become inseparably linked in her life-writing, has been justified by various critics and social scientists. Sara Mill quotes the words of Macdonnell in her *Discourse*, "...discourses differ with the kinds of institutions and social practices in which they take shape and with the positions of those who speak and those whom they address" (9). She adds:

> Thus a discourse is not a disembodied collection of statements, but groupings of utterances or sentences, statements which are enacted within a social context, which are determined by that social context and which contribute

> to the way that social context continues its existence. Institutions and social context, therefore, play an important determining role in the development, maintenance and circulation of discourses. (10)

The predicament of the marginalised women either does not find space or has minimal representation in the writings of men. Even the First Wave and the Second Wave feminists turned a blind eye towards the issues concerning the marginalised women. Though advancement in science and technology and increased education and employment opportunities have minimised the intensity of gender discrimination, it is an incontrovertible fact that women throughout the world, still have to struggle for their individual rights in the society. In such a social scenario, the study of the status of the marginalised women and the humiliation and subjugation endured by them and the challenges encountered by them in their everyday life due to the dominant class and the patriarchal society, gains significance. The autoethnographical narrative of Bama is an authentic manifestation of the predicament of the marginalised womenfolk in our country. It brings to the fore, the multi-domain marginalisation of the Dalit women. Dalit women are hard-pressed and they exist below the margins – in lower echelons than the menfolk of their community.

Women are always treated secondary to men and they are considered inferior to men in the family, society and religion. The Dalit women, whether educated or uneducated, living in villages or cities, employed or unemployed, invariably have to endure the torments of double marginalisation – as Dalits and as women. In the course of her weave, Bama documents the plight of the women of her community, their everyday struggle to earn their livelihood, their ethos, their endurance, resilience, and their hope for a better life. The "ethno" factors – their low caste and the patriarchal society – relegate them even below the margins, lower than their menfolk and make them victims of marginalisation in various domains such as familial, social and religious. In the course of her documentation, Bama records the customs and habits of their community – their every day ordeals, their marriage, child birth, their ceremonies and festivals.

Bama's *Sangati* is a precise record on the predicament of Dalit women as the victims of domestic violence and twofold discrimination – as women and as Dalits in all the domains. The narrator, Pathima, says that discrimination starts right from the birth of the children. Boys are treated specially and are given more care and attention than the girls. When the boy baby cries, instantly he is picked up and fed. He is breast-fed for a longer duration than the girl babies. When they grow up also they are given more respect and given first preference. Pathima's 'Patti' says, "If you are born to this world, it is best you were born a man. Born as woman what good do we get?" (*SE* 6-7). Girl children are trained from their childhood to obey the menfolk, and they are conditioned that they are ignorant and are inferior to their men. The little girl Maikkanni's life reveals that the ordeal for the women starts even during their childhood: "The day Maikkanni learnt to walk, she started to work as well" (70). In addition to looking after the siblings, the girl children have to work in their capacity as daily wagers. Pathima's Patti affirms: "Once you are born a woman, can you go and confront a group of four and five men? Should you even do it?... What do we know about justice? From your ancestors' times it has been agreed that what the men say is right" (28-29).

Women's health is given least importance, though they are the pillars of the family. In giving birth to children also, "women rarely go into hospitals, but deliver their children at home in a makeshift way" (*SE* 36). They don't enjoy such privileges as special care, nursing, special food and so on, that the upper caste women enjoy during pregnancy and after childbirth. When women happen to die, during childbirth or after that, the men immediately will have a second marriage. The men will force the women to undergo birth control measures rather than sterilising themselves. Hence, women have to bear the burden of their whole family. Thus Pathima says: "As it is, the families keep going only because of the women" (36).

The autoethnography of Bama is the mimetic representation of the family life of Dalits. Bama brings forth the horrors of domestic violence. The women, however dutiful and selfless, are victimised by their husbands, who think that they have every right to thrash their wives. It is not uncommon to see the husbands brutally attacking their wives for no reason. Nobody can question them because the husbands are considered as their masters and saviours. Tormenting and thrashing one's wife is common and an everyday occurrence in almost all the households. A man has all the rights over the woman, even to kill her. Nobody has the authority to question him, as he can say, "She is my wife, I can beat her or even kill her if I want" (10-11). Thus the men in the Dalit community assert their superiority over their women. When Pathima reflects on the reason for the daily routine of menfolk drinking and thrashing their wives in the streets, she wonders "whether all that violence was because there was nowhere else for them to exert their male pride or to show off their authority. All that suppressed anger was vented when they came home and beat up their wives to a pulp" (65). The study of human nature reveals:

> All individuals seek some level of control over their environment. Without control we are less than human, dependent upon others and alienated from society and from ourselves. But people seek different *degrees* of control.... At work we may not be boss, but there are always niches in which we can exercise control; there are people lower down the line who may be subject to our authority and influence. (Edgar 139)

She also justifies the act of lower caste women exhibiting obscenities in the streets when there is a quarrel. It is the woman who looks after the entire household as the husband most often drinks and spends money for his pleasure: "So, on top of all this, why must she submit to being beaten and stamped upon for no rhyme or reason? That's why she quarrels with him. If he shows his strength of muscle, she reveals her sharpness of her tongue. Because she can't hit him back, she curses him roundly. What else can she do?" (67). She reveals the bitter truth that their "lives are unceasingly tedious. When they are so frustrated by all this, they are driven to venting their bitterness by quarrelling and shouting" (68). The narrator does not fail to point out that only a very few women quarrel with their men like this, while others "put up with all that violence and suffer a life of hellish torment. On the one side she is worn out with physical toil, on the other, she is beaten until she is left with only a half or a quarter life" (67). Thus, domestic violence can be seen at its extreme harsh level in their families.

A woman is tutored for generations to believe that she is under the protection of a man. She has to live according to his whims and fancies. Pathima observes: "A woman's body, mind, feelings, words and deeds and her entire life are under his control and domination. And we too have accepted what they want us to believe - that this is actually the right way, that our happiness lies in being enslaved to men" (68). The women have to listen to their husbands even to exercise their democratic rights. Pathima's mother says, "I voted as your Ayya [father] told me to" (98). Commenting on the ignorance of women voting for two or more parties, a man remarks: "These are completely ignorant donkeys. They should never have been allowed to vote" (100). The words of Pathima are revelatory: "It is by repeating that to us that they have made us as useless as rotten egg. Nowadays women can take up all sorts of responsibilities. But just as they fooled us and took away our rights within our homes, they have also marginalised us in the world outside" (104). Her mother also reiterates the effect of the centuries-old conditioning on women: "We've believed what they told us repeatedly – that we are useless chickens scratching about in the rubbish – and now we have no confidence in ourselves" (104).

In *Sangati,* Bama shows that, despite their hard work and earning on their own amidst many hardships, these women are taken for granted in all spheres. The narrator blames: "...because of our caste and because of our poverty, every fellow treats us with contempt. If ever there is a problem or disturbance, everyone, starting with the police, chooses to blame and humiliate the women of our community" (*SE* 66). Women are vulnerable for abuse and are stigmatised not only by men but also by other women. It is frustrating that "....

women did not show any pity or compassion towards other women" (40). While a woman will be publicly tried and punished cruelly if she is found guilty of misbehaviour, a man is allowed to go scot-free for the same guilt. The case of Mariamma, the victim of domestic violence and gender and caste discrimination exposes this fate of the lower caste women. Pathima laments: "If a women is slandered, that's always her fate. People won't consider whether the accusation is true or not, nor will they allow the woman to speak out" (42). As our former President K.R. Narayanan rightly stated: "In parts of rural India forms of sadism seem to be earmarked for dalit women. From the time of Draupadi our womenfolk had been subjected to public disrobing and humiliation as means of vendetta – individual, social or political" (Narayanan 6).

Mariamma's life is a case in point. Her modesty was thrown to public criticism by an upper caste man who tried to misbehave with her. The village elders never compromise when it comes to honour and modesty. In the meeting of the village folks, the village "nattamai" (the village elder) says: "Here is a case where our entire community's reputation is at risk. In a village where there are many caste-communities, if someone of our caste behaves disgracefully, then it brings shame on all of us. As it is, we paraiyas are treated with contempt" (*SE* 21). Women have no say in such meetings and they are not even allowed to speak or give their opinion: "'Do you women have any sense at all? What are you muttering about here, when we men are talking seriously? Go home all of you'. They added a couple of obscenities, scolded us roundly and drove us off" (21). The women need to maintain silence and be docile, otherwise, the men will shout, "Will you she – donkeys get out of here or do we have to stamp on you? The more we drive the witches away, the more they come back and make trouble" (23). The women know very well that it is "one justice for men and quite another for women" (24). Mariamma was fined Rs.200 and Manikkam Rs.100. As Liam Gearon rightly comments:

> The exploitation of low-caste laborers and the rigid assignment of demeaning occupations on the basis of caste keep lower-caste populations in a position of economic and

> physical vulnerability. The triple burden of caste, class, and gender effectively ensures that lower-caste women are the farthest removed from legal protections. (80)

Mariamma stands as a testimony to this. The women are shrewd enough to understand the reason behind their menfolk's domineering attitude towards them. The men are able to show their strength and valiance only before their women and not in front of the upper caste men. Their helplessness makes them behave wildly with their women. As Susaiamma observes correctly: "They never allow us to sit down at the village meetings.... But it's only to us that they will brag. Ask them just to stand up to the 'mudalaali' (employer). Not a bit, they will cover their mouths and their backsides and run scared" (*SE* 24). The village "nattamai" ended his "proceedings" with an implied warning only to the women: "It is you female chicks who ought to be humble and modest. A man may do hundred things and still get away with it. You girls should consider what you are left with, in your bellies" (26). The arrogance of a male dominant society is brought out in this autoethnography.

In the patriarchal society, even to speak what they think as right is regarded as a mark of disrespect. When Pathima talks about what was "really chafing" inside her mind, her Patti says: "Whether it is right or wrong, it is better for women not to open their mouths. You just try speaking out about what you believe is right. You will only get kicked and beaten and tramped on for your pains.... It's the same throughout the world. Women are not given that kind of respect'" (29). Even in children's play, boys took the lead role and "they were the ones in authority" (31). In their village, the men never allowed women to take part in plays or skits put on festival days. The men themselves did the roles of women. They are not allowed to go anywhere as they wish, even to the cinema. They go for their work in the fields or as domestic servants and apart from that they have to "try really hard" (13) even to go to the church. Women are so used to this patriarchal bondage that they find safety and security in this system and are diffident to come out of it. As Pathima's grandmother puts it: "... 'what these men say makes sense too. Can we go about as freely as they do, after all? Some wicked fellow or other is waiting to rape us'"

(14). A woman becomes an easy prey for the lust, treachery and cunning of man. Whatever work the women do, wherever they go, they are paid less than the men. They have to fight with the natural villains like wild animals which pose a threat to them when they collect firewood or work in the fields and human villains at home like their drunken father, husband or brother, and at the outside society like their upper caste masters. Even if they fall ill they cannot sit at home, as they have to earn for their daily livelihood.

The narrator says: "I could see that in some ways I was lucky to be a paraichi. On the other hand, I could not help remembering the number of times I was sorry and ashamed that I was born into this community" (113). She does not fail to highlight the rights the womenfolk enjoy in the dalit community which are denied to the upper caste women. Dalit women take part in all the activities hand in hand with men. They even accompany their men to graveyard and do the rituals when there is a death. Unlike the upper caste Hindu women, they need not suffer widowhood after the husband's death. They have the freedom even to remarry. Nevertheless, she has to endure more problems as a woman and as a Dalit. She shares her unpleasant experiences as an educated Dalit woman looking for jobs: "... even with an education one has to face many difficulties when trying to earn a livelihood. Being a Dalit creates a problem. On top of that, being a Dalit woman makes it more difficult" (119-120). In the narrator's experience, the greatest of all the problems, "is trying to live alone as an unmarried Dalit woman" (120). She finds it difficult to get a rented house because of all these factors which dog her down throughout her life. Gail Omvedt in her *Dalit Visions,* exposes the patriarchal nature of Hinduism by citing Panditha Ramabai "who was the first to proclaim, with great clarity, backed by her personal refusal to remain a Hindu, that the Sanskritic core of Hinduism was irrevocably and essentially anti-woman" (26). Panditha Ramabai observes: "Those who diligently and impartially read Sanskrit literature in the original, cannot fail to recognize the law-giver Manu as one of those hundreds who have done their best to make women hateful beings in the world's eye" (qtd. in 27). The lives of women portrayed in *Sangati* illustrate this.

In *Sangati*, the narrator says that the women are often possessed by 'peys' (spirits). The people have strong belief in all these supernatural existence and mostly women are the victims to these "peys". The narrator wonders, "... how a man could even strike at a 'pey' bravely, while a woman is easily caught and becomes its prey. And even among women, I never heard of upper-caste women becoming possessed or dancing in a frenzy. The peys always seem set on women from the pallar, paraiyar, chakkilyar, and koravar communities" (*SE* 57-58). The narrator analyses the reasons for such possessions that the women are torn to pieces mentally and physically inside and outside the house. They have to work tirelessly at home as well as at the fields, bearing the harassment of the menfolk. She perceives: "Women are overwhelmed and crushed by their own disgust, boredom, and exhaustion, because of all this. The stronger ones somehow manage to survive all this. The ones who don't have the mental strength are totally oppressed; they succumb to mental ill-health and act as if they are possessed by peys" (59). But the menfolk, though oppressed in the external world, have their freedom at home. They are the masters and the law making authorities who have the entire control over their family and their womenfolk. They find pleasure in controlling and ruling over their womenfolk. Christophe Jaffrelot aptly notes that Indian society has "obsession [with] small differences, especially at the lowest level of the social scale, where each individual feels the need, more than elsewhere, for someone lower in status than himself" (37) The Dalit men satiates this basic human need by subjugating their womenfolk.

Bama authentically points out that even their conversion to Christianity, which advocates liberal humanism, does not guarantee their freedom from discrimination. The Dalit women have to endure more marginalisation than the men of their community in the religious domain also. Among the Dalits, the paraiyas alone became Christians hoping that their conversion would result in their emancipation. But on many occasions, in the autoethnography, women could be seen in quaims on their decision to become Christians: "Why on earth paraiyas alone became Christians, I don't know, but because they did so at that time, now it works out that they get no concessions from the government whatsoever" (*SE* 5). The villagers will seek the help of temple priests or "pujaris" to recover from illness. The ignorant people will be warned by the church priests against going to these "pujaris" as it will be a mortal sin, having joined the Christian faith. They will threaten them by saying, "you will definitely go to hell forever" (14). These ignorant women who want to get solace in some way or other instantly comes out with solution: "...if you feel worried about it, you can always go to confession after you've been to the pujari, get a pardon and take communion" (14). Their conversion to Christianity does make a difference in their life style, customs and habits. As Dalit Christians, they celebrate the weddings integrating "tali-tying" (central rite in the wedding ceremony) and communion in the church.

Among the other Dalit communities like Pallar and Chakkiliyaar, a marriage can be ended and the couples are free to marry again at their will. But the Paraiya community is deprived of this privilege also as Pathima's mother comments: "... it seems that it was a mistake that we ever became Christians" (97). The narrator agrees: "'Had we stayed as Hindus, our women would have had the chance of divorce at least. But in everything else, we are all in the same position" (97). Their dream of getting freedom from their oppression and discrimination in the name of caste does not materialise, even after they become Christians. Even in the church, only the lower caste women need to sweep and keep the church clean, so that the other castes "march in grandly and sit down before anyone else" (119). The grip of caste is so powerful that even conversion to a religion that promises equality of all classes cannot wipe it out. When these women go and complain to the nuns, they are told that they will gain merit by sweeping the church and God will bless them specially. But the village women could sense: "How they fool us in the name of God! Why don't those people need God's blessing too?" (119). In her interview, Bama states: "In reality, there is no difference between Hindus and Christians in the way they treat Dalits. The only difference between the two is that while Hinduism is basically hierarchical, Christianity claims to be caste-free, but in practice it preserves the caste hierarchy" (Azhagarasan 146). It is only the Dalit women who have to carry their offerings to the priest and not the men. Bama puts the multi-domain marginalisation of Dalit women in a nutshell:

> The position of women is both pitiful and humiliating, really. In the fields they have to escape from upper-caste men's molestations. At church they must lick the priest's shoes and be his slaves while he threatens them with tales of God, Heaven, and Hell. Even when they go to their own homes, before they have had a chance to cook some kanji or lie down and rest a little, they have to submit themselves to their husbands' torment. (*SE* 35)

Thus, through her autoethnography, Bama exposes the predicament of the Dalit women, beset by the "ethno" factors, caste and patriarchy, which prove to be an impediment to their emancipation. As Malathi Maitri remarks: "Family, Society, Community, Religion and Constitution – All these five institutions oppress the existence of women.... It is only the most backward and marginalised women who bear the brunt of the Hindu culture" (53).

It is significant to note that Bama highlights the inherent human nature to combat the life's challenges, the "ethno" factors, with the weapon of the "auto" factor – the power of the self. The "auto" factor within the narrator transcends the limitations caused by the "ethno" factors, namely, caste/race and patriarchy. The self-introspection and self-analysis of the narrator result in self awareness which is indispensable for the emancipation from the tentacles of the "ethno" factors. As Carolyn Ellis in her "Autoethnography, Personal Narrative, Reflexivity: Researcher as Subject", succinctly puts it: "Autoethnography provides an avenue for doing something meaningful for yourself and the world..." (207). In her journey towards self-realisation, the narrator, Pathima, not only get deliverance for herself, but also paves the way for the deliverance of her community from the marginalised predicament. The evolution of the right attitude and the radical transformation in her outlook are manifested in her autoethnography. There is a transformation from her befuddled state of mind entrapped by the clutches of casteism to the state of tranquillity and she becomes an enlightened individual with fervour to empower their community.

Bama in her Preface says:

> *Sangati,* which has at its theme the growth, decline, culture, and liveliness of Dalit women, changed me as well. Even in times of trouble, boredom, and depression, the urge grew to demolish the troubles and to live happily. To bounce like a ball that has been hit became my deepest desire and not to curl up and collapse because of the blow. (vii)

The optimistic self which aspires for, the so far denied equality is revealed in Bama. Being a self-realised soul, Bama has "resolved to write about Dalit women, especially about those who stood up to protest against the atrocities ... not simply about the victims" (Azhagarasan 151). She asks, "You know who were the narrators in my stories?" and emphatically replies, "My amma and my paatti" (151). She does not merely analyse the root cause of the multi-domain marginalisation of the women of her community, its gravity and its impacts, she also comes out with an effective solution to the pursuing problem. According to her, it is meaningless to expect the government or others to redress this: "We must take up the challenge ourselves .... We must stand up for ourselves and declare that we too are human beings like everyone else. If we believe that someone else is going to come and uplift us, then we are doomed to remain where we are, forever" (*SE* 66). She wants the Dalit women to realise the "auto" factors in themselves, particularly their self-esteem and the potential of their self: "But if only we were to realize that we too have self-worth, honour, and self-respect; we could manage our own lives on our own way" (68). Pathima, the narrator, is resolute:

> We must be strong. We must show by our own resolute lives that we believe ardently in our independence. I told myself that we must never allow our minds to be worn out, damaged and broken in the belief that this is our fate. Just as we work hard so long as there is strength in our bodies, so too, must we strengthen our hearts and minds in order to survive. (59)

Similar to the physical strength, what is more imperative is mental strength. Bama also ventures to resolve the age-old discrimination found between the girl-boy children in the patriarchal society. She affirms:

> We must bring up our girls to think in these new ways from an early age. We should educate boys and girls alike, showing no difference between them as they grow into adults. We should give our girls the freedom we give our boys. If we rear our children like this from the time they are babies, women will reveal their strength. Then there will come a day when men and women will live as one with no difference between them; with equal rights. Then injustices, violence and inequalities will come to an end, and the saying will come true that 'Women can make and women can break'. I am hopeful that such a time will come soon. (123)

Her vision of creating an egalitarian society is succinctly summed up in her Afterword to *Karukku:* "... I have also been crushed by the growing violence, cruelties and repressive measures directed towards Dalits in recent times. Beyond all this there stands firm a fierce anger that wants to break down everything that obstructs the creation of an equal and just society, and an unshakable belief in that goal" (106). She reinforces the same desire in *Sangati* through Pathima: "And I don't like to hide my identity and pretend I belong to a different caste. The question beats away in my word; Why should I tell a lie and live a false life?" (*SE* 120-121). The proposition of "caste identity" theory proves to be relevant here: "*Caste Identity* theory is a clarion call to all lower castes to be conscious of their own caste as caste which is no way inferior to any higher castes" (Chowdhury 18). The benefit of this caste identity is that it "asserts your dignity. With sense of dignity the low castes together can valiantly fight with enthusiasm" (18). Like in Marxism, where "the class consciousness of the proletariat is a vital step forward in their advance to classless society... in a caste society, caste consciousness of the low caste" (19) is a vital move. This identity can be used as a "strategic weapon to emphasise castes at the initial stages to achieve casteless society in the ultimate stage" (19). Pathima declares her caste loudly.

She has no inhibition to assert her identity: "I often get angry enough to shout it out aloud: I am a paraichi; yes I am a paraichi" (*SE* 120-121).

Compared to the upper caste women, Dalit women, according to Bama, face more problems in the social domain like taking a house for renting: "I have to struggle so hard because I'm a woman. And exactly like that, my people are punished constantly for the simple fact of having been born as Dalits. Is it our fault that we are Dalits? On top of that, just because I am a woman, I have to battle specially hard" (121-122). At least she could live a less-problematic life, with her "little education" (122) and earning. But the women of her community are illiterate. She says: "... when I think of the women from my community who can't tell 'a' from 'aa' and bend low to receive endless blows at home and at work, I am filled with frustration" (122). Though Bama feels sorry for their plight, she is of the conviction that they have a strong will to survive. Though buffeted by heavy odds in life, these women manage to pull along with their indomitable spirit.

Bama's observation of the girls of her community stands as a testimony: "In our streets the girls hardly ever enjoy a period of childhood.... Yet, in spite of all their suffering and pain one cannot but be delighted by their sparkling words, their firm head, and their bubbling laughter" (75). She reiterates that she is not an isolated individual but the representative of the women of her community: "Today when I say, 'I', it includes people like me. All these things together form our collective identity and help us all to act together. I cannot claim for myself the identity of an individual, a Dalit woman, I am part of a collective awareness. I carry their voices" (qtd. in Azhagarasan 151). The autoethnography of Bama brings to the fore the fact that, "Over the years, the Dalit women themselves have constructed an identity about their lives and struggles. This identity deals about their multiples roles and problems faced as an individual, in the family, at work places, in the religious sphere and in the Dalit and wider society" (Louis 130).

The fact that the life-writing of Bama is not merely restricted to her personal accounts but an authentic representation of the people of her community is explicitly seen in *Sangati: Events.* Thus, it is more autoethnographical than mere autobiographical. As Nadia Santiago succinctly expresses: "Autoethnography, ... is well suited to topics that seek an understanding of how people understand and negotiate (or renegotiate) their identities. It also is not for everyone. Those who have a passion for looking within and the courage to re-examine an intense emotional past may want to give it a try." Bama exudes this passion, re-live and re-examine such emotional past and attain self-awareness and identity. She is able to achieve empowerment in her life with the self-realisation and determination to lead her life. Thus, the autoethnography reveals the equanimity achieved by her retarded by the "ethno" factors but transcended by the powerful "auto" factors of self-introspection and explication. Her self-discovery not only redeems her but also serves to enlighten the other marginalised. McIlveen is right in demanding that, "Rather than a self-absorbed rendering, an autoethnography should produce a narrative that is authentic and thus enable the reader to deeply grasp the experience and interpretation of this one interesting case." Bama's *Sangati: Events* is an outstanding testimony to this.

WORKS CITED

Ambedkar. B.R. *Ambedkar: Autobiographical Notes*. Pondicherry: Navayana, 2003.

Azhagarasan, R. "I am Part of a Collective Awareness: An Interview with Bama." *Vanmam: Vendetta*. By Bama. Trans. Malini Seshadri. New Delhi: Oxford U. Press, 2008.142-161.

Bama. *Sangati: Events.* Trans. Lakshmi Holmström. New Delhi: Oxford UP, 2005. Trans. from Tamil *Sangati.*

______Afterword. *Karukku*. Trans. Lakshmi Holmström. Chennai: Macmillan India Limited, 2000. 105-106.

______Preface. *Karukku*. Trans. Lakshmi Holmström. Chennai: Macmillan India Limited, 2000. xiii-xiv.

Chowdhury, Singha. S. "'Caste Identity' is the only Right Road to Caste War & Revolution." *Dalit Voice* 1-15 May. 2009: 17-22.

Clifford, James. "On Ethnographic Authority." *A Cultural Studies Reader: History, Theory, Practice.* Ed. Jessica Munns, and Gita Rajan. London: Longman, 1995. 258-283.

Dallmayr, Fred. *Beyond Orientalism: Essays on Cross-cultural Encounter*. Albany: State University of New York, 1996.

Edgar, Donald. *Introduction to Australian Society: A Sociological Perspective*. Australia: Prentice Hall, 1980.

"Ethnography." Def. Johnston. R.J. *The Dictionary of Human Geography*. Eds. R.J. Derek Gregory, Geraldine Pratt and Michael Watts. USA: Blackwell Publishers Inc., 2000.

Ellis, Carolyn. *The Ethnographic I: A Methodological Novel About Autoethnography*. CA: Altamira Press-Rowman & Littlefield, 2004. *books.google.co.in*.

_______ and Arthur P. Bochner. "Autoethnography, Personal Narrative, Reflexivity: Researcher as Subject." *Collecting and Interpreting Qualitative Materials*. Eds. Norman K. Denzin and Yvonna S. Lincoln. California: Sage Publications, 2003, *book.google.co.in*

Gearon, Liam. ed. *Human Rights & Religion: A Reader*. Brighton: Sussex Academic Press, 2002. 77-83.

Holmström. Lakshmi. Introduction. *Sangati: Events*. By Bama. Trans. Lakshmi Holmström. New Delhi: Oxford UP, 2005. xi-xxiii.

Jaffrelot, Christophe, *Dr. Ambedkar and Untouchability: Analysing and Fighting Caste*. Delhi: Permanent Black, 2005.

Louis, Prakash. *Political Sociology of Dalit Assertion*. New Delhi: Gyan Publishing House, 2003.

Maithri, Malathi. *Nam Thanthayarai Kolvatheppadi. [How to Kill our Fathers]*. Trans. Mine. Chennai: Pulam, 2008.

McIlveen P. "Autoethnography as a method for Reflexive Research and Practice in Vocational Psychology." *Australian Journal of Career Development*. (2008): 13-20.

Mills, Sara. *Discourse*. London: Routledge, 2004.

Nagarajan, Rema. "It's an Exclusive Story". *Times of India 28* March 2009, Chennai. ed.: 2 Pr

Narayanan, K.R. *A Dalit President Speaks*. Chennai : Dalit Media Network, 2000.

Omvedt, Gail. *Dalit Visions*. 1995; rpt. New Delhi: Orient Longman Private Ltd, 2006.

Porter, Noah. "CMA Methodology: Autoethnography." 2004.

Russel, Catherine. "Autoethnography: Journeys of the Self." Excerpt from *Experimental Ethnography*. *n*.p.: Duke UP, 1999.

Santiago, Nadia. "Autoethnography: Research from within." *San Jose Scholarly / Examiner.com*.

Vucinich et al. Chennai: Orient Longman, 2007. ix-xvi.

Vucinich, Janet. Translator's Preface. *Government Brahmana*. By Aravind Malagatti. Trans.

Wall, Sarah. "An Autoethnography on Learning About Autoethnography." *International Journal of Qualitative Methods*. 5 (2). Article 9. June 2006.

8

A Culture of Violence: A Study of Kishwar Desai's *Witness the Night* and Githa Hariharan's *Fugitive Histories*

— Aparna Sundaram

The nineties ushered in an era of change that redefined the ethos of the country. In this atmosphere of change it is important to note how women's lives have been transformed. Today, women are a part of almost all spheres of activity and there is an overall sense of empowerment among them. The reality of the situation is however complex and dichotomous as women on the one hand are empowered through education and financial independence but on the other hand they have to constantly battle with the deep-rooted traditional beliefs and practices that are detrimental to their ability to attain their true potential as individuals on their own right. This paper aims to analyse one such issue—violence perpetrated against women.

'Violence against women', is a phrase that has become so commonplace in the modern discourse that it fails to make an impact on anyone who hears or reads it. This goes on to show how the society has dismally failed its women even though they have become greater participants in the building of the new India. Bharti Ray and Aparna Basu place violence against women as one of the foremost issues that are of concern for women in contemporary India (xiii-xiv). This paper will be exploring this very aspect which is an ugly truth, an open secret that dents the buoyancy of India's spectacular growth in the twenty-first century. The status of women can be the indicator of the real progress of a nation.

The paper will be analysing acts of violence against women under the following points of focus, namely,

- Right to be born—female infanticide and foeticide.
- A matter of (dis)honour—honour killings / violence in the name of honour.
- A woman's body as a battlefield—rape and sexual assault during conflicts.

Kishwar Desai's *Witness the Night* (2010) and Githa Hariharan's *Fugitive Histories* (2009) are the two novels that the paper will study to explore these issues. The two writers are important literary voices of contemporary times who lend their perspective to important feminist issues that are plaguing the nation and hampering the growth of women. Desai's *Witness the Night* deals with female infanticide and foeticide and violence against women. *Fugitive Histories* deals with the complexities of religious identities in India and the repercussions of the Gujarat riots on the lives on women as their bodies became battlefields where men fought their wars.

The paper will set out to establish that there exists a culture of violence against women in our country and unravel the many layers of regressive ideas and practices behind the veneer of a progressive nation in the twenty-first century.

Kishwar Desai (b.1957 had an illustrious career in media as a journalist, scriptwriter, TV anchor, producer and the head of a TV channel. She began her writing career with the book *Darlingji: The True Love Story of Nargis and Sunil Dutt* published in 2007. *Witness the Night* (2010) is her first work of fiction which was in the long list of the Man Asian Literary Prize. Recently the book won her the prestigious Costa Book Award for First Novel for 2010. With an arresting writing style, Desai has created a commendable thriller in her debut novel. Her deep social conscience is revealed in the novel as she highlights the plight of girl children in a highly prejudiced upper class Punjabi society. She currently lives in London, Delhi and Goa.

Githa Hariharan (b.1954) is one of the most important novelists and writers in contemporary India. Her fiction reflects sensitive and contentious issues that have taken centre stage in the society which makes her an important social commentator of our times. Subtlety is her forte with which she achieves moments of literary brilliance. Born in Coimbatore, she grew up in Bombay and Manila. She worked as a writer in television and later as an editor and freelance writer. Her first novel, *The Thousand Faces of Night* (1992) won the Commonwealth Writers' Prize in 1993. Her other novels include *The Ghosts of Vasu Master* (1994), *When Dreams Travel* (1999), *In Times of Siege* (2003), and *Fugitive Histories* (2009). She is a visiting professor in many Western universities and is currently a scholar-in-residence in Jamia Milia Islamia University in Delhi.

The two novels *Witness the Night* and *Fugitive Histories* are significant contributions to literature and society in the way they have effectively depicted the various facets of Indian womanhood and the myriad challenges involved in liberating women from the patriarchal shackles. The important feminist issue that comes to the forefront while reading these novels is violence against women which is truly reflective of the times that we live in.

In the twenty-first century, one of the worst forms of human rights abuse is the unending perpetration of violence against women. On the International Women's Day in 2008, the UN Secretary General Ban Ki-Moon said that: "Violence against women and girls continues unabated in every continent, country and culture. It has taken a devastating toll on women's lives, on their families and on society as a whole. Most societies prohibit such violence—yet the reality is that too often, it is covered up or tacitly condoned" (qtd. in "Facts & Figures"). Throughout the world women are being subject to various forms of violence meted out to them by known and unknown males. Fran Hosken argues that violence against women is perpetrated "with an astonishing consensus among the men in the world" (qtd. in Mohanty 178). As much as women have reasons to celebrate their emancipation there are equally compelling reasons for women to be concerned because of their vulnerability to violence. Women have and are still suffering domestic violence, sexual harassment, rape and sexual violence, harmful traditional practices like genital mutilation, honour killings, female foeticide and infanticide and dowry deaths. Women suffer violence at the hands of the very same people who are supposed to love them like fathers, husbands, lovers, boyfriends and relatives. Everyday numerous women are battered, molested, raped, and murdered around the world. Most of these incidents go unreported. Sustained campaigns by feminists against sexual violence since 1970s have prompted the United Nations to recognise "violence against women and girl children as a violation of human rights" (Radford 170).

In a country like India that is largely rooted in patriarchal traditions and mores, women have always been living in shackles in the form of regressive attitudes and ideas that curb their freedom. Indian women are just as vulnerable to violence as women elsewhere. Media reports are replete with news of violence against women in some form or the other. There is a pervasive culture of violence against women in the country cutting across regional boundaries. Ruth Vanita believes that "For every one reported police rape taken up by women's groups in India, there are hundreds of unreported routine marital rapes: for every case of severe wife-beating there are hundreds of more routinized, less severe violence ..." (530). Female infanticide/ foeticide, dowry deaths, rape and sexual assaults, honour killings, domestic violence, sexual harassment are some of the forms of violence that women face in India today. Feminists and women's groups have been fighting a hard battle in India to introduce and amend legislations with regards to violence against women. The Prevention of Domestic Violence Act of 2005 is an example. This law has many challenges when it comes to its implementation but still it is a step forward for women to take legal recourse for an atrocity that went unquestioned. Domestic violence which incapacitates women and crushes their physical and emotional well-being, was considered a personal matter till recently, until feminists brought it to the public space. This paper will focus on three forms of violence namely female foeticide / infanticide, honour killings and rape / sexual assault during conflicts.

Female foeticide and infanticide—killing of infant girls or female foetuses because they are girls—is a practice that is quite prevalent in India in varying degrees in urban and rural areas. This is a practice that reveals the deep-rooted prejudices and age-old beliefs, gender inequality and misogyny that exist in the society. 'May you be the mother of a hundred sons' is a common blessing given to women in India (Bumiller 10). The idea that giving birth to a son is a privilege and a girl is a curse is deeply ingrained in the Indian psyche. Sudhir Kakkar states that: "The preference for a son when a child is born is as old as Indian society itself. Vedic verses pray that sons will be followed by more male offspring, never by females" (8). The *Atharva Veda* states that: "The birth of a girl, grant elsewhere, here grant a son" (qtd. in Kakar 8).

One of the reasons for son-preference can be attributed to the Hindu belief that a son has to light the funeral pyre for the parents to go to heaven. Dowry is another important reason that forces mothers and fathers to kill their own infant daughters. A woman "who pines for a son becomes disheartened at seeing the birth of a girl. She begs for the pardon from the family members as if she has committed a crime" (Malladi 10). Julie Rajan is of the opinion that: "Even women are culturally ingrained to value their own gender with low regard, as the value of the male gender is tied closely to a woman's social and political power". Over the years the girl child has come to mean a 'burden' for the family because of the money involved in her upbringing and arranging her marriage. But even in many urban centres this despicable practice is carrying on in spite of the parents being educated and where there is a greater chance for the daughters to become independent. Bumiller who extensively researched this practice in the eighties in Bombay and rural Tamilnadu says that: "Most of the educated, well off-women of Bombay were of course trying to avoid the astronomical cost of dowries in India, but among the rich, who could afford the cost of any number of weddings, a stronger motive seemed to be to avoid the social embarrassment of having daughters but no sons" (114).

The sex ratios in the in the country suggests that female foeticide and infanticide is happening at an alarming rate that has led to a great paucity of women which is harmful for the growth of any society. According to the Census 2001, the all India sex ratio is 933 females per 1000 males. Haryana is the state with the lowest sex ratio with 861 females (*A Handbook*). "2001 census informed us that we had 60 lakh missing girls", says Thekaekara about the numerous infant girls and foetuses that were not given a chance to be born in India. Comparatively, Census 2011 suggests that the all India sex ratio is 940 females per 1000 males while Haryana's sex ratio has seen a marginal increase with 877. However the worrying scenario emerges from the child sex ratio (from ages 0-6) that suggests the prevalence of female foeticide and infanticide. The all India ratio is 914, while Haryana has recorded 830 ("Provisional Population Totals"). Manjula Padmanabhan in her novel *Escape* (2008) has envisaged a futuristic society bereft of women which may become possible if the killing of girl children continues.

Technological advances have only made female foeticide easy and convenient for those parents who crave for a son and can do away with an unwanted daughter in her foetal stage itself. In the seventies and eighties, procedures like amniocentesis and chorionic villus sampling (CVS), which were performed to detect defects in the child, were used extensively to find the sex of the child and consequently led to abortion if it was a female (Bumiller 115). It was usually the third daughter who was forced to die as parents made peace with raising one or even two girls (Karlekar 314). The ultrasound scan, which is a non-invasive and easy method to detect the sex of the child, is the modern day's answer to the continuing menace of female foeticide. Private clinics mushroomed in urban areas like Bombay which used to lure people with ads that stated: "Better 500 rupees now than 500,000 rupees later", indicating the huge dowries to be paid for a daughter's marriage (Bumiller 115). There was a huge uproar among feminists in Bombay in the eighties against this inhuman practice. The parliament passed the Pre-natal Diagnostic Practices (Regular and Prevention of Misuse) Act in 1994 which followed a similar law enacted by the state of Maharashtra in 1988 (Menon 279). Laws did not deter many families from opting for sex selective abortions nor doctors and medical practitioners from performing these procedures.

Female infanticide is another way of getting rid of a girl child. Tandon and Sharma describe it as "a deliberate and intentional act of killing a female child within one year of its birth either directly by using poisonous organic and inorganic chemicals or indirectly by deliberate neglect to feed the infant by either one of the parents or other family members of neighbours or by the midwife" (3). The female infants would be fed poison or the husk of rice in order to kill them for being born as girls. This practice was prevalent among some communities in rural Tamilnadu, Punjab, Rajastan, Gujarat and UP (Tandon and Sharma 3). Mariaye, a woman from a poor family in rural Tamilnadu who killed her infant daughter told Bumiller: "' Actually, I have done the right thing. Why should a child suffer like me?'" (102).

It is within this premise—that of wanting a male child and abhorring the birth of a girl—that Kishwar Desai's novel *Witness the Night* lies. The novel is a severe indictment of a society that treats its women in such a contemptible manner. At the heart of the hard-hitting narrative, is the tragic tale of fourteen year old Durga who was a victim of gross injustice meted out to her because she was a girl. Set in Jallundur, the novel traces the travails of social worker, Simran, as she traverses through a dangerous and corrupt world of policemen and politicians in the pursuit of justice for Durga who is a suspect in the murder of her entire family.

Durga was the daughter of wealthy Punjabi Sikh parents who were well respected in Jallundur, Punjab, as philanthropists. The family clearly preferred sons to daughters as was the case in many families in the region. Durga and her older sister Sharada knew that they were unwanted right from the beginning. Their parents adopted the father's nephews to raise as their sons because they did not have their own. Desai's idea of using the word "Boys" with a capital letter in all of Durga's narratives was deliberate to indicate the importance given to them in the Atwal family. Durga and her sister's world was clearly defined by their gender with little or no freedom or space to call their own. Any misdemeanours from the side of their brothers were completely tolerated but the same was not the case for Durga and Sharada. They only had each other for solace in a hostile atmosphere filled with people who did not want them in the first place. Durga always used to pine for love: "Someone would love me, someone would hold me close" (Desai 16). It was this loveless existence that drove an unsuspecting Durga into the arms of a sexual predator who used her to his own ends and later led her to be embroiled in the murder of her whole family.

Desai reveals in the course of the novel that both Durga and Sharada were supposed to have died just after birth. In her narrative, Durga called herself "the child who should have never been born anyway" (18). Their family wanted to kill them because they were girls. They were fed opium and buried but somehow they did not die and were allowed to live because the family thought they were witches. Durga gives a detailed account of the attempts by her family to kill Sharada after she was born:

> At first they gave her opium and put her in a pot of milk and twirled it around. Miraculously, the milk turned to butter and the crying child still lived. The opium did not put her to sleep.... Finally my grandmother picked up courage and instructed the wretched girl be buried in a clay pot in the earth at night. Unfortunately for her the dogs dug her out... (82)

She later imagined her own attempted killing:

> I imagined myself—a tiny child as yet not even able to suckle—being fed opium. I probably went to sleep, and they may have thought I was dead. It was only when they began to bury me in the ground that my sudden shriek made Amla run because she thought I was a ghost. I can still feel the earth being shovelled onto me. Sometimes in my nightmares the mud descends on my face, handfuls of dirt are shoved into my mouth and in my eyes. Breathless, I gulp for air and fight the bed sheets. (156-157)

The life that the sisters lived was fraught with hatred, prejudice and complete lack of love. Sharada once found skeletal remains of an infant in the fields behind their bungalow which made the sisters realise that there were many others before them who had to die because they were born girls. In a heart-wrenching part in the novel, Durga looked at a tiny bone and asked her sister: "Did she have a name?...I'd like to pretend she had a name, and a chance to grow up.... These little babies...no one even remembers them.... They could have been our sisters" (138-139; 3rd ellipsis in orig.). The girls cried for their dead sisters. Durga even kept the bones of an infant hand in her pencil box as a reminder of a sister that she was not allowed to have.

The so-called philanthropic parents of Durga even ran many clinics and hospitals in the city where sex determination and sex selective abortions were carried out in large numbers. They wanted to "help" other couples from having unwanted daughters. They also wanted to abort the female foetus of their daughter-in-law, Binny, who escaped to her family in UK and gave birth to her daughter. When Durga heard this news that a girl was born in her family in a loving, safe and secure environment, she said: "I don't know if you understand how important this is for me, for us" (122).

Punjab, the state in which this novel is set, has a dismal record in terms of sex ratio and incidence of sex selective abortions. Among the Sikh population, the sex ratio is 893 women per 1,000 males (*A Handbook*). According to the 2011 Census, Punjab has a sex ratio of 893 while the child sex ratio is 846. The urbanised capital city of Chandigarh, has an appalling sex ratio of 818 and a child sex ratio of 867 ("Provisional Population Totals").

In *Witness the Night*, Kishwar Desai also touches upon the issue of honour killings, another harmful traditional practice that is detrimental to a woman's freedom. It is largely reported to be taking place in countries like Pakistan, Turkey, Jordan, Syria, Egypt, Lebanon, Iran, Yemen, Morocco and India ("Facts & Figures" 4) which are primarily traditional societies. Honour killings—an act that has no honour in it—is the killing of women who would defy the rigid and conservative strictures about sexual conduct and relationship with the opposite sex based on misplaced ideas about a woman's chastity and purity. The heinous crime of honour killing is committed because, "In many societies, rape victims, women suspected of engaging in premarital sex, and women accused of adultery have been murdered by their relatives because the violation of a woman's chastity is viewed as an affront to the family's honour" ("Facts & Figures" 4). There have been numerous instances of fathers, brothers and uncles killing young girls for these transgressions because they believe that in the chastity of the girls rests the honour of the family. A girl must, at any cost, preserve her chastity and virginity and the family takes pride in giving her away in marriage to a 'suitable' male with her virginity intact. No such thing is of course expected of men. A man does not necessarily carry the honour of the family on himself nor do his transgressions in anyway prove to dishonour his family.

Most families tolerate men's sexual misdemeanours as a male prerogative. As Simone de Beauvoir says: "Patriarchal civilization dedicated women to chastity; it recognized more or less openly the right of the male to sexual freedom" (395). According to R. S. Shrivastava, "Norms of sexual behaviour are much more stringent in case of women. They are considered to be the 'symbols' of honour of their family or community. Sexual 'purity' in case of women is to be maintained at all cost, while the males enjoy relative flexibility in sexual attitudes and conduct" (173). Most honour killings are endorsed by the families and communities and are carried out with their collusion. It is important to note that a small percentage of men are also victims of honour killings for having relationships with girls from different communities or religions—killed by the girls' families. United Nations Population Fund estimates that the annual worldwide number of honour killing may be as high as 5,000 women ("Facts & Figures" 4).

In India the practice of honour killings is prevalent in parts of UP, Haryana and Punjab. In the past year alone many cases of honour killings came to light in the media. In urban and modern Delhi, a nineteen year old girl Asha and her twenty year-old boyfriend were murdered by her family last year by the girl's family. The reason was that the boy was from a lower social class (Rahlan). In May 2010, in Allahabad, UP, an eighteen year-old girl was murdered by her own brother because she became pregnant while she was unmarried (Joseph). In Punjab, a prominent politician Bibi Jagir Kaur is facing trial for allegedly killing her daughter Harpreet Kaur for marrying a man from a lower social stratum (Swami). Honour killings are prevalent in the west among the Asian and Middle Eastern immigrant population (Chesler).

In *Witness the Night* Durga's sister Sharada, a sixteen year old teenager, fell in love with her tutor, Harpreet, hired to teach both the girls. Harpreet's good looks, charm and compassion towards the girls won the heart of Sharada. She became pregnant and very naively began to dream of eloping with him till one day she was caught by her family members. Sharada had violated all the norms laid down for her by her conservative family by not only falling in love with a man from a lower caste but also becoming sexually involved with him. In the novel, Simran concludes that Sharada "has crossed the lakshman rekha. In a tradition-bound small town like Jullundur, sex outside marriage was taboo. Only the tribal family elders could decide who a woman could marry and sleep with" (103-104). Sharada's act was a clearly an affront to the honour of the Atwal family and their reputation.

Sharada was forcibly taken away from home by her family, kept in isolation and beaten and tortured till her child was born. Her son was taken away from her and was being raised by her 'son-starved' parents as their own. Later she was shifted to a mental asylum and was treated for diseases that she never had. After a period of unnecessary treatment involving drugs, medication and electric shocks, Sharada lost her mind. She lost her ability to speak and think and the only way she communicated with the world was through some unintelligible sounds. She became a mere shell of her former beautiful and intelligent self. Durga painfully narrates Sharada's pitiful state in the novel: "Her lying on that bed, handcuffed to the side, not even allowed any clothes or food, a long chain keeping her from wandering too far away...she would be like that for days, her faeces mixed with menstrual blood lining the floor till someone came and cleaned it up. Why did they do this to her? Her own family, her own flesh and blood?" (166). When Simran found Sharada, she described her thus:

> Her clothes, just a long kaftan, had ridden up her legs, revealing scabs and scars from old wounds. Her hand, chained to the bed, fluttered weakly, twisting like a white butterfly. She was pale, paler that anyone I had ever seen; even her hair was white. She was only twenty years old, and the mother of a young son, but she looked like she was a frail woman of sixty. Her skin hung in emaciated strings from her bones. What a price to pay for one summer of love. (118)

Sharada was not killed in the name of honour but in decimating her and maiming her for life, they had come very close to killing her. In the end as Durga was recuperating from her own trauma, she was trying to help Sharada make sense of the world that she was lost to.

The Atwal family's attitude in the novel reflects the attitude of the modern Indian society that still holds on to archaic ideas that places women in a secondary position and makes them victims of cruel and gruesome acts in the name of upholding traditions and family honour.

Rape is a violent crime against a woman that violates her physically, mentally and emotionally. Rape is being used as a weapon by men to assert power over women for centuries. Susan Brownmiller states that: "Man's discovery that genitilia could serve as a weapon in prehistoric times, along with the use of fire and the first crude stone axe. From prehistoric times to the present, I believe, rape has played a critical function. It is nothing more or less than a conscious process of intimidation by which all men keep women in a state of fear". Among traditional societies in some parts of rural India and Pakistan, women are raped as a punishment for the wrongdoing of the men in their families. Rape is used as a form of control in rural areas (Rosa 42). In India people often judge the rape victims saying that she 'asked for it' because of the way she dressed or behaved. Even in the twenty-first century there is no sign of decline in the number of rape cases that are reported. According to *A Handbook of Statistical Indicators on Indian Women 2007*, the number of reported rapes in 2001 was 16075 which went up to 15847 in 2003 and in 2006 it became 19348. There may be so many cases that go unreported because of the stigma attached to it. A rape victim is victimised many times over during the course of getting justice, in facing the stigma of the society and dealing with her own mental trauma.

Rape has become a vicious form of attack during conflicts. Amrita Basu says that: "Thanks to feminist scholarship, we have come to recognize the political significance of the violence that is enacted in the domestic sphere and its corollary, the rape of women as an instrument of warfare" (265). In an ethnic conflict, the fighting is always been between two groups of warring men and one of the ways to attack each other is to violate the bodies of their women. Men consider women as part of their wealth and property and identify greatly with their possessions and an attack like rape on women is considered a great affront to men's honour. R.S. Shrivastava believes: "Since the symbol of honour and prestige of a family or community resides in women, they are the first to be targeted in any situation of conflict between two groups. During war times the women of the vanquished side are considered to be the legitimate possession of the victors" (173). Wars between men are fought on the bodies of women thereby making women's bodies battlefields to settle scores. Looking back at history, the partition of India was witness to numerous rapes and gang rapes of women on both sides of the border. Fearing rape many women committed suicide before attackers could reach them or the men in their families killed them to protect their honour. They believed that it was better for women to die that to be raped by other men.

During times of war and conflicts women are doubly vulnerable because they may be killed or raped or both. Even in the past two decades, when the world has seen some of the bloodiest ethnic conflicts in the Balkan region and in many countries in Africa, it was women who suffered unspeakable sexual violence. "Women's bodies have become part of the battleground for those who use terror as a tactic of war—they are raped, abducted, humiliated and made to undergo forced pregnancy, sexual abuse and slavery.... Violence against women during or after armed conflicts is reported in every international or non-international war zone" ("Facts & Figures" 7). According to "Facts & Figures", 70 per cent of the victims in recent conflicts have been non-combatants—women and children. In Rwanda half million women were raped during the 1994 genocide, in Bosnia–Herzegovina and Croatia sixty thousand were raped and sixty four thousand women were rape victims of the civil war in Sierra Leone (7). There are rape wards in some hospitals in Africa where rape victims get treated for brutalities that were inflicted on their bodies. Little girls to women of any age are vulnerable to rape during conflicts when there is an absolute break down of human values.

Communal riots have a long history in India right from the Partition to the post-Babri Masjid demolition riots in the early nineties, which proves that in some parts of India the Hindu-Muslim coexistence has been an uneasy one. In the beginning of the twenty-first century, one of the worst communal riots happened in the Gujarat in which around two thousand Muslims were killed. The riots began as retaliation to the burning of a train in the town of Godhra in which 59 people belonging to the Hindu community, who were travelling from the temple town of Ayodhya, were killed. The ensuing large-scale riots that happened between February 28, 2002 and March 02, 2002 were aimed at Muslims, their lives and properties (Khetan).

Women paid a heavy price during the riots as they were sexually brutalised by rampaging mobs. These stories went largely unreported or underreported in the media. Sayeda Hameed et al. who went to Gujarat in March 2002 on a fact finding mission reported that:

> There is compelling evidence of sexual violence against women. These crimes have been grossly underreported and the exact extent of these crimes—in rural and urban areas—demands further investigation. Among the women surviving in relief camps, are many who have suffered the

> most bestial forms of sexual violence—including rape, gang rape, mass rape, stripping, insertion of objects into their body, molestations. A majority of rape victims have been burnt alive (4).

Many women were raped and murdered and those who survived found it difficult to file FIRs to report the crimes. One thing that came to light after the riots was the collusion of the state and its indifference. Even after nine years, many rape victims of the Gujarat riots are yet to get justice. These women face multiple problems of displacement, loss of livelihood and families. Above that they also have to cope with the trauma of rape. The following is an account of a rape survivor, Sultani:

> On the afternoon of February 28th, to escape the violent mob, about 40 of us got on to a tempo, wanting to escape Kalol. My husband Feroze was driving the tempo…A mob was lying in wait…. The tempo overturned. As we got out they started attacking us. People started running in all directions. Some of us ran towards the river. I fell behind as I was carrying my son, Faizan. The men caught me from behind and threw me on the ground. Faizan fell from my arms and started crying. My clothes were stripped off by the men and I was left stark naked. One by one, men raped me. All the while I could hear my son crying. I lost count after three. They then cut my foot with a sharp weapon and left me there.
>
> (Hameed et al. 6)

Githa Hariharan's *Fugitive Histories* deals with religious identities in India and questions whether one can be a-religious. The author has etched some memorable characters like Azad, an artist who died heart-broken as he watched his fellow citizens kill each other in the name of religion. Mala, his wife is one of the important characters in the novel who believed in the ideology of humanism and in blurring the religious or other divisions that exist in the society. Sara their daughter, in search of herself, found her calling in helping others, especially Yasmin, who is a displaced victim of the Gujarat riots. Hariharan brings to life the sufferings of women during conflict as their bodies became battlegrounds.

Sara visited Ahmedabad with her friend to speak to the survivors of the riots in connection with a documentary film. She came across many women who have seen and experienced the horrors of the riots as their bodies were plundered by the frenzied mobs. One of the women, Zuleikha narrated to Sara: "Those girls were screaming, they were begging us to remove the stumps of wood that had been pushed into them. Each one was crying, 'Me first, remove mine first'. I'll never forget their screams" (Hariharan 160). Many victims of the riots lived on measly sums earned through sewing and embroidering and among the women there was a wonderful sisterhood which helped in alleviating their collective pain and suffering.

Yasmin was a seventeen year-old who lived quite happily with her parents and brother till the riots happened after which their peaceful life was shattered. Her brother never returned from college and the family was unable to trace him even after three years and he was presumed dead. She was almost raped by a few men but was fortunately let off because they were more interested in acquiring their house. When the attackers came to their house,

> Ammi and Yasmin hid on the roof among boxes and sacks stored behind the water tank...Yasmin is flat on the floor, its smoky dark though its not yet night. There must be something sharp in his hand. She can feel it on he inner thigh like a nail tearing the cloth of the salwar, piercing the flesh underneath, then sliding down...Ammi covers Yasmin's body with hers. Ammi's begging words make a breathless mess of a prayer. (Hariharan 145).

Her father's shop was burnt and they received many threats like "*Muslims Quit India—or we will fuck your mothers*" (Hariharan 138), after which they left the only home she had ever known. This message also shows that the way one group of men want to attack another is through the bodies of their women. The family moved to a cramped flat in another area of the city which was considered 'safe'.

Yasmin was fortunate enough to escape rape but the trauma of that incident and the stories of rapes she heard around her coloured every waking moment of her life. Fear was a constant as Yasmin walked to and from school trying hard to pass her final exams that she failed once. She was constantly bombarded with words like "*careful, alert, guarding against, taking care, anything can happen*" (Hariharan 123) by her parents; words that said that she was not safe. Her journey—walking distance—from school was an ordeal as she tried not to catch any attention and reach home safely. On her way home she thinks that "...being safe is the most important thing of all. Only being safe can help her to be free" (Hariharan 148). Yasmin's fear is an unsettling and disturbing aspect that comes out of the novel. Hariharan effectively brings out Yasmin's fear in the following lines:

> They can't see the feeling trapped inside her, fighting its way out. This is not a simple feeling. It does not have a name, something small and easy to say, like fear or anger or sadness. It is a little of this, a little of that. Sometimes the feeling changes so fast from one to the other that she needs to check the dupatta around her head and shoulders again, tighten it once more (149).

It shows that even after the riots are over, a woman's life and safety cannot be taken for granted. It is as though Yasmin's already fragile and makeshift existence was under constant threat of being destroyed.

The novel ends on an optimistic note as Yasmin's parents reluctantly agree to send her to Bombay to join college under Sara's care. The triumphant moment of the novel is when Yasmin's mother declares that her daughter will not wear the *burqa* as women of her generation did: "She is not going to be like us.... The angry ones on both sides want to put our daughters in burqas so they can prove their point. Did their burqas keep our women safe five years ago?" (227). She envisages a free and independent life for her daughter.

The subject of violence perpetrated against women discussed and analysed in this paper through a general understanding of the issues and the literary works affirm the fact that there is a culture of violence against women that exists in the country as well as the world at large. From the time of her birth, or even in the womb, a girl is subject to a continuous and sustained assault on her physical, mental and emotional being. Violence against women remains unabated even in the twenty-first century. The need of the hour is to debate, discuss and most importantly, act in order to stop this gross violation of one half of the population. As Shashi Deshpande says: "...often there are no limits to human cruelty. And cruelty had to be opposed. To be silent is to abet it" (85). By raising these issues in their novels, the two writers Kishwar Desai and Githa Hariharan have raised their voices against violence perpetrated by men on women. Through their writing they have raised some critical questions pertaining to Indian women's lives in the twenty-first century. These writers' contribution to literature and society as a whole is very significant for this very reason.

The protagonists discussed in this paper, Durga and Yasmin, both in their teens, are representatives of the present generation. Durga, an unwanted daughter of conservative parents, and Yasmin, a girl scarred by the violence of Gujarat riots, both dared to hope to have a better life for themselves—a life in which they will not be constantly battling issues that are detrimental to their freedom to choose a life of their own. If they have to stake claim to the new world, partake in the progress of India and assert their identities as confident individuals, then it must be in an atmosphere of change. It is extremely important for an attitudinal change to set in that would implore men to look at women as thinking, feeling individuals and not as fragile beings who can be attacked and violated for fulfilling their own needs. The society should not allow another girl to think as Durga did: "I often wondered what life would have been like if I had been loved and wanted and cared for. If I had a mother who did not hate me because I was a girl" (Desai 190).

The culture of violence against women is extremely pernicious for their growth and consequently for the progress of the country itself. If and only if the country can free its women from the clutches of violence can the women citizens call themselves truly free and the nation call itself progressive in the real sense of the word.

Works Cited

A Handbook of Statistical Indicators on Indian Women 2007. Ministry of Women and Child Development, Government of India. <http:wcd.nic.in>

Basu, Amrita. "Engendering Communal Violence: Men as Victims and Women as Agents". *Invented Identities: The Interplay of Gender, Religion and Politics in India*. Eds. Julia Leslie and Mary McGee. New Delhi: OUP, 2000. 265-285.

Brownmiller, Susan. *Against Our Will: Men, Women and Rape*. New York: Simon and Shester, 1975. "Excerpt from Chapter one". *Susanbrownmiller.com*.

Bumiller, Elisabeth. *May You Be the Mother of a Hundred Sons: A journey Among the Women in India*. New Delhi: Penguin, 1991.

Chesler, Phyllis. "Are Honour Killing Simply Domestic Violence?" *The Middle East Quarterly*.Spring(2009).61-69.*TheMiddleEastQuarterly*. <www.meforum.org/2067/are-honour-killings-simply-domestic-violence>

De Beauvoir, Simone. *The Second Sex*. Trans and ed. H.M. Parshley. Middlesex: Penguin, 1972.

Deshpande, Shashi "Why I am a Feminist". *Writing From the Margin and Other Essays*. New Delhi: Penguin, 2003. 82-85..

Desai, Kishwar. *Witness the Night*. New Delhi: Harper Collins, 2010.

"Facts&Figures" onVAW.*unifem.org*.UNWomen.<www.unifem.org/gender_issues/violence_against_women/facts_figures.php.>

Hameed, Syeda et al. "Gujarat Riots -The Impact on Women: How the Gujarat Masscre Affected the Minority Woman? The Survivors Speak." *Infochangeindia.org*. Centre for Communication and Developmental Studies.

Hariharan, Githa. *Fugitive Histories*. New Delhi: Penguin, 2009.

Joseph, Ammu. "No Honour in Murder". *Infochangeindia.org*. Centre for Communication and Developmental Studies.

Kakar, Sudhir. *The Essential Writing of Sudhir Kakar*. Comp. T.G. Vaidyanathan. New Delhi: OUP, 2001.

Karlekar, Malavika. "Domestic Violence". *Handbook of Indian Sociology*. Ed. Veena Das. New Delhi: OUP, 2004. 308-330.

Khetan, Ashish. "Twice Burnt Still Simmering". *Tehelka*. 4.43. (2007). *Tehelka.com*.

Mohanty, Chandra Talpade. "Under Western Eyes: Feminist Scholarship and Colonial Discourses". *Contemporary Postcolonial Theory: A Reader*. Ed. Padmini Mongia. New Delhi: OUP, 1997, 172-197.

"Provisional Population Totals- Census 2011: Punjab". *Census of India.* Government of India: Ministry of Home Affairs. n.d. Web. 02 May 11. <http: //censusindia. gov.in /2011-prov-results/data_files/punjab/ Provisional Population Result Punjab2.pdf>

Radford, Jill. "Theorizing commonalities and differences: Sexual violence, law and feminist activism in India and the UK". *Women, violence and strategies for action: Feminist research, policy and practice.* Eds. Jill Radford, Melissa Friedberg and Lynne Harne. Buckingham: Open University Press, 2000. 167-184.

Rahlan, Anisha. "Delhi Honour Killing: What Happened that Night". *Rediff.com.* 18 June 10.

Ray, Bharti and Aparna Basu. "Introduction". *From Independence Towards Freedom: Indian Women Since 1947.* New Delhi: OUP, 2000.

Rajan, Julie. "An Assessment of Human Rights Violation Against Women in Modern-Day India as a Result of Son Preference". *Sawnet.org.* South Asian Women's Network. <http://sawnet.org/articles/ Son_Preference.htm>

Rosa, Kumudhini. *Women of South Asia.* Colombo: Gala Academic Press, 1995.

Shrivatsa, R.S. "Women Empowerment: Some Critical Issues". *Modernity, Feminism and Women Empowerment.* Eds. Asha Avasthi and A.K. Shrivastava. Jaipur: Rawat Publications, 2001. 172-181.

Subbama, Malladi. *Women in Changing Society.* Hyderabad: Malladi Subbama Trust, 1994.

Swami, Praveen. "The Case of a Mother and a Daughter". *Frontline.* 17.22 (2000). *Hinduonnet.com.*

Tandon, Snehlata and Renu Sharma. "Female Foeticide and Infanticide in India: An Analysis of Crimes Against Girl Children". *International Journal of Criminal Justice Sciences.* 1.1(2006). *South Asian Society of Criminology & Victimology.* Web. 13 Jan11.

Thekaekara, Mari Marcel. "Sixty Years of Women's Struggle for Freedom?". *Infochangeindia.org.* Centre for Communication and Developmental Studies. 07 Mar 08. Web. 13 Jan 11.

Vanita, Ruth. "Thinking Beyond Gender in India". *Gender and Politics in India.* Ed. Nivedita Menon. New Delhi: OUP, 2003. 529-539.

9

House Divided against itself: Frictions and Fusions in Githa Hariharan's *In Times of Siege* and *Fugitive Histories*

— C. Amutha Charu Sheela

> "Who does this land belong to?" *(Fugitive Histories* 164)
>
> What makes a fanatic? A Fundamentalist?
> What makes communities that have lived together?
> for years suddenly discover a latent hatred for each other?
> *(In Times of Siege* 129)

These questions which arose from the cleft, wounded and bleeding heart of the Indian subcontinent as a result of the Partition and the religious riots that occurred in its aftermath still retain their urgency.

The Partition was an earth-shattering event in the annals of India's history that irrevocably altered the lives of millions. Even today its spectral presence haunts Hindu-Muslim relations, continues to widen the communal divide and ignites religio-cultural tensions in the country. Echoes of the Partition can be seen in each and every instance of communal and fundamentalist violence that has taken place since. Hindu-Muslim strife has been on the ascendancy since the 1980s. The destruction of Babri Masjid at Ayodhya in 1992 triggered widespread violence against Muslim's throughout India. In 2002 India witnessed some of the worst communal clashes ever seen in recent times, with the Gujarat state government being accused of sponsoring the terrorism against Muslims. It is against this fractious backdrop that *In Times of Siege* and *Fugitive Histories* were written. *In Times of Siege* was written shortly after BJP-Hindu right wing party formed the central government in 1999 and *Fugitive Histories* was written after the Gujarat carnage.

Contemporary women writers in Indian English writing have made significant contributions to literature. Many writers have won international awards. Their writings no longer portray the stereotypical images of women as a submissive housewife, doting mother, village girl waiting for her prince or women revolting against women. Their writings deconstruct myths that degrade women. Githa Hariharan is one such writer whose discourse shows resistance and questions every aspect of social order. *In Times of Siege* is her fourth novel and *Fugitive Histories* is the most recent one. Her first novel *The Thousand Faces of Night* won the Commonwealth Writers Prize in 1993. She then published her short stories collection *The Art of Dying* and her two novels *The Ghost of Vasu Master* and *When Dreams Travel*. When the Hindu-Muslim violence escalated, she along with her women writer friends set up a movement for secularism. She edited *Southern Harvest Stories* and also co-edited *Sorry Best Friend*, a collection of secular stories. Her stories deal with inequalities, power struggles and women asserting their identity. She observes, "All my novels and stories look at power politics in some way or the other. Fiction has a thousand ways of giving us a new take on the dynamics of power relations" (Pratham Books). Her novels straddle fear, love, caste, violence, and identity. Through an analysis of the novels *In Times of Siege* and *Fugitive Histories* this paper examines different aspects which include recasting history, question of secularism, identity and violence and other narratological models.

Recasting History

Indian English fictions of 1980's and 1990's have witnessed a steep increase in the publication of historical novels. Their writings question "some of the assumptions of that period, some choices and decisions ... it enters into a dialogue with the contemporary political reality and thus may become an expression of dissent, intellectual, disagreement and intervention in the understanding of political reality and political trends and as such seek to warn the intelligent reader" (Jain 92). In a similar manner, Hariharan uses both novels as a platform to reevaluate the pressing issues relating to controversial events in contemporary India. As the novel *In Times of Siege* unfolds it reflects the present-day tortured face of India where human rights are violated, and there are attacks on people who cherish secular ideals. The story centres on the middle-aged Professor, Shiv Murthy, who is leading a peaceful and contented life as an academic at a distance education university. His wife is on a visit to Seattle to be with their daughter. His childhood friend Sumathi's daughter, Meena, who is studying in Kamala Nehru University, comes to stay in his house when she fractures her leg, as he is her local guardian. One fine morning, Shiv finds him amidst sea of troubles when his medieval history lesson irks the Hindu fundamentalist group - Ithihas Suraksha Manch. It is Meena who induces Shiv to act and not to compromise on his stand. Taking help from Meena and her friends he decides to stand firm by the values he upholds and not succumb to pressure from the fundamentalists.

The glaringly obvious parallels between Ithihas Suraksha Manch and Hindutva fundamentalist groups are very hard to overlook. They underscore the manipulations of history attempted in 1999 when BJP was in power in the central government. The National Council of Education Research and Training was directed to revise certain passages which were considered to be pseudo– secular and rewrite the school history text books with versions that conformed to the ideology of Hindutva. The inconvenient facts such as Gandhi being assassinated by an RSS activitist were glossed over. In a similar move, the historical Indus Valley Civilization was replaced by mythical Indus Saraswathi Valley Civilization. Kai Friese notes in the *NewYork Times* that many important dates were missing in the history textbooks and that it was full of distorted and uncorroborated facts such as "India itself was the original home of the Aryans. The Aryans were an indigenous race and the creators of the Vedas" (15) Hariharan's novel *In Times of Siege* is a narrative emplotment of this controversial revision of history text books initiated by the BJP government and the tussle between the secular historians and fundamental political agents. Her protagonist Dr. Shiv Murthy's medieval history course module on Basava, twelfth century finance minister in Vijayanagar Empire was targeted by Hindu fundamentalists. His module picturizes Basava as a social revolutionary who created a "community that sought to exclude no one –not women, not the lowest, most polluting castes.... All were equal in that they were Veera shaivas; warriors of Siva" (ITOS 60). Many people got excited and took part in Basava's egalitarian dream. The story goes that the proposed marriage between a brahmin and a cobbler acted as the catalyst to destroy the whole city. Basava left the place and died in exile. Over the years he was remembered as a mystic poet and saint and it is this face of Basava as a religious figure that the Ithihas Suraksha Manch wants the historian to project and not as a "man obsessed with upsetting tradition. A dangerous man, a threat to structure, stability, religion." (87).

The demonizers feel Shiv is exaggerating the caste system in our country and is biased against brahmins and temple priests. Caste is the central fault line and the root cause of all violence in India. Hinduism believes in varnashrama. Caste hierarchical, inegalitarian structure is widely accepted. As Francesca Orsini puts it, "The ideal Indian society, the varna system, seemed to ward off the mirage of equality, the dangers of class conflict and the evil of materialism ... to reassert India's claims to superiority (qtd. in Srinivasan 98). In the violence that followed Partition, all the castes, upper caste, middle and lower class Hindus were united in orchestrating a united Hindu front against Muslims. The right wing Hindutva party wants to project India's past as a glorious, unified, homogeneous Hindu past. So they "fear that our Indian history will force people see that our past, like our present has always been critical of social divisions that masquerade as religion and tradition ... they whitewash historical figures (and) they seize history" (97) and plan to perpetrate a fictitious and homogeneous

> golden Hindu history that will legitimize their programme of one language, one religion, one nation (*ITOS* 93).

Thus Hariharan captures vividly the Hindutva-inspired party attempts at rewriting of history which runs counter to their ideologies. She asserts that any attempt to homogenize history must be opposed as one should not yield to institutional pressure and political groups.

In Times of Siege highlights the unpalatable truth that there is frequently bias and prejudice in the way history is presented:

> Vested interests....History as armor. History as propaganda, history as battleground. History as the seed of hatred. History in the hands of the mob. Conspiracy theories, rightist conspiracies, leftist conspiracies (132).

Rafiq Zakaria, scholar,writer, and diplomat admits histories can be distorted to suit particular ideologies. He says, "Facts have many facets and historical figures are complex. Everything depends on how one looks at them." It is reassuring that such distortions raise stiff opposition from certain quarters of historians. There is often wide disagreement among historians over the way history should be written. Under these circumstances when novelists blend fact with fiction they should be acutely aware of the purpose of invoking the past in their fiction. Hariharan firmly asserts the central premise of the novel:

> It is the right of a people to a complex, pluralistic history. It is true that history is not an indisputable body of knowledge. But history itself shows us that attempts to rectify it have all too often been camouflage for the doctoring of history.
>
> (*ITOS* 170)

Another ongoing controversy in the Indian historiography is the difficulty in separating history from myth and religion. In ancient India there was no systematic way of writing history. It was mixed with myth and religion. A.K. Warder laments the encroachment of *kavya* (literary writing) on the field of *ithihasa* (historical writing), the substitution of aesthetic truth for historical truth in presenting history (Dhar 63). It continued for several centuries. It is presented from the Hindu's point of view which is similar to the *Ramayana* and the *Mahabharata* in which fact and fiction are inseparable. Things changed with the arrival of the Mughals and the British. Indian historians started to develop historiographies which are free from myths and religion. Hariharan has handled the Basava story well. She has drawn her sources from A.K. Ramanujan's translations of Basava's verses in *Speaking of Siva* and Kamil V. Zvelebil's *Lords of the Meeting Rivers: Devotional Poems of Basavanna*. Hindu watchdogs want only that mythical, saintly-faced Basavanna who was sent "to the earth by Lord Siva himself to do his work among men" (*ITOS* 91) remain and not be the iconoclast of the twelfth century. They charge Shiv with presenting Basava as an ordinary poet and resort to violence by damaging all university property to show their anger. Hariharan asserts the need for clarity:

> separating history and myth, pulling apart history and legend. Deciding which chunks of history will keep the myth earth bound; which slivers of myth will cast light and insight, on dull historical fragments. The two have to be torn apart, their links disentangled, to see who is who then coaxed into embrace again to understand the composite reality. Approaching the whole, the heterogeneous truth that demands the coupling of conflicting narratives, requires the participation of one body (*ITOS* 87).

In recent times Indian socio-political life has been dominated by instances of fundamentalist–inspired violence and protest. The most horrendous act of religious vandalism which caused shockwaves was the demolition of Babri Masjid in 1992 by an unruly mob who believed that it was constructed on the birth place of Lord Rama, a Hindu God. In 2007 when the ruling DMK in Tamil Nadu gave the green signal to dredge Sethu Samudra channel in Rameswaram between India and Sri Lanka, the right-wing fundamentalists posed stiff resistance. They believed that such construction would damage the mythical bridge built by Lord Rama when he went to Sri Lanka to bring back his wife Sita who was abducted by the demon king Ravana. The project has been shelved. Had the project been continued Indian ships would not have had to take a detour, thus saving millions of rupees. As long as people do not have the analytical ability to differentiate between history and myth the right–wing exploitation of people's religious sentiments will continue, enabling vested interests to block developmental activities.

Fugitive Histories explores the events of historical significance that tore the secular fabric of India. This is not merely a story: in the novel Hariharan blends chronicles, registers the accounts of the event by the affected parties and interviews with eyewitnesses. She registers her views about Gujarat carnage and life in the aftermath of the riots in the city of Ahmedabad. The grim spectre of Gujarat is brought before our eyes when Nina, one of the women characters, reads her documents:

> On 27th February 2002 the Sabarmathi Express was attacked in Godhra station in Gujarat and two of its carriages set on fire. The train was carrying 'Hindu-activists' on their way back from Ayodhya. Godhra is a 'Muslim locality'. In the days and weeks that followed, the Muslims in Gujarat became the target of brutal violence. The statements of survivors, eye witnesses and relief workers suggest that state officials and the police connived with the attackers (*FH* 42).

The happenings are seen through the eyes of women. Mostly the story is woven around Mala, a Hindu–brahmin. She marries Azad, a Muslim artist, against the wishes of her parents. This is not an unusual story, but through their relationship she is able to portray the nature of the human relationship which is biased, prejudiced, divided yet connected. Hariharan, in an interview to *The Hindu* says, "Regardless of what we say, we all have at some point given reason to certain prejudices or experienced them." After Azad's death, when Mala is leafing through the sketches of Azad, her thoughts travel back and forth allowing the readers a glimpse of what has happened in her life and what is happening now.

In the second part of the novel, Sara, Mala's daughter, becomes the narrator. She works as a social worker in Mumbai, who tries to carve a niche in her job. She decides to seize the opportunity when her friend invites her to Ahmedabad, the recent venue of carnage to write a script for a documentary on the mayhem. Yasmin is another woman who recounts the state orchestrated violence against the Muslims. Hariharan does not stop with merely registering the events; she goes one step ahead and tries to find out the epicenter of this hatred towards each other and probes why the two communities started to move away from each other. The reasons are numerous, but Partition could be the founding trauma for crimes against humanity in the name of religion. Those who did not personally experience the Partition were not fully aware of this catastrophic divide. So it was thought that such divisions would never recur and it had become a thing of the past. But the riots which were sparked off after the destruction of Babri Masjid and post-Godhra make us acutely aware of the ghostly presence of Partition which looms large even today. As critic Priya Kumar observes, "Memories of partition of violence have inevitably seeped into their consciousness, shaping and informing their self-definitions and ways of being in the world especially for the populations of those regions that were directly impacted by the event" (94).

Scholars opine this has happened because we have forgotten the Partition trauma as a result of amnesia. They hope the acts of remembering through reading novels, eyewitness accounts, reports, films and short stories would prevent such mishaps in the future. It gives a healing touch to the wounded hearts and thus promotes reconciliation. Some scholars are of the view this act of remembrance might induce the victims to take revenge by consolidating group identities. Right wing groups have been using Partition stories to avenge it in the present. Writers who record the testimonies of the survivors of the trauma should show utmost responsibility. Literary narratives can visualize a bright future for the disparate religious people by living together peacefully.

Writing fiction out of a recent upheaval is a daunting task especially when the theme deals with sensitive issues such as communal clashes. In *Fugitive Histories* as Khushwant Singh notes, "Hariharan writes with anguish, pain and anger about what is happening to our country". She makes the reader think, realize, reflect and react as she states in her website, "Our work has to reflect the troubled times we are living in. The battering rams are at the door and we have to think of protecting the cushion writer's space. You do not need Rushdiesque example of fatwa to understand the threats."

Secularism under Threat

Githa Hariharan uses fiction to explore through history the burning issue of secularism, the foundation of modern India, which is under threat of late. With the rise of the right wing Hindutva parties and other fundamentalists groups, the threat to Indian secularism is frightening. Brenda Cossman and Ratna Kapur in their book titled *Secularisms Last Sigh*, an allusion to Salman Rushdie's *The Moor's Last Sigh*, give voice to Indian secularism which is in a state of crisis:

> On 6th December 1992.... The RSS, BJP and VHP combined impaled the cause of secularism on the trishul (Shiva's spear) of Hindutva ideology. With their bare hands and teeth they annihilated the 500 years of bricks and mortar that held together a simple mosque – the Babri-masjid. Within minutes, the mobs of the Hindu right had left the ancient structure in ruins and the remaining rubbles occasionally belching clouds of smoke and dust as if gasping for the last breath of secularism. The mosque lay belly up, harpooned with saffron flags and swarmed by the apostles of the God squad ebullient in their victory over tolerance, faith and the secular ideal (1999: XI).

The graphic description in this paragraph sounds the death of Indian secularism.

In these two novels she laments the erosion of secularism. In *Times of Siege* attack on Shiv is not an attack on some history professor, who had projected Basava in an ordinary manner, but it is an attack on human rights, intelligent freedom and on a person who wishes to cherish secular ideas. The terms, "fundoo, fundamentalist. Fascist, obscurantist. Terrorist." ((*ITOS* 57), which are used by Meena's (his ward's) generation, with ease show how this fundamentalism "garden variety hate mongers" has occupied our own backyard.

This secular hooliganism is not new. It has been around for quite some time. Few more examples given by Amar, Meena's friend – like Campaigns against Christians, the murder of Australian missionary, Graham Staines and his two children.... The attacks on artist M.F. Husssain, for painting Hindu goddesses in the nude.... Teachers in Goa having their faces blackened for setting politically incorrect exams and the recall of a volume on the freedom struggle.... The disruption of the shooting of a film on the plight of Hindu widows in Banaras (100) show how the stormtroopers indulge in suppression of free expression.

Besides an excoriating revision of history, Hariharan also touches religious conversion and questions why the majority Hindus agitate. Since inegalitarianism prevailed in Hinduism, nineteenth century Christian missionaries lured lower caste Hindus and tribals to Christianity. In post-independent India conversions have met with stiff opposition though the Indian Constitution says, "One has the right to profess, practice and propagates religion as a fundamental right". Hindu right wing considers religious conversions as a threat to Hinduism. So it unleashed violence against those who try to proselytize as in the case of gruesome murder of Graham Staines, an Australian missionary working in Orissa, and his two sons by Hindu fundamentalist in 2000. "In more recent history, trying to understand the violence in Gujarat in February 2002 it is important to remember that the initial threat was perceived from the conversion of tribal groups to Christianity and the bleeding of Hinduism" (Srinivasan 70). Hindu violence, that is, brutality and violence against the lower caste Hindus by the upper caste Hindus, is prior to Hindu–Muslim violence. Using violence to establish their dominance against the lower castes might have turned into hatred and aggression against the external threats from Muslims and Christians. They are identified as foreigners, invaders, aliens, strangers etc. In *In Times of Siege* Dr.Arya, a religious bigot, stages his protest in the department meeting when one of his key paragraphs which raises questionable statements are cut and slashed. The paragraph vividly portrays Muslims as invaders: "Lakhs of foreigners found their way to India during these thousands of years, but they all suffered humiliating defeat. Some of them we digested. When we were disunited, we failed to recognize who were our own and who were foreigners and we were unable to digest them" (*ITOS* 19). In *Fugitive Histories* Yasmin who narrates the sabotage laments, "We are strangers" (165). Slogans raised against Muslims such as, "Muslims Quit India" (132) illustrate their status as foreigners in India.

The same phrase 'Quit India' which was used by Gandhi against the British is now being used by Hindu fundamentalist groups to flush out the Muslims away from India. According to Hindu fundamentalists, Hindus, irrespective of their caste, locality, place, are the sons of the soil, original inhabitants and the true guardian angels of its rich cultural heritage. Sikhs, Jains and Buddhists are identified as Indians since the origin of their faith has its roots in India whereas for Christians and Muslims, their holy places lie outside the boundaries of India. Since their customs, habits, religious faiths are entirely different from the native culture, they are considered as foreigners. Thus the right wing Hindutva party BJP tries to promote nationalism around Pan-Indian Hindu identity. Hariharan feels constructing nationalism around Hindutva is dangerous. When Shiv's supporters stage a demonstration against pseudo–secularists' interference in academic affairs, erudite historian Amir Qureishi echoes Hariharan's opinion on stage: "The nationalism practiced by these sullen, resentful, intolerant men is different from the nationalism of the freedom struggle. This new brand of nationalism is monstrous" (*ITOS* 133). Dr. Arya who is listening to the fiery speeches of the supporters of Dr. Shiv in support of secularism, questions their loyalty to India by branding them as foreign lovers. Anybody speaks for secular ideals and against their ideology is looked upon as outsiders. Priya Kumar claims: "The construction of insiders and outsiders, natives and aliens, citizens and foreigners has been fundamental to the Hindu rights programme for consolidating India as a Hindu-Nation"(57). So construction of Hindu-Indian Rashtra denies a space for Muslims and identity as Indians because of foreign tag attached to them.

The authors of *Khaki Shorts and Saffron Flags* note:

> At the heart of Hindustan lies the myth of a continuous thousand-year old struggle of Hindus against Muslims as the structuring principle of Indian history. Both communities are assumed to have been homogenous blocs of Hindu patriot's, heroically resisting invariably tyrannical,' foreign' Muslim rulers...(2).

In *In Times of Siege* Shiv remembers his visit to Hampi, glorious medieval Hindu Kingdom, showpiece of Hindu, which has been plundered, razed to the ground by Muslim Kingdom. He takes an auto to visit the site. When he is looking at the ruins along with the auto driver Suban, a Muslim hesitatingly says, "It must have been beautiful. They shouldn't have broken it down". By 'they' he meant "Muslims, ancestors" (*ITOS* 159). It appears to Shiv that Suban who is the namesake of one of the Deccan Sultans appears to render an apology for this ghastly deed done by his ancestors Muslims. Shiv realizes that the driver identifies him with a religious group and "makes him a custodian of mythicized Hindu past". ((ITOS 159) This act of taking sides, feeling sorry for this destruction done by his forefathers expressed to the representative of the other side clearly shows, the Muslims started to think of them as foreigners. The clash between these two civilizations which is construed in Indian history as taking place for so many centuries runs contrary to the version of accepted academic histories. Kakar recognizes the basic fabric of India as syncretic. Thus:

> The story of Hindu- Muslim relations takes on different hues depending on the color of the ideological lenses through which it is viewed. For these liberal historians or one with leftist leanings, the story is bathed in a roseate glow of the pre-colonial golden age of Hindu-Muslim amity. For these liberal story tellers, the tale is of a commingling and flowering of a composite cultural tradition, especially in art, music and architecture.... To the conservative Hindu nationalist ... the rift between the two communities is a fundamental fact of Indian history.... The composite civilization, according to this view, was limited to small sections of the population around the courts and to court patronized arts like music and architecture (19-20).

V.S. Naipaul in his interview to *Outlook* magazine millennium special issue discounts the notion that Indian culture is fluid and syncretic. He says, "To say that India has a secular character is being historically unsound. Dangerous or not, Hindu militancy is a corrective to the history I have been talking about. It is a creative force and will be so. Islam can't reconcile with it". This stance echoes BJP's ideology which detests the implication that Hinduism is a syncretistic religious tradition.

Hariharan deftly reveals how these right wing communalists have indoctrinated the people's heads so many of them have become paranoid. When Jyoti Meena's friend feels she is getting fearful Meena consoles her saying, "This paranoia is nothing when compared to theirs". She further adds, "During the 1993 riots in Mumbai, some people drove their cars on to Chowpatty Beach and shone their headlights into the sea. They were actually trying to ward off an imminent Iranian Invasion" (*ITOS* 149).

Thus Hindu right wing people want to render the minority of external origin and project Hindu religious beliefs, customs and practices as national culture. But these people are generous enough to lend those minorities some space in their ancestral land as long as they accept the Hindu culture and tradition:

"Muslims and Christians are welcome so long as they conform to the dominant Brahminical Hindu culture – in the more benign version of Hindu majoritarian politics" (Kumar 58). In *In Times of Siege* Hariharan upholds the same view in one of the many hate letters written to Dr. Shiv which says, "The truth is that these minorities will be safe in India only if share our vision of our country and culture. Then we won't mind accommodating two more gods (Allah and Christ) along with our thirty three crore Gods and Goddesses" (*ITOS* 118). Rushdie also expresses concisely Hindu majoritarian politics which does not allow the minorities to claim their rights. In *Moor's Last Sigh* Raman Fielding rhetorically speaks which echoes Hindu-Nationalist ideologies. He speaks, "In India every community must have its place, its leisure activity –art etcetra — all Christians Parsies, Jains, Sikhs, Buddhists, Jews, Mughals. We accept this. This too is part of our ideology of Ram Rajya, rule of Lord Rama. Only when other communities are usurping our Hindu places, when minority seeks to dictate to majority, then we say that the small must also accept to bend and move before the big"(260)– which seems to be a veiled threat to the minorities.

Why do Hindus agitate? Why do they consider the Muslim as an invader, an arch rival? The familiar charge which is leveled against the Muslims is all Indian Muslims are Pakistanis at heart. After the Partition majority Muslims have migrated to Pakistan. Only a very few stayed back. The Hindutva group considers them as the enemy within. So the Indian Muslims are constantly under pressure to prove their loyalty to India. The Hindu fundamentalists in the process of Hinduization wanted to cleanse India of these minorities. In Gujarat riots the Muslims were constantly referred to as Pakistanis and a spate of atrocities were inflicted in order to expel them from the country. In *Fugitive Histories* Hariharan provides an evocative instance where Muslims are identified with Pakistanis and boundaries are demarcated. One of the women narrates fearfully how these people were threatened by the murders to go back to Pakistan at the time of genocide. She is wondering why they have to go back to Pakistan. "'We were already scared because we kept hearing terrible things on the loud speakers,' the woman called Razia is saying. She wipes the sweat on her face with her dupatta. 'Go to Pakistan! Go back to Pakistan! Why should we go to Pakistan?'" (*FH* 157). These innocent victims didn't cross the Indian border. They went, "across the city, across the border" (116), shifted their space, to start a fresh new life without any new fear. "They had to quit their neighbourhood, their India. They found a safe house in a Muslim neighbourhood" (138). Nina tells Sara as they cross a highway, "They call this a border .... And some call this area mini Pakistan" (110). Anthropologists Deepak Mehta and Roma Chatterjee in their ethnographic work which deals with people who live in Dharavi the biggest slum in Bombay, says they come across certain areas which are marked as 'Indo-Pakistan border' after the 1992-93 riots. Hariharan emphasizes this in *Fugutive Histories* when the police tell them, "You better learn to protect yourselves if you want to live in Hindustsn... (160) — the real death-knell for Indian secularism.

Another reason why a majority of the Hindus agitate is majority of Hindus who constitute 82 per cent of the population feel that their rights are curbed in the name of secular state while all the religious minorities are enjoying all the privileges and they have been pushed to minority status. Article one states: "Nothing shall prevent the state from making any special provision for the advancement of any socially and educationally backward classes of citizens or for the scheduled castes and scheduled tribes (Constitution of India 2000:22). The Indian citizen is subject to different civil codes according to the community or religion he belongs. Hindu traditionalists accuses the successive Congress governments for their unjustified bias against Hindus by banning certain unacceptable Hindu practices whereas pampering the minorities by giving monetary benefits to build educational institutions, subsidized Haj travel to Mecca etc. Hariharan in *In Times of Siege* clearly brings out this paradox through Arya who raises their issues in the dept. meeting. He accuses, "Today, apart from Muslims, even Christians, Parsis and other foreighners are also recognized as minority communities. But in many of the states the Hindus have been reduced to a minority and the Muslims, Christians or Sikhs are in a majority" (19). ISM leader's leaflet charges the secularists and rationalists for not criticizing other religions. "People feel free to revile Hinduism with impunity, but they do not dare criticize Islam because then the swords would be out" (100). With the unearthing of mind-boggling treasure-trove at Padmanabasamy temple in Thiruvananthapuram, the predictable clamour is now at peak pitch. Call for nationalizing all temple property and utilizing the funds for public purposes raises hue and cry from Hindu traditionalists. They retaliate by asking, "Why not subject churches, mosques, masjids, madrasas, gurudwaras, Jains temples and all places of worship to assess their inventory and make that suggestion wholly secular? Hindutva demands uniform civil law which might produce great harmony." Hariharan touches at heart how the Government treats the citizens of post-independent India and exposes the hypocrisy of secular religious freedom practised in this country.

In *In Times of Siege* secular professor Dr. Shivmurthi's daughter Tara's letter from USA indicates the hands of external forces in fueling the Hindu revivalist sentiments. It reads: "It's sort of weird and embarrassing to explain why you have written something against our temples and priests and all that. It's only after coming to the US that many of us have learnt to appreciate Indian traditions" (Githa Hariharan 2003:112). It appears that Tara has consolidated her Indian identity after going to US. Many Indians abroad feel Hinduism is being discriminated. Every major religion in the world has its own nation state to support: "Look at Israel; it plays for the Jews, of course. The United States is clearly a Christian country ....The Vatican, the church of the Catholics, even has status at the U.N. The Muslim states ... band together in foreign policy through institutions such as the Arab League and others. It is natural therefore for Hindus abroad to ask: who plays for Hinduism?" (T.N. Srinivasan 16). Hinduism has more than a billion followers who are predominantly in India. So they see India following secularism as a threat. This constellation of factors produces a backlash among the Hindus.

Identity and Violence

In both novels Hariharan reiterates the fact that the illusion of singular identity nurtures violence. Of late civilizational or religious partitioning seems to be on the rise. People do have multiple identities as Asian, Indian, Tamilian, doctor etc. It is very important to identify ourselves with others in various possible ways for a peaceful living. In a parliamentary debate about the riots against Sikhs after Gandhi's assassination by her Sikh bodyguard, the Indian Prime Minister, Manmohan Singh, told the Indian parliament, "I have no hesitation in apologizing not only to the Sikh community but to the whole Indian nation because what took place in 1984 is the negation of the concept of nationhood and what is enshrined in our constitution" (qtd in Sen, Amartya 168). Here, Manmohan Singh's multiple identities, as Prime Minister of India, Leader of the Congress party, member of the Sikh community and citizen of India are very much in prominence. There are many identities other than religious identity that are crucial for a person's relationship with other people who belong to different backgrounds in a country like India which is a pluralistic culture.

Hariharan in *In Times of Siege* criticizes the ISM Ithihas Suraksha Munch which tries to homogenize the identity of Indian nation and this proves to be dangerous. Since Arya the religious bigot, has designated all Muslims as foreigners Mrs. Khan's, Muslim secretary in the department, identity is fixed in the religious context. Now she has to wrestle with "the new status thrust upon her Muslim Mrs. Khan, Foreign Mrs. Khan. Mrs. Khan, a woman who has travelled leagues from her grandmother's lives to work in an office and make a modest contribution to the family income. Now she is being pushed back to square one, to the old diminishing religious identity" (*ITOS* 22). Because of her newly discovered identity as a foreigner by Arya all her other identities seem to fade away and suddenly she has become different. Seeds of hatred have been sown along the communal lines by Arya. Later Shiv's office is attacked by Arya, which leads to war of words in the media between secular academicians and pseudo-secularists. This Hindu zealotry visualizes a Hindu India without any warring essences. They believe everyone has only one identity that Indians are Indians, Africans are Africans which will never change. But actually identity fluctuates. It keeps changing. In the text the historian Quereishi avers: "Identities are never permanent. This obsession with identity uses the past to legitimize the political requirements of the present" (132). Even Amar laments the fact that everyone wants to tame this manifold divisions in the world. Amar and Meena believe the world is diversely different. She ends up asking, "Can't we have more than one voice or one identity? (142). Amartya Sen articulates stating, "The world frequently taken to be a collection of religions [or of 'civilizations or culture'] ignoring the other identities that people have and value, involving class, gender, profession, language, science, morals, and politics" (Amartya Sen xvi)

After partition Muslims became minorities in India and they had to renounce much of their secular identity in order to become a true Muslim. This loss or transformation of secular identity into a more religious one is represented in *Fugitive Histories.* Asad is a secular Muslim, marries a Hindu brahmin. They want to bring up their children in a secular manner. They are not bothered about their religious identity. He asks his children not to "worry about whether you were Indian, Muslim or Muslim Indian or part Hindu or atheist by default, it was enough just being you?" (*FH* 102). But this secular Indian Muslim's heart, his idealism was broken in the month when Gujarat burst into flames. Many people thought communal holocaust similar to the act of Partition would never reoccur and it has been far removed from their memory. Asad regrets that they have been idiots to think gruesome violence will not strike again.

Sara, his daughter, remembers his last words which seem to be an angry challenge against those who try to impose solitary identity: "You had nothing to fight for, now you do. There's battle going on. A war. The enemy wants to tell people whether they are Muslims or Hindu or Christian or something else, as if people no longer know themselves. Let's see how you do in the new war" (*FH* 100). Finally at the end of the war his son Samar loses his battle. He has given up everything which his parents try to inculcate in him when he is growing up. Mala's worst fears, whether they have finally become Christian, Hindu or Muslim, even if they do not believe, have come true. Samar is happy to be seen as a Muslim because he feels the world wants to identify them along the religious lines. Even Asad at the end in his war against sectarian people throughout his life has become tired of being a different Muslim, a moderate, modern and reasonable Muslim because the world wants them to be "demon Muslim" (*FH* 201). Samar and Asad's stand seem to justify Samuel Huntington's thesis, *The Clash of Civilization,* which classifies the humanity into discrete and distinct civilizations and their relationship between different human beings can be seen in terms of relations between different civilizations. Hariharan, through Mala, poetically brings out how hatred has been fed into the minds of children, though not open but in an insidious manner when they eat, drink, comb their hair or play:

> Don't use left hand like a bazaar Christian!
> Don't showoff like an uncultured Punjabi!
> Don't part your hair on the side like a Muslim!
> Push the f-a-a-a-t slaving pa a-ri-aah out of the game!
> You are the stupid pariah this time; you're thrown out of the game! (*FH* 203)

But Mala has survived this prejudice. Sara, Asad's daughter, too has won the war. Though Sara has plural identities to choose from she is indeed happy to be the daughter of mixed parentage. She says, "How glad I am that I am a hybrid" (*FH* 184). But Samar and Asad have become victims. Sen strongly advocates, "The main hope of harmony in our troubled world lies in the plurality of our identities, which cut across each single hardened line of vehement division that allegedly cannot be resisted" (Sen Amartya, 16). After September 11 attacks Muslims around the world are looked at sceptically and suspiciously. They have been placed on the divisive lines. The word Muslim is immediately linked to terrorism, terrorist or jihadist. Samar grieves at how the world looks at him:

"Whatever I am, whatever I believe and however I live, I am an M. Samar too is just another Muslim, a potential terrorist" (*FH* 206). Sikhand notes, "Islamaphobia has today become a fashion in large circles and demands for justice to Muslims who are quickly branded as 'communal' and anti-national by those who see Islamist terrorism in a political vacuum" (Kumar 233). Hariharan's description about Muslims ghettoization, parents not willing to send their children to schools, missing names in the list point out a growing sense of alienation and insecurity among Muslims.

To focus on just one identity is to deny the various other identities that a person who happens to be a Muslim has. Sen is of the view neglecting multivarious identities of people makes the world more flammable. He warns, "Violence is fomented by the imposition of singular and belligerent identities on gullible people, championed by proficient artisans of terror" (Amartya Sen, 2). This is what happened in Gujarat. Thousands of innocent Muslims were massacred by angry mob in retaliation to the burning of train carrying Hindu pilgrims by supposedly Muslim rioters. These mobs knew their targets well. The level of sexual violence was appalling. Everything was staged in connivance with the police as the state government, headed by Narendra Modi, watched as a silent spectator. A committee called 'Concerned Citizens Tribunal' was formed to conduct an enquiry. Findings declared, "There seems to be a clear target in the overall destruction –lives maimed and brutally snuffed out, the community crippled economically, religious and cultural symbols debased and all signs of growth and modernity erased" (Srivatsava 13). *Fugitive Histories* captures this beastly behavior of blood thirsty human hunters. Nasreen, one of the victims, narrates the fearful morning: "They had swords, pipes, hockey sticks, soda–lemon bottles, saffron flags, all kinds of sharp weapons. They had petrol bombs and gas cylinders. They broke the dargah down, the street and gas cylinder. They came to our houses, they were shouting, 'Kill them, cut them, burn them alive! Then they blasted apart our lives'" (158). They are identified as people who wore saffron cloth around their necks ...". They knew what they were doing, they were like an army with a plan. They knew which shops was Muslim, which godowns were Muslim, which restaurants and hotels were Muslims" (159). Hariharan registers the mutilating effects of violence and trauma on the bodies and memories of survivors with profound sorrow, despair, rage and disillusionment. She feels words are inadequate to depict the genocide

Major political parties try to accuse the BJP right wing as fascist. Many populists try to project BJP government as Hitler's Nazi-style government. Even in *In Times of Siege* Hariharan links fascism and Hindu fundamentalism. Meena, Hariharan's mouthpiece, observes, "The link between fascism and the ugly faces of Hinduism unveiling themselves around is the regimentation of thought and brutal repression of culture". The analogy drawn between Hindu fundamentalism and Hitler's Germany is inappropriate and far-fetched. Mukesh Williams and Rohit Wanchoo, authors of *Representing India, Literature, Politics and Identities*, cite some reasons in support of this argument. First of all in Germany, the German fascists, the ruling party, mobilized their nation and waged a war against the minority Jews. It is not possible for the Indian government to wage a war because of the huge Muslim population in India. India's Muslim population is the third largest in the world. Secondly, if such things happen all the Muslim countries in the world will wage a war against India. Thirdly, Jews were not rulers of any country and they were only the victims of persecution by the ruling class. But in India, Muslims were the powerful rulers for many centuries. So now the Hindu revivalists feel it is their time to avenge their sufferings at the hands of Muslim rulers. Muslims have not undergone any persecution, instead they have been protected under minority laws by the government.

Hariharan's novels depict the changing status of women in India. Women are shown as opening the windows and breaking the barriers. In her interview to Joel Kuorrti she says, "Certainly all my books in some sense or the other deal with the plight of women, they do place women's lives in the foreground" (25). In *In Times of Siege* Meena is the voice of Hariharan. She is the one who forces Shiv to fight against the pseudo-secularists: "What is the plan of section? How do we beat your fundoos at their game?" (97). She is portrayed as a girl matriarch. She garners support for Shiv by arranging a big really which includes people from 'Secular Women Against Patriarchy' (SWAP); Forum Against Hindu Terrorism (FAHT) People's Association of Secular scientists(PASS) who carry placards: "STOP TALIBANISATION OF INDIA to HISTORY DESTROYED to WHO'S AFRAID OF THE MUNCH"? (145). She belongs to the newer generation which is aware of the current Indian political scenario: "Don't get batteries made by those murderers Union Carbide" (*FH* 48). The cast around her leg does not immobilize her whereas only Shiv feels he is being wrapped by a cast which prevents his free movement. Her brief stay in Shiv's house is the history of doing. In *Fugitive Histories* it is women who do not succumb to the external religious pressure. Sara and Mala have become successful in not falling a prey to religious forces whereas Asad and Samar have bonded superficially with communal forces. When Abba, Yasmin's father has his own doubts in sending his daughter to college it is her mother Ammi who jettisons her religious constraints when she announces that she is going to send her daughter to college without burqas. Here Hariharan gives an open invitation to all the women to defy all the barriers which deny them their identity. Ammi sounds hard when she says, "The angry ones on both sides want to put our daughters in burqas so they can prove their point.... Did the burqas keep our women safe five years ago?" (*FH* 227). She also indirectly tells the reader all these religious identities will prevent them from joining the secular mainstream.

Change in the women's attitude and their development is shown through three generations of women. Bala, Mala's grandmother, is hysterical. She was never let out in this male-dominated world. So she went within. Mala defies her family tradition and comes out to marry Asad, a Muslim guy. Sara, the author's muse, who is glad to be simply an Indian, wants to establish her own identity by carving out a place for herself in her field of work.

Prospects for Peace

In Times of Siege laments the erosion of Nehruvian secularism which Indian state has adopted as its ideology post-independence. Nehru saw religion as a major deterrent factor for India's development. Nehru, who was a rationalist, identifies secularism as the only approach which would guarantee the development of a truly integrated nation. He said that he did not mean "absence of religion, but putting religion on a different plane from that of normal political and social life. Any other approach in India would mean the breaking up of India" (Nehru 331). He thought religion should be withdrawn from the public sphere and relegated to the private space in a gradual manner. He thought of the separation between church and state as a gradual process and the different personal law provisions for the majority community and the minorities would be gradually be phased out in favour of Uniform Civil Code. This is one of the basic reasons for Hindu fundamentalism. Hindu fundamentalists believe the fundamental rights of majority Hindus are being suppressed and oppressed in the native land by the government in the name of secularism to protect minorities. One of the BJP's leaders, L.K. Advani, in his speech in the parliament in 1990 spoke of his party's secular policy: "The BJP believes that the state in India has always been a civil institution which respects all religions equally and makes no discrimination between one culture and the other on the grounds of language, caste, or religion" BJP believes that no religion or caste should receive special treatment. It endorses Gandhiji's notion "Sarva dharma sambhava" – all religions should be treated equally.

In *In Times of Siege* Shiv's father, who is a freedom fighter, metaphorically stands for India's secularism, and believes the struggle for freedom did not end in 1947. "In fact, the burdens of the new world – the travails of a free India– sat heavy on his shoulders" (*ITOS* 32). He went missing on his way back home after attending Congress workers' meeting at Indore. It symbolically says India's secularism too has gone missing. His ending too like Basava's ending is controversial. Nobody knows what has happened to them at the end. The vandalism of ISM in Shiv's room and written attacks on Shiv make him to conclude, "Nehru, the symbol of independent India, his father believed so passionately in, is losing his charm" (188). Nehru has been shown the door and Hindu theology is in. The auto driver who accompanies Shiv on his visit to Hampi has become silent and withdrew into suspicious silence on his return trip after Shiv tries to explain to him that they do not belong to two different sides. It is of no use. Shiv realizes Gandhi, Nehru, Ambedkar and Bose's vision of syncretic nationhood has been shattered by the politics of divisiveness and intolerance. Shiv can hear his father's ghost, which is very much saddened by the rise of sectarian forces, questioning him, "What kind of country poisons the minds of children, of its youth? And did we fight for freedom so we could divide this teeming, hungry house forever?" (*ITOS* 160).

In *Fugitive Histories* Hariharan pins her hope in Gandhiji's radical secularism. Gandhiji feels, in order to protect the Indian civilization from the evils of Western civilization, it is essential to return to the native roots that is religion. Here religion is not specific to any particular religion but the universal religion. Gandhiji says, "Religion is dear to me and my first complaint is that India is becoming irreligious. Here I am not thinking of the Hindu, the Mahomedan or the Zoroastrian religion but that religion which underlies all religions. We are turning away from God" (Gandhi 42). Sara comes to Sabarmathi Ashram, the resting place of Gandhiji, the abode of peace. He seems to be a missing person there. But Sara imagines the presence of his ghost there. She cannot understand why the ghost is resting quietly doing nothing to stop the violence. He is singing the song "Ishwar Allah tere naam. Sabko sanmati de Bhagvan" which is highly relevant to the current political situation. To Sara only Gandhiji seems to sing this song, others including the birds, his messengers of peace, have not joined him because she assumes it is of no use singing this song now as everyone has forgotten this famous song which looks at all as one. Hariharan sarcastically pronounces how the world has started looking at the difference.

The mob which assassinated him in 1948 now comes to the abode of peace to kill the ghost. He whispers in Sara's ears: "In the dictionary of Sathyagraha, there is no enemy" (*FH* 176). Sathyagraha or passive resistance was Gandhiji's one of the weapons used in his fight against colonialism Here he suggests the best way to deal with communal conflict is through Sathyagraha. He adds, if the Hindus want the Muslim to stop cow slaughter, then they should come forward to sacrifice themselves. "This is Sathyagraha, this is equity, even as, if I want my brother to redress a grievance, I must do so by taking upon my head a certain amount of sacrifice and not by inflicting injury on him. I may not demand it as of rights. My only right against my brother is that I can offer myself as a sacrifice" (Gandhi 260). He informs his decision to Sara that he will not give up his fight against violence and his belief in ahimsa and non-violence. Finally the ghost fades away with tears in its eyes. Through Sara's interaction with Gandhiji's ghost Hariharan drives home the point that sathyagraha, ahimsa and non-violence remain the powerful weapons to combat the enemy, that is, religious fundamentalism.

Through these novels Hariharan attemps to convey the spirit of tolerance, the dominating factor in India struggle for independence, that has been eroded. Both Nehru's and Gandhiji's idea on secularism is based upon the idea of tolerance. But who has to tolerate who, that is the question. The word 'tolerance' itself is intolerable to many people. Tolerance is advocated only when inequality exists in a society. Nandy would have it, "Tolerance is an ideal whereas its origin is rooted in inequality" (Srivatsava 40). Gandhiji feels it is the duty of the majority population to tolerate the minority: "till... communal jealousies or preferences become a thing of the past, minorities who suspect the motives of majorities must be allowed their way" (Gandhi 267). He set his own example by undergoing fasting to stop the communal violence that erupted after partition. He became a martyr as his stance towards Muslims wrought the wrath of the Hindu fundamentalists who killed him.

The attack on Shiv for nurturing liberal ideas shows the intolerant attitude of the Hindu fundamentalists. Artists M.F.Hussain's death in exile and banning of books is today's India which is intolerant of late. Is there any possibility of peaceful co-existence? Hariharan has reposed her faith in the younger generation. In *In Times of Siege* Shiv hands over his father's walking stick to Meena which symbolically conveys that the future generation is entrusted with the duty of safeguarding secularism that the previous generation of Nehru, Gandhi and Shiv's father had dreamt of.

Sara in *Fugitive Histories* can see a "bright moving spot in the middle of the gloom" (121). A little boy and his sister race to Yasmin and her friend Sultana. Those Muslim children are helping their father who is making kites for Hindus for their festivals. The little girl informs Yasmin, "They are for Hindus. She tells her. For their festivals" (122). The poor people care less about religion because as long as someone else provides them work to feed their family, work is meant more to them than religion. Hariharan's novel underscores the idea how the people want to live in peace without taking revenge. "After each riot there's a whole lot of construction .... We are citizens. We will stay and fight.... Riots happen, and then people forget. Life carries on. People carry on" (*FH* 233) – all the above conversations by the affected people show how they yearn to lead a normal life. They want to forget and move ahead. Gujarat carnage is difficult to forget but dangerous to remember because it might incite violence. "If Muslims, Hindus and Sikhs have to live together in peace and amity, it is important they leave behind these events as something most traumatic, something tragic but something most unfortunate which ought not to have happened" (Kumar 92). Such a forgetting is very important for peaceful co existence. As Sen rightly says, "The prospects of peace in the contemporary world may well lie in the recognition of the plurality of our affiliations and in the use of reasoning as common inhabitants of a wide world, rather than making us into inmates rigidly incarcerated in little container" (Amartya Sen xvii).

Works Cited

Cossman Brenda and Ratna Kapur, *Secularism's Last Sigh?: Hindutva and the Misrule of Law,* New Delhi: Oxford University Press, 1999

Dhar, Tej.N *History fiction interface in Indian English Novel: Mulk Raj Anand, Nayantara Sahgal, Salman Rushdie, Sashi Tharoor, O.V. Vijayan,* Prestige: New Delhi, 1999.

Friese, Kai, "Hijacking India's History," *NewYork Times* (December 30, 2002), 15.

Gandhi, Mohandas Karamchand, *The Essential Writings of Mahatma Gandhi*, ed. Raghavan Iyer, NewDelhi: Oxford University Press, 1993.

______*Hind Swaraj and Other Writings*, ed. Anthony J. Parel,. Cambridge: University Press, 1997

Hariharan, Githa *The Double Burden: The Continual Contesting of Tradition and Modernity*, Interviewed by Joel Kourrti, New Delhi, 3 February 2000.

Hariharan, Githa *In Times of Siege* New Delhi: Penguin, 2003.

______*Fugitive Histories* New Delhi: Penguin, 2009.

Huntington, Samuel, *The Clash of Civilizations and the Remaking of the World Order,* New York: Simon & Schuster, 1996.

Kakar, Sudhir, *The Colours of Violence*, New Delhi: Viking, 1995.

Kumar, Priya, *limiting Secularism:The Ethics of Coexistence in Indian Literature and Films,* The University of Minnest: 2008.

Mehta, Deepak et.al *Boundaries, Names, Alterities: A Case Study of a Communal Riot in Dharavi Bombay*, Berkley: University of California Press, 2001.

Naipaul, V.S. *Christianity Didn't Damage India Like Islam*, Interviewed by Tarun Tejpal, *Outlook India, Millennium Special*, November 15, 1999.

Nehru, Jawaharlal, *Jawaharlal Nehru: An Anthology,* Sarvepalli Gopal, New Delhi: Oxford University Press, 1980.

Rushdie, Salman, *The Moor's Last Sigh*, London: Jonathan Cape, 1995.

Sen, Amartya *Identity and Violence: The Illusion of Destiny*, London: Penguin Group, 2006.

Srinivasan, T.N., *Future of Secularism*, New Delhi: Oxford University Press, 2007.

Srivastava, Neelam, *Secularism in the Post colonial Indian Novel,* London: Routledge: 2007.

Tapan, Basu et.al. *Khaki Shorts and Saffron Flags – A Critique of the Hindu Right*, New Delhi: Orient Longman, 1993.

Williams, Mukesh, et.al. *Representing India, Literature, Politics and Identities*, New Delhi: Oxford University Press, 2008.

Zakaria, Rafiq Interview by *The Indian Express* December, 1991: 19.

pratham books. org/2009/07/event/*githa hariharan*/fugitive/*html*

www.githahariharan.com/books/in times of siege.html

http://www.thehindu.com/2009/09/15/stories/

10

Towards a Confusion: A Study of Woman's Search for Identity in Anjum Hasan's *Neti, Neti—Not This, Not This*

— P. Karkhuzhali

> It is a world where many people feel intensified levels of insecurity as the life they once led is being contested and changed at the same time.
>
> —*Catarina Kinnvall*

This paper explores a young liberated woman's journey of rediscovering herself in the age of globalization. In the developing nations, within the past two decades, globalization has created a tremendous impact on the lives of women. Although it has created a large number of employment opportunities and a sense of liberation among them, it has had some negative impact on their lives. They experience a sense of loss, estrangement, restlessness and weariness. An attempt has been made to disclose the tensions, dilemmas and dissatisfactions experienced by women in the age of globalization and their search for self as represented in Anjum Hasan's *Neti, Neti—Not This, Not This*.

"She talks about an almost unexplored phenomena — Indians moving to other national towns" (*Tehelka* Oct 17, 2009). Anjum Hasan, one of the finest contemporary novelists, depicts the socio-cultural life of the vast country like India and the different cultures co-exist within it by portraying the life of an individual. *Neti, Neti—Not This, Not This* depicts the life of the 25 five-year-old Sophie Das and her search for identity. She has left Shillong, her home town, for Bangalore in search of better future and confronted with harsh realities of life. She soon experiences a sense of loss and estrangement in the fast-moving materialistic city like Bangalore. In short, it is not a story of a young girl attaining personal freedom but the representation of a young woman's struggle to rediscover herself in a fast-moving world. An attempt will be made to provide a theoretical explanation of globalization, culture and identity.

In human history, generally the beginning of a new century represents a symbolic change in the lives of human beings. The twenty-first century is no exception. The present century is experiencing tremendous changes in economic, social, cultural and political spheres which are often referred to as 'globalization'. It is a dynamic process of liberation and international integration of markets and technology. Often the term 'globalization' is associated with 'economic globalization' which indicates the process of production distribution and consumption of goods and services. In other words, it refers to the free flow of goods, services, capital, labour, information etc. Fredric Jameson defines globalization as:

> The concept of globalization reflects the sense of an immense enlargement of world communication, as well as of the horizon of a world market, both of which seem far more tangible and immediate than in earlier stages of modernity.
>
> (qtd. in Steger 10)

In this globalized era, everything moves fast and distance shrinks in a very impressive manner. James Mittelsman refers to this aspect of globalization as, "Globalization compresses the time and space aspects of social relations" (qtd. in Steger 10). In *Post-Colonial Studies: the Key Concepts,* globalization is defined as:

> Globalization is the process whereby individual lives and local communities are affected by economic and cultural forces that operate world-wide. In effect it is the process of the world becoming a single place.
>
> (Ashcroft 100)

The above words indicate that globalization has brought massive changes not only in the economic sphere, but also in the socio-cultural values of human lives. Like the two faces of the coin, globalization has both positive and negative effects on the people of third world countries. In India, on one hand, globalization has opened up enormous employment opportunities, introduced new technologies, information services and thereby improves the financial status and livelihood of people. On the other side, it widens the gap between haves and have-nots and becomes a threat to socio-cultural values of Indian society.

Robert J. Lieber and Ruth E. Weisberg in *"Globalization, Culture and Identities in Crisis"* remark:

> We find that in an increasingly globalized world, culture has become a central arena of contestation. Culture takes on this pivotal position not only because of its intrinsic significance, but precisely because it has become so bound up with the most fundamental questions of human Identity in its many dimensions: personal, ethnic, religious, social and national. (275)

Since indigenous culture is viewed as authentic, pure and unchanging, it is believed that the effects of globalization damage and destroy the sanctity and the uniqueness of the indigenous culture. In essence, it is viewed as a form of domination of the main stream people over the indigenous people in which the indigenous culture is ruined by the western culture. In the contemporary globalized world, culture has emerged as a central domain for debate. It has become a difficult task to resolve the issues related to culture. As Robert J. Lieber and Ruth E. Weisberg point out:

> Other issues on the globalization agenda, especially economic problems of trade, aid, investment and poverty, are more readily subject to negotiation and compromise. But precisely because culture has become a signifier for other more deep-seated and intractable issues, the problems it poses are harder to resolve. (291)

Hence, in the Third World countries like India, the rapid transformation of economic, social and cultural spheres intensify the notion that the traditional culture is 'under threat'.

Another important aspect of globalization is migration. There is an uneven development within the country due to globalization in recent decades. Certain parts of the country are benefited by modernization and the rest remained unchanged. As Catarina Kinnvall in "Globalization and Religious Nationalism: Self, Identity, and the Search for Ontological Security" remarks, "a number of factors related to globalization seem to increase the gaps between those who have reaped the benefits of the global market and those who have been left behind" (742). As a result, people from under developed sites move to other places to seek better economic opportunities. Venay Gidwani and K. Sivaramakrishnan in "Circular Migration and the Spaces of Cultural Assertion" point out that both Marxist and Marginalist identify the uneven spatial development of capitalist economy as the motive force of migration (189).

In a totally new circumstance, the migrants experience a sense of loss, fear, insecurity and self-alienation. As Catarina Kinnvall comments:

> Migration... is both a structural and a psychological process. It is often characterized by a sense of powerlessness and dependence as insecurity is increasing among many migrants. This is frequently mixed with an acute anxiety about their new circumstances and strong feelings of homelessness. (747)

The term 'home' always associated with a sense of security. Whereas,' homelessness' denotes loss, fear and insecurity. In order to experience a secure feeling, the migrant should rediscover his/herself and redefine his/her identity in the new circumstances.

One of the notable features of globalization is its high demand of employment opportunities for women. They have started entering into a number of new professions which are exclusively meant for men. Like men, they migrate to new places in search of new opportunities and experience sense of loss, anxiety and alienation. It is this struggle of a woman to rediscover her identity in the age of globalization is fore grounded in this paper.

Neti Neti is a novel of a young liberated woman from Shillong who lost herself in the midst of new materialistic and money-minded city like Bangalore.

> The book *Neti Neti* tells the story of 25-year-old Sophie Das, who has moved from Shillong to Bangalore. Here, she and her friends explore the city's many facets: its nightlife and call centres, the rock concerts and homes of the newly rich. But the young woman soon begins to feel alienated in the "money-mad city.
>
> (*The Hindu*, Oct. 22, 2010)

It is a portrayal of a young woman's journey of rediscovering herself in the globalized world. It discloses the process of rejecting everything in order to search the ultimate happiness. The protagonist Sophie Das has left Shillong, a rural quiet hill town, and migrated to Bangalore with the hope of getting an editing job in a publishing house. She doesn't get what she expects; instead she gets a job in BPO transcribing Hollywood movie subtitles.

The novel opens with an overwhelming experience of Sophie Das, a young Shillong girl, in an urban, chaotic, materialistic city like Bangalore. For the first time, she feels liberated and independent in the new city. In her apartment, "She could cook what she liked, smoke to her heart's content, put every object exactly where she wanted it to be and know it would not move unless she moved it. For the first time in her life she was free" (*Neti, Neti* 30). But on the other side, she finds it difficult to maintain a smooth relationship with her conservative landlord. He often admonishes her for her unruly behaviour. "the scolding she got always had a moral edge to it. He would not mind, for instance, if the boys hung out underwear to dry, whereas in her case it implied a shocking looseness of character" (19). On seeing her new curtain Mr. Bhatt delivers "a lecture on the idiocy of those who shopped without comparing prices" (19). She is often rebuked for coming home any time at night, smoking on the balcony in full public view, and for letting her bad-mannered friends into her apartment. Mr. Bhatt's intruding behaviour snatches away her privacy from her and intensifies her restlessness and uneasiness. Hence, it is evident that her apartment which should have helped her to develop a sense of belongingness turns out to be alienating.

Sophie's total rejection of Western style of living is exposed through her habit of newspaper reading. The newspaper depicts the ostentatious and pretentious ways of living of the rich in the city. For instance:

> She would read them, furious at people who described their beach holidays, their self-designed bungalows, and their favourite night clubs. She ground her teeth learning about wine appreciation evenings in swanky hotels, salsa competitions, champagne brunches and tips on where to get the best lounge furniture. Massive idiots, she would say out loud to those who considered going on cruise trips in the Mediterranean de rigueur, to those who were standing up in restaurants and telling the chef he had made a mess of the osso bucco, to those who swore by their Blanco shoes. (24)

Since they have been influenced by western culture, they make an attempt to construct their identity and seek their happiness mainly through external exploration. Her total rejection of these kinds of show-offs strongly exhibits her search for self and true happiness.

A series of events encountered by Sophie Das in a lifeless materialistic city contribute to her sense of loss and fear. She experiences an oppressive environment in the metropolitan city and fears that traffic jams, accidents, gorgeous night clubs, late night parties would drown her. For instance:

> Sophie was obsessed with traffic accidents. She recognized well the sickening, explosive crunch of a bike spinning out of its rider's control and hitting the road, an SUV colliding with a scooter, a lorry crumpling a small car like a ball of paper. She'd seen people die on these streets, or knocked unconscious, or with their legs gone. ...Nobody else seemed to think much about it, while Sophie had to work hard to

> suppress the idea, when she was out, that in the end everyone on the roads simply *wanted* to die. (38)

Another important facet of the city which deepens her insecure feeling is The prevalence of mindless consumer culture. She witnesses a death of a child in a shopping mall and the bereavement of the child's parents.

> Got herself a coffee, found an empty table, poured a sachet of sugar into her cup, stirred it, blew on it, took a sip and shut her eyes. Her claustrophobia had given way to an intense sadness. She tried to focus on the matter of the gifts before the shops closed but all she could think of now was the dead child, the murdered, secret brother of Mani's and the unmoved and un moveable car onto which he had fallen. (74)

Sophie's encounters with constant road accidents, people defaulting on loans, the death of a child in a shopping mall due to mindless consumerism and finally the murder committed by Ringo Saar make her feel insecured and alienated in the chaotic metropolitan city. "Sophie Das is somebody who moves from a place of security to a place unknown, a phenomenon that could be replicated anywhere" (*The Hindu,* Oct. 22, 2010).

Immediately after her migration to Bangalore, she has been disembedded from her cuisine, language, soothing hilly region etc. Neither her travels nor her encounters with a series of incidents give her a sense of belongingness. She completely lost herself and experiences a sense of homelessness, alienation, existential fears, insecurity, loss and despair in a new location. Giddens in *Modernity and Self Identity: Self and Society in the late Modern Age* says:

> Globalization tends to break down the protective framework of the small community and of tradition replacing these with many larger, impersonal organizations. The individual feels bereft and alone in a world in which she or he lacks the psychological support and the sense of security provided by more traditional settings. (33)

It is at such times of homelessness and alienation; she tries to restore her lost self and security by reconstructing or redefining her identity. She strives to recreate her identity by reestablishing connections with her past through nostalgia. As Catarina Kinnvall remarks:

> Going back to an imagined past by using reconstructed symbols and cultural reference points is, in other words, a response to the destabilizing effects of changing patterns of global mobility and migration. It is an attempt to recreate a lost sense of security. (744)

There are various ways of connecting with the past, but the most important way is remembering. Since Sophie Das feels out of place, often she connects herself with her past through her memories. Her delightful encounters with Mani, the grandson of her landlord reminds Sophie of her attraction with her baby sister Mukulika, "She remembered her fascination with her baby sister and something from those years, some residue of tenderness and amusement, flared up in her" (20). Her moral tussles with Mr. Bhatt remind Sophie of her school moral science classes. Throughout the novel she clings on to three books. *Swami and Friends*, *Vivekananda: Awakener of Modern India* and *Madame Bovary*. The memories associated with these books take her back to "Shillong, her home town" away from her "present home". Through memory she traces her identity and completeness which is too fragile to call her own. The construction and reconstruction of her identity through her memories provides her a sense of security to her insecure life in the city.

Ironing is yet another way Sophie uses to withdraw herself from an imperfect world into a flawless universe. "She started to smooth out a pair of cotton trousers. Ironing was her peculiar obsession - a way of withdrawing from a faulty world into a perfectionist's universe" (78). She attempts to seek pleasure through minor things as all the major things in the city ruin her peace and happiness.

> Sophie had learnt to content herself with the minor things, therefore - the smell of flowers coming from pushcarts late

> in the evening, the view of a palm tree from an open window, the corners of certain pubs, the pleasure of seeing one's things neatly arranged in a room. (36)

Giddens refers to ontological security as:

> Person's fundamental sense of safety in the world and includes a basic trust of other people. Obtaining such trust becomes necessary in order for a person to maintain a sense of psychological well-being and avoid existential anxiety.
>
> (qtd. in Kinnvall 746)

In a cosmopolitan city like Bangalore, one can feel the sense of absence and insecurity. Sophie is no exception to it. She frequently experiences a sense of loss and absence, but in the company of Swami, she feels the presence and experiences a sense of security. She gifts him one of her favourite books *Swami and Friends* as he has once reflected the fictional Swami of the novel. Both the fictional character and her boyfriend Swami strive to escape from the intractable adult world of rules and responsibilities. Sophie loves his laid-back nature and his laziness. They both share their comments on the stupidity and crazy attitude of the people in the metropolitan city. Sophie's intimacy with Swami starts diminishing as he joins a call-centre job and becomes one in the frenzy. She hopes that his reading of *Swami and Friends* would bring some changes in him and she could possess him wholeheartedly.

> Sophie believed that if he did, some kind of irreversible mutation would take place in Swami - the same that had taken place in her when she read *Swami and Friends* at the age of nine.... He might become more like that Swami and less like the Swami that was hardening, leaving his sangfroid behind. It was all because of that call centre he'd joined, thought Sophie for the hundredth time. (37)

Hence, it is evident that once again she is left alone in the lifeless materialistic city. All her efforts to reconstruct her identity yield no desirable result. Moreover, she lacks the feeling of recognized kinship which provides a sense of security to people in a new location. Gayatri Chakravorty Spivak points out, "In the field of rational analysis, a feeling of recognized kinship is more desirable than nationalism" (773). As she lacks the feeling of recognized kinship, she decides to go back to Shillong for a week to recreate her lost identity and happiness. She misses the beauty of her quiet rural hill town and longs for it.

> Waking up early on a winter morning and watching through the frost on the windows two boys in jackets and mufflers kicking a ball around in the football field and an occasional taxi rolling out through the morning mist. And then continuing to stand there and freeze as the light slowly changed and the yellow cast of morning deepened, and sunlight transformed the air of ancient sadness that hung over the scene - the lonely shouts of the boyos, the milky mist, the cold, sleeping houses on the hill - into an ordinary morning. Bangalore, on the other hand, possessed a great zest for ugliness. Everyone just wanted to obscure the view, blot out the sky, erase the gaps. (35-36)

When she shares her thought of going home for a week with her boss Maya and her boy friend Swami, she experiences a sudden and strange sense of happiness, "'I'm going to Shillong for a week,' "she said evenly, trying, as she'd done with Maya, to suppress the sudden, absurd sense of happiness" (66). On her journey from Bangalore to Shillong, she thinks, "'I won't go back to India'" (181). This statement of Sophie indicates her eagerness to rest herself in peace away from the chaotic world and also reminds that north-east is often not considered as part of India.

Sophie's overwhelming happiness to find her peaceful life in Shillong turns upside down. The life which she finds in her home town is not what she wants. She believes that her calm and unruffled home would remain unchanged, but all her hopes and dreams about her home town shattered down as it becomes a smaller reflection of Bangalore. Her parents' relationship is not what she imagined to be. They want to live the rest of their lives in their separate spiritual ways. Her sister also lives in her own world of imagination. Internet cafes, Westernized values, people's obsession with Bob Dylan and the chaos it creates in the quiet hilly town intensify her sense of loss. Neither her town nor her home seems to console her. Even the beauty of her hilly town which she misses is not enough to comfort her. She feels that "She was alone from now on. She was her own context" (236). It is only after Ribor's rejection of Sophie's love and affection for him that she understands the concept of dharma-karma which her mother has been talking about. "Everyone has a duty in life, sometimes you may think your duty is taking you on the wrong path, but even then you have to do your duty first and think of the consequences afterwards. You can't be happy all the time, but you can do your duty" (258). She realizes that the life is offering far more than what it takes away from her. It is with this insight she returns to Bangalore. Her new attitude towards life offers a resolution for her confused state of mind.

> She felt fine. Nothing frightened her anymore - not walking into a shop in a plush mall, trying on clothes and then buying nothing. Not waking up in the middle of the night and being unable to go back to sleep. Not seeing a man crushed to death on the street. (278).

Thus Anjum Hasan's *Neti, Neti—Not This, Not This* is a story of alienation and homelessness. It discloses the dilemmas of a young Indian woman and her search for self and identity in the face of globalization. Away from 'home' – Shillong, in a foreign land – Bangalore, Sophie experiences a sense of loss and lacks the protective cocoons of home. Her confrontations with constant road accidents, glitzy shopping malls, late night parties and mindless consumerism make her feel insecure in a globalized cosmopolitan city. She wishes to go back to Shillong for a week to escape from the oppressive environment of the metropolitan city, but unfortunately all her attempts to recreate her lost identity and happiness prove to be a failure as Shillong becomes a smaller reflection of Bangalore. As a result Sophie decides to negotiate with her new life in the metropolitan city, "I don't want to feel the knife edge of anything ever pressing into me again" (287). Hence, Anjum Hasan's *Neti, Neti—Not This, Not This* exposes the struggles of a young liberated Indian woman to recreate or redefine her lost self and identity in the new phase of globalization.

Works Cited

Ashcroft, Bill., Gareth, Griffiths, and Tiffin, Helen. *Post-Colonial Studies: the Key Concepts.* 2nd ed. London and New York: Routledge, 2007.

Giddens, A. *Modernity and self-identity: Self and society in the late modern age.* Cambridge: Cambridge University Press, 1991.

Gidwani, Vinay, Sivaramakrishnan K. "Circular Migration and the Spaces of Cultural Assertion." *Annals of the Association of American Geographers* 93.1 (Mar. 2003): 186-213.

Hasan, Anjum. *Neti, Neti-Not This, Not This*. New Delhi: Roli Books Pvt. Ltd, 2009.

"Importance of Elsewhere". *Tehelka Magazine*, 17 Oct. 2009: 6.41.

Kinnvall, Catarina. "Globalization and Religious Nationalism: Self, Identity, and the Search for Ontological Security." *Political Psychology* 25.5 (Oct., 2004): 741- 767.

Lieber, Robert J., Weisberg, Ruth E. "Globalization, Culture, and Identities in Crisis". *International Journal of Politics, Culture, and Society* 16.2 (Winter 2002): 273-296.

Spivak, Gayatri Chakravorty. "Acting Bits/Identity Talks". *Critical Inquiry* 18 (Summer 1992):773. Staff Reporter. "A Reading that Resonated". *The Hindu*, 22 Oct. 2010.

Steger, Manfred B. *Globalization: A Very Short Introduction*. United States: Oxford University Press, 2003.

11

Silencing Ethics as Disempowering Features of Women's Articulation in Anita Nair's *Ladies Coupe*

— Vennila Ramanathan

Drucilla Cornell's 'Ethical Feminism' envisions a world "peopled by individuals, sexed differently, a world beyond castration" (131). In *Beyond Accommodation*, she states that the goal of ethical feminism is not just to demand power for women but to redefine the fundamental concepts of women including power. Further, she argues that the legal laws formulated on a strong ethical basis "should provide us with the moral and psychic space through which we come to terms with even the not yet dreamt of meanings of our sex" (xxv). She believes that one can have a glimpse of a woman as a free individual when the cultural, psychic and legal laws terminate the inequality between men and women over the issue of sexual freedom. For a true transformation to women, she states in the Introduction to *Beyond Accommodation:*

> My argument in *Beyond Accommodation* is that we cannot transform our place in the world without challenging the culturally imposed limits to the feminine within sexual difference, and that we cannot truly challenge these limits without contesting the so-called bedrock of civilization of sexual differentiation imposed through normalized heterosexuality. (xxxii)

One of the patriarchal norms that limits women's freedom is in the area of social practice of communication. It governs the cultural, social and psychological expressions of women. This article analyzes how Anita Nair's heroine transgresses sexual ethics that restrict the conduct of women exclusively in Indian societies in her *Ladies Coupe.* It also focuses on the strained relationship between the mother and daughter and wife and husband, which issues forth due to lack of social practice of communication. Anita Nair points out the flaw in the feminine practice of communication which is given a free play in the male world. Her novel centres on this kind of inequality between men and women, and she tries to find a way out for her heroine Akhila who was prevented by her mother from acting in accordance with her desire.

There is always a difference between the moral voice of women and the moral voice of men. In the gender hierarchy, men enjoy the freedom of self-assertion which, according to Drucilla Cornell is "a masculine identity" (132). She defines the "masculine identified values" as freedom over love and the desire for intimacy. Very few women in well-developed societies could exercise these 'masculine identified values'. Patriarchal domination has silenced most of the women till this day by drawing out norms considered as taboos for women. It is an obvious fact that patriarchal norms prevent women from expressing or acting in accordance with their sexuality. These norms have created an invisible gap in the feminine practice of social communication. In "In a Different Voice," Carol Gilligan observes the general finding of the studies on sex-role stereotypes: "It is believed that the capacity for autonomous thinking, clear decision making and responsible action are the qualities associated with masculinity but considered undesirable as attributes of the feminine self" (482). In this work she traces the difference between the moral voice of women and the moral voice of men. Cornell comments that Gilligan has "tentatively and speculatively explored the reason for the devaluation of women's moral voice..." (135), trying to legitimate women's speech and experience as valuable. She points out that devaluation will surely lead to silencing as per the communication studies. In support of Gilligan's argument, she states: "So we value freedom as self-assertion over love because self-assertion, and not intimacy, love and care, are associated with a masculine identity. It is that privileging of the masculine as the only legitimate that Gilligan asks us to question" (136). This observation implies the necessity for women to rise against patriarchal norms that bind them with the rules for feminine conversation. For the same reason Drucilla Cornell calls for reformative cultural, psychological and legal laws. She says: "Inarticulateness before sexual difference is obviously part of the crisis of female adolescence that has gotten so much attention in the press recently" (xxvii). In *Reviving Ophelia: Saving the Selves of Adolescent Girls*, Mary Pipher describes how girls in early adolescence "crash and burn in a social and developmental Bermuda Triangle" (19). She states: "Their voices have gone underground—their speech is more tentative and less articulate" (20). But this is not the problem faced by adolescent girls alone. Even empowered women belonging to aristocratic societies do not freely express the injustice caused to them by their husbands. The condition is worse with female children who are harassed by the sexual advances of older male members of the family. They do not know to communicate the violent behavior of these men to their closest ones. For the same reason, mothers too fail to transmit to their daughters what it means to be a woman.

Newspapers report on the silent resistance of teenagers against rape attempts. Domestic violence against women has become a commonplace subject in news headlines. Such news comes to light when the harassment reaches its climax. The biggest problem with abuse lies in the fact that women do not speak about it freely to anyone due to various social constraints. An article titled 'Web of Support' published in *Sunday Times of India*, insists upon the necessity for women to claim rights through revealing the injustice caused by men, either husbands or strangers. Shahjahan who launched a website in 2008 to help women communicate all kinds of abuses says:

> I want them to speak out against injustice.... Many of us are proud to send our daughters abroad after marriage.

> But then communication becomes difficult. I hope this site will help girls who are far from home to pick up the courage to speak out, feel that they are not alone.
>
> (*Sunday Times of India*)

According to Cornell, the problem lies on "the conventional meanings we consciously and unconsciously rely on to make up the background of our world..." (xxx). Hence this article probes the problems that arise due to the gaps in the social practice of feminine communication and how women find out solutions to these in Anita Nair's *Ladies Coupe.*

With the strained relationship between Akhilandeshwari, the heroine and her mother as the main vein of the story, this novel projects women's inability to communicate with others on the injustice caused to them by men. As the novel proceeds, readers are given to understand Akhila's venture to find a solution to the question that has been with her all her life through an exchange of different perspectives on life from the other women in the coupe. Akhila has so long taken up the masquerade of femininity, but as she gets older she realizes the mistake of it because she perceives that it has robbed her of her freedom.

Anita Nair projects the rule of patriarchal norms upon sexuality and kinship patterns through the narration of each of the women in the coupe. Akhila, brought up in the Agraharam of brahmins, finds it difficult to communicate her desire for marriage to her mother and family members. Her mother could sense her daughter's feelings but she pretends as if she has not understood her daughter's feelings for the sake of making her the only responsible earning member of the family. Akhila, aged 45 years, with unrequited desires to escape into the vast arena of life and experience, pondering over the past, intends upon getting herself connected to the future. After her mother's death and the bitter experiences with her married sister and brothers, she decides to run away somewhere, perhaps to the land's end. With all hunger for life and experience, she dreams of escape from the practical world into a vast space where no restrictions would constrain her life. Her dream comes true when she finds herself with five women in a ladies coupe on the Kanyakumari Express. Beneath her name she finds the names of five women – SheelaVasudevan, Prabha Devi, Janaki Prabhakar, Margaret Paulraj and Marikolunthu – and she wonders who they are going to be and what their lives would be like. They all exchange greetings except Marikolunthu whose poor attire conveys her socio-economic status to them. As the train starts moving, their conversation focuses on the definition of happiness. Akhila expresses her intention to learn from their experience of the possibility of a woman to have a happy life without a man. She finds it interesting to know a new definition of a successful life from each one of them.

Her conversation with each one of them throws light on the truth that they have been silenced by the male members around them who cling on to the patriarchal norms to their convenience. The striking feature of their conversation focuses on the point that they could freely open up their hearts to totally strange ladies other than their kith and kin. They feel secure from all psychological taboos. Another interesting fact is that they all belonged to different age groups.

Akhila can very easily empathize with the psychological suppression of Janaki from her account of her life. When young, Janaki, as was the condition of the girls of her age, didn't know what to expect of marriage though she had been groomed to reach the destination of it. Her mother and aunts had taught her all the skills of marriage but they had not communicated to her of the sexual acts. Anita Nair focuses on all the arts a girl is taught in her girlhood with an implication that she is not taught of the intricacies of marriage because of a psychological taboo. She says: "...she wasn't expected to know what it really meant to be married, and neither was she curious about it. It would come to her as it had to her mother, she thought" (25). She expresses the limited freedom of speech that women have regarding sex in the communication of Janaki's aunts: "He is your husband and you must accept whatever he does" (25).

However, Janaki cannot accept her husband soon after her marriage, and it is not shyness but "strangeness" (25) she feels whenever her husband comes close to her as she has been brought up in a society that frowns upon women in the company of men. For the same reasons, Nair says that their marriage remains "unconsummated for more than two months" (25). She overcomes her revulsion fearing that her husband would go looking for it elsewhere if she doesn't co-operate with him. On reaching womanhood, she can realize the "tensile connection" that is there between most couples "who have been married a long time" (31-32). Her difficulty in understanding this relationship as companionship or friendship or a mere complicity that springs between people who share a bed, a child and a life, perhaps is due to her lack of social communication with the other women of her age. Her intimacy with her husband grows as she starts realizing that she is his wife and "it was the sharing that counted" (27).

"Emotions are for the young; the elderly have no use for them" (33) says Nair. Janaki could never express her emotions in her youth and old age as well. On an occasion when her husband is addressing her 'mummy', and giving an exalted picture of hers to their daughter-in-law, she feel like screaming aloud: "I am your wife. Remember, you used to call me Janu once. Wife, Darling, Sweetheart. And if you find it hard saying those, call me woman, but don't call me Mummy" (34). But Janaki cannot scream as she has to feign the feminine virtues of being a "composed and contented woman" (35). Nair points out that Janaki is less articulate in spite of her willing efforts to share her feelings with her husband: "Some nights they talked. Random pieces of conversation.About their son. A neighbour. Or, perhaps a film they had seen earlier that night. Sometimes they slipped into reminiscences. Memories that were dicephalous" (26). However she can feel a friendly love for her husband at the exhaustive phase of her married life after receiving her son's taunting accusations of her smugness.

Her failure to communicate the right feelings to her son creates a "suppressed dislike" (36) in him. Though she understands the tensed nature of her son, she fails to express her dislike of him and the same becomes the reason for her detachment from him. Nair voices her innermost thought on alienation: "When you get to a certain age, nothing matters but your serenity" (33). Janaki, immersing herself into a pool of emotions, describes Akhila as a person hiding behind "such a stiff armour of control that most people must be in awe" (41) of her.

Anita Nair throws her accusation against patriarchy for contriving "such a stiff armour of control" into the consciousness of young girls. When Akhila was young, she could sense the scanning eyes of Subramani Iyer, her neighbour in the Agraharam, deep into her georgette half-sari. As a girl, she couldn't discuss Subramani Iyer's behaviour with his wife and daughter though they were friendly with her. She hears similar experience from Sheela, a young girl travelling with her in the same coupe. When Sheela's grandmother warned her daughter against the danger of allowing her granddaughter to play badminton with the neighbourhood uncle, Naazar, she didn't dare to speak openly about Celine's pregnancy through her father's friend. Though Sheela was just five years old then, she could understand her grandmother's implication. In her teenage she could sense the same danger through Naazar too. Once when she went to Hasina's home, Naazar attempted to wipe the line of sweat on her upper lip and another time, he knotted the loose bows of her blouse meticulously. Sheela, couldn't protest against his actions but she stopped her visits to Hasina's house. Hasina, her mother and Sheela could pass their censure against the malicious actions of Naazar through an exchange of glances, but all the three do not attempt to voice against him. When Naazar knotted her bows, she could merely feel "her breath lodge in her throat and when she saw the hurt in Hasina and her mother's eyes, shame wrapped itself around her" (66). Shame, a garment forced upon femininity by patriarchy, becomes the most powerful weapon of men to escape from legal laws.

Patriarchal norms determine and restrict the moral voice of women. Anita Nair portrays them as the lynchpin of Akhila's life. Moulded by these norms, Akhila feels guilty to dream of a life of her own on becoming the head of her family after her father's death. When her brothers find jobs, she waits for them to speak about her marriage. She swallows her hurt and anger against her family members when none speaks about her life.

The worst punishment to those women who transgress the norms of patriarchy is excommunication. Sarasa Mami, Subramani Iyer's wife, takes revenge against these norms by initiating her daughter, Jaya, into prostitution after her husband's death when she fails to receive help from the Brahmin community. When Akhila's mother prevents her from talking to Jaya and her mother at a stop, she taunts her mother blaming the "brahmin cronies who have ostracized that poor woman and her family" (83). Further, she tells her that it could have been them standing like that if her father's job was not given to them. Akhila justifies Sarasa Mami's decision to her mother: "Do you realize it could have been us standing there, Amma?" (83). Anita Nair aptly describes the condition of femininity in the grip of patriarchy: "Akhilandeswari. Mistress of all worlds. Master of none" (84). Akhila can never become the real master of her family in spite of heading it after her father's death. Nair portrays patriarchy's attempts to destabilize femininity confining it under the terms like society, virtues and nobility. Transgressing these rules would cause havoc to women. Nair says: "To do so would be entering a dangerous territory" (85).

From Margaret's Shanthi's experience, Akhila realizes that a woman doesn't really need a man's companion. Margaret, a gold medalist in MSc Chemistry feels despondent after her marriage with Ebenezer Paulraj. Her hatred against him is on the upsurge when she is forced by him to agree to an abortion. Moreover, her mother's advice on the responsibility of a woman to keep the marriage happy, forces her to succumb to a melancholic disposition. Hence she decides to remain quiet in spite of her husband's rampant behaviour in front of his coterie. Nair underscores the pathetic condition of all the suppressed women in India through the expression of Margaret's thoughts:

> Besides there was the stigma of divorce. No one had ever been divorced in my family. What God had put together, no man or woman had cast asunder. In respectable families such as ours, no one gave up on their marriage. They grit their teeth and worked harder to preserve it. If I left Ebenezer Paulraj, I would have to be prepared to lose my family as well. (113)

Driven to abject hatred against him for his forcible transformation of her appearance and his persuasion of her to go in for medical termination of her first pregnancy, she vows to incapacitate him from all enjoyment. Her art of communication fails with the doctor who asks after her health on terminating her pregnancy, as she becomes bereft of any expression after the nipping up of her unseen baby at its budding stage. Her husband's supreme powers upon her and his despicable coterie become the target of her rebellion. She decides to make use of Ebenezer's weakness for food as her silent anti-patriarchal weapon which can never be sensed by Ebenezer or her own family members. She appeases his palatable tongue with food items fried in ghee and very soon she can see him become a quiet and easy man avoiding the coterie or defaced books. Her tantalizing effect on "his appetite for food and occasionally for sex" (134) draws his attention once again to herself. She experiences the ultimate happiness after giving birth to a girl baby. From her narration of her personal life, Akhila realizes that love is a wild beast that needs domestication.

To her Margaret's idea of love appears to be a watered down love. She recalls her irretrievable love for Hari, a train mate whom she had refused to marry because of the significant age difference between them. When she had stayed a night with Hari at a holiday resort, it hurt her to hear the stinging remarks of the workers of her elderly look. All of a sudden she felt bereft and alone on the train after having listened to

Margaret's bitter experience. She regrets her mistake of having given up Hari and starts believing that "life would toss forth a second chance" (155) as it had done for Janaki and for Margaret in a "convoluted way" (155).

Through the narration of Prabha Devi, Anita Nair cautions those women who engage in rapport with patriarchy through an adoption of norms and behavior exclusively used by males. Nair's focus in *Ladies Coupe* is on the linguistic and ethical barriers that suppress the conscience of women, preventing them from acting as men. Terms and expressions used by men are not expected to be used by women. In this novel, Nair suggests that terms like 'sex' and 'condom' are considered as obscene terms when used by a woman. Prabha Devi's expression of thoughts regarding pregnancy and sex is despised by her husband, Jagdeesh. He is flabbergasted upon her insistence on making him wear a condom to avoid pregnancy. He stiffens in shame and embarrassment and ponders: "What kind of a woman was she? Sex was something a man and a woman did beneath the covers of the night and a thin sheet. It was not a topic of conversation" (179). The unspoken conversation between Prabha Devi and her daughter reveals the terribly possessive and domineering attitude of patriarchy:

> 'Daughter,' I'll have to say, 'show him you are incapable of doing anything beyond the periphery of your home and he will manage your life.... He will pet you and cosset you at first, for after all, you are appealing to the male in him to protect and safeguard. But it will be only a matter of days before he turns into a tyrant who will want to control your every thought'. (188)

For her, a complete submission of her body to him merely meant a dutiful acceptance of her role in his life when it is "a mere satiation of a bodily need" (194) for him. Lack of communication deepens her withdrawal from her husband. She fails to convey her sensual desires to him for the fear of losing her respect. Thus fear disallows her to utter her innate sexual desires to him.

Akhila's friend Karpagam spells out the need to rise against patriarchy in order to live a life of complete happiness. Her advice to Akhila to live a life of her own pronounces the necessity to get rid of fear against patriarchy. She asks: "Who made these laws anyway? Some man who couldn't bear the thought that in spite of his death, his wife continued to be attractive to other men" (202).

From Prabha Devi's life, Akhila learns that she has to triumph over her innate timidity and reprimand tradition. She learns more from Marikolunthu's life about the art of swimming into the current of ocean instead of being cast away on its banks. Marikolunthu's drastic accusation against patriarchy and her description of it as a cruel world for women stuns her. She was born and brought up at Palur near Kancheepuram in Tamil Nadu. Her poor origin drives her to work as a maid at the Chettiar Kottai, the richest family of that village though her mother regrets of stealing her childhood. The gloomy phase of her life begins when she is raped by Murugesan, one of Chettiar's family members, at the mango grove on the night before Pongal.Victimized by social restrictions on femininity, she dares not to speak of her rape to anyone including her dearest mother. Constrained by the innate fear to voice out the injustice caused to her, she pretends that nothing had happened to her. But her pregnancy compels her to divulge the beastly act of Murugesan to her mother and Sujathaakka, the daughter-in-law of the Chettiar. For no fault of hers, everyone expects her to be ashamed of what has happened. Further, they refuse to accept her accusation against Murugesan whose affluence and his status in the Chettiar's family has silenced everyone. From then onwards, her hatred against her own child and the world of affluent men cannot be understood by the women around her.

Her account of the close relationship she has with Sujathaakka and her husband in the Chettiar's family in her later days as a "surrogate housewife," "surrogate mother" and "surrogate lover" (268) and her desire to be "the real thing" (268) to her son Muthu whom she has disowned because of her hatred against Murugesan in the past brings in a change in the attitude of Akhila. She decides that she wouldn't let her family use her anymore. She discovers a new woman in her craving to break the boundaries drawn around the life of a spinster by patriarchy.

Transmission of the knowledge of feminine sexual difference from one generation of women to the next generation still remains a taboo in most of the Indian societies as it could not be spoken. As long as there is a psychological taboo that dissuades women from speaking openly on the problems related to puberty, pregnancy, rape, sex abuse and so on, women can never represent themselves as empowered beings.

Nair's women in *Ladies Coupe* are not convey their problems related to sex and kinship either to their mothers or their husbands. Though Akhila's companions on the Kanyakumari Express share their personal experiences with her, she stays totally immune to the social practice of communication and she doesn't convey her carnal desires to anyone of them till the end of the novel. This throws light on the fact that there is always the difficulty of intergenerational relationships between women preventing them from conveying their ideas on sexual pleasure. Cornell quotes Irigaray regarding this: "Feminine pleasure has to remain inarticulate in language, in its own language, if it is not to threaten the underpinnings of logical operations..." (156).

Nair's heroine represents the spinsters in most sections of Indian society in her narration of her desires and in the description of despondent moments. In her case, it is a representation culminating in action. The restrictions inscribed as psychological taboos in the conscience of spinsters or widows in most of the Indian societies are easily flouted by most bachelors and even those who have supposedly embraced celibacy. Nair's heroine transgresses all these restrictions by seducing a young man whom she had met on Kanyakumari beach. Swamped totally by lust, she discovers that it is the "energy that defines life" (274). She feels a purgation of her past when her sexual need is satiated. Drucilla Cornell points out that it is a mistake to contrast representation against the act of communicative practice: "Representation has often been mistakenly contrasted to the focus in other strands of discourse theory or communication as action. But representation is inseparable from action". (xxxi) According to Cornell "representation is inseparable from action" and it "is not just about rendering things visible" (xxxi). Nair's heroine represents unconventional women who plunge into action though it may not be welcome to all women.

Women's limited usage of language to communicate meaning will not be sufficient to transmit and generate more ideas on female sexuality to the future generations of women. All problems that issue forth from patriarchal domination upon women can be redressed if women cease to be inarticulate. Akhila could have enunciated her desire for marriage to her mother and brothers at the right time. Jaya could have rebelled against her mother for initiating her into prostitution. Janaki's inarticulateness before her husband and son had prevented her from expressing her anguish. Margaret Shanthi could have had her first baby through an articulation of her desire to both her husband and parents. Marikolunthu could have revealed Murugesan's rape of her on the same day of that accident. All these women failed to communicate and lost an opportunity to thereby establish individuality before and after the miseries fell upon them.

Cornell discusses that "freedom is not a static condition women achieve once and for all" (xxvii). She argues that it is not absolutely foreclosed to us by male domination. In her view "it is a process of struggle we engage in, in part by resignifying the personas of femininity, and the meanings given to our 'sex', so to express and represent who we are in our singularity and in the complexity of our other basic identifications" (xxvii). True transformation to women will occur only if they challenge the patriarchal norms through an articulation of their feelings and emotions without feigning the feminine virtues. Through a description of negative norms that mute women, Anita Nair implies the importance of breaking the moral and psychic limitations that handicap feminine sexuality.

WORKS CITED

Cornell, Drucilla. *Beyond Accommodation: Ethical Feminism, Deconstruction and the Law*. Boston: Rowman and Littlefield Publishers, Inc., 1999.

Gilligan, Carol. "In a Different Voice: Women's Conceptions of Self and of Morality." *Harvard Educational Review* 47 (1977): 481-517.

Nair, Anita. *Ladies Coupe: A Novel in Parts*. New Delhi: Penguin Books, 2001.

Pipher, Mary. *Reviving Ophelia: Saving the Selves of Adolescent Girls*. New York: Ballantine Books, 1994.

Shahjahan, C.J. 'Web of Support.' *Sunday Times of India*, Chennai, January 23, 2011.

12

'Taboos to be Tasted': Analysis of the Select Short Stories of Githa Hariharan

— G. Kalvikkarasi

> It is far harder to kill a phantom than reality.
>
> —Virginia Woolf

Githa Hariharan's *The Art of Dying* is a collection of short stories which acts as a critique of the decadent values and the false consensus with which her characters live in their world. Her trajectories are towards the subconscious state of the characters which are displayed with more frenzy and appropriation. The internalization of ill-conceived cultural notions, the unbalanced social order and the stereotypical perspectives distort their conceptualization of self. But the paradigmatic shift occurs only on the verge of their death. There is reconceptualisation of the self and the art of living is revealed to them in the shadow of death. The seven select short stories of Githa Hariharan are analysed for the power relations of patriarchal authority.

"The Remains of the Feast" is a poignant tale of an old woman who desperately tries to live, on hearing about her impending death. Her last two months are reserved for 'remembering the taboos to be tasted' (15). The old woman wields courage to act upon her fatal life and expresses her frenzy against the irrational ideologies of the community. This story unfolds the psychodynamics of the great grandmother.

The story is narrated by the passive observer, the great granddaughter Ratna who bridges the generations by the simple act of attending to the old woman Rukmani's 'unexpected and inappropriate demands'. Rukmani, a village-bred brahmin woman is 90 years old at the time of her death. She is picturised as a docile woman "who signed the papers my father has brought with a thumbprint", "giggling like a little girl, flippant about her only child's death" (9). Githa Hariharan fixes her in the subjective position of a woman whose life was culturally determined and her value systems were what she has internalized in her orthodox stance. Her internalization conditions her needs, wants and desires and thereby defines her whole life. But this is contradictory to her real self and leads to split perception or madness.

The strange relationship between the dying woman and the great grand daughter starts with the sudden demand of cakes by the old woman from the Christian shop. Ratna was surprised by these demands but she satisfied the cravings of Rukmani. The cravings slowly become monstrously open, "Varied and unpredictable", "laughable and urgent" (13). Her demands were for lemon tarts, garlic, aerated drinks, fruit cakes laced with brandy, bhel puri and chilli bonda and her list extended to raw onions, fried bread, chickens and goats.

Her exasperation shows that she did not have the liberty to choose her food and some food was forbidden to her orthodox Brahmin family. But the struggle is not for food alone but to taste many other taboos which were denied to her. She subverts her internal oppression in the form of outburst of insanity. As Phyllis Chesler remarks:

> Neither genuine madwoman, nor women who are hospitalized for conditioned female behavior, are powerful revolutionaries. Their insights and behavior are as debilitating (for social reasons) as they are profound. Such women act alone, according to the rules that make no sense and are contrary to their culture. Their behavior is mad because it represents a socially powerless individual's attempt to unite body and feeling. (229)

But are these demands mere fumblings to communicate her great losses? Her speech has slowly descended into a rant and ended in schizophrenia. Her split self dangled between the social constructions of gender and caste with that of her real self. Shoshana Felman makes an insightful remark in "Woman and Madness: The Critical Phallacy" about the moral dilemma of such people:

> Quite the opposite of rebellion, Madness is an impasse confronting those whom cultural conditioning has deprived of the very means of protest or self affirmation. (8)

The worsening health and emotional chaos results in her admission into the hospital. From her deathbed, she rushes crashing the IV pole, screaming at others to bring a red sari with wide border of gold. The age old convention of shedding her fancied dress because of her widowhood and to wear the pale brown sari, "the widow's weeds", was loathsome to her. The old woman passes away. The author subtly brings in a subtext when Ratna clears the wardrobe and arranges the books in a row like a row of soldiers, evoking her great grandmother's irrepressible, child-like spirit.

The structure of the story is symmetrical and shows the progressive evolution of the woman through the three generations in the story. Ratna acts as the representative of modern woman with greater self assertion. She aids her great grandmother in her final rigidity and role reversal thus breaking the myth of the conservative woman. Like several other women writers' texts, the structuring principle of this text relies on "the exploration of the points of view which madness and dreams offer, or the points of view of freaks, children, women which leads to the rejection of adequacy of normal attitudes, beliefs and behavior" (Katherine Wheeler 3).

If the agony of Rukmani is the result of internalization, the story "Reprieve" shows Nagaraj paying the reparation for denigrating the subjectivity of his wife Mangala on the anvils of death. After the death of Mangala, the retired advocate comes to Mumbai to live with his son and daughter-in-law. His stay evokes the memories of Mangala and his life with her for 50 married years. Like a defendant, he now thinks and argues about his role play as a husband.

Mangala is a patient, pleasant hardworking woman who runs the machinery of a 30-member household but whose components are decided by Rao. Mangala without any choice of her habitat or her way of rearing the family fits herself and painstakingly builds it. As Kathleen Wheeler remarks:

> The patriarchal attitudes to sex, work, art and play are questioned by submerging ourselves into the forms which unconsciously structure and people our imaginations from our earliest childhood. (13)

Nagaraj now feels he has missed 'something finer, more essential' in his pursuit of justice. He senses the intimacy of his son and daughter-in-law and he realizes that he never cared for Mangala's way of life.

> It seemed to him that Mangala had talked only about the children or the many problems of the household. Had she wondered about his cases? His life away from and independent of the household? Had she been lonely or too busy or tired or vacuous to care? (46)

His reminiscences about the romantic glances and the radiant smile of Mangala which happened years ago are vividly picturised by the author. He had no laxities in his professional life; but he failed to even understand if she lived comfortably well or found her life difficult. With the gnawing guilt, he screams "Mangala" and falls into the "dark safety of the outstretched arms" (47).

The story deals with the physical and mental isolation of the couple living in the same house. Her moments of happiness or anguish are unknown to him. Nagaraj does not deliberately dismiss her but his internalization of the patriarchal authority results in his taking Mangala's life for granted while maintaining his grand act as a lawyer. This makes him insensitive to her life. Further it shows the man's stereotyped response which has stunted his role as a sensible husband. Betty Friedan's remarks in *The Feminine Mystique* reflect the other side of male psychology:

> How could we ever really know or love each other as long as we play those roles that kept us from knowing or being ourselves? Were not men as well as women still locked in lonely isolation, alienation no matter. ...It seemed to me men were not the real enemy, the fellow victims suffering from outmoded masculine mystique that made them feel unnecessarily inadequate....(521)

Mangala lives in a world which is defined and circumscribed on men's terms. Her psychic disintegration is completely absent in the story which indicates lack of communication and companionship between them. There is no hysterical shriek or walkout. But Nagaraj pays for his callous attitude by his mental derangement. The power relationship subsumes the niceties of life. Githa Hariharan creates an atmosphere of the mock court session staging the argument between Nagaraj's insensitive practicality and the feminine sensitivity of Mangala, the sacrificial woman. The author experiments with the theme of split subjectivity and shows the victim suffering on the blurring borders of the real and the conventional self creating the psychic space of hallucination.

The story "Forefathers" begins with intense subtextual intricacies in the narration of a simple incident. Here the young boy is the victim of patriarchal authority. The young college boy anxiously tries to predict his father's death by the probability of hitting the crow. Slowly the story unfolds with the revelation of his father's personality through the eyes of the protagonist, the young boy. He lives in a flat which was his father's kingdom. He has to nurse his invalid father. The father, the lawmaker would often summon him either for the bedpan, dish tray or plain summons with a question; "Sit here, do you want me to die alone" (54).

The young boy is tired of his father's demanding behavior and wears a mask that absorbs "the sharpest sarcasm and angriest of tears" (52). He is even summoned to perform like a circus monkey to entertain the guests. Kate Miller in her *Sexual Politics* observes that the principles of patriarchy appear to be twofold: men shall dominate female: older male shall dominate younger. However just as with any human institution there is distance between the real and the ideal... (25). One can see the same power struggle being introduced by Githa Hariharan in this story.

The young protagonist sleeps huddled together with his two sisters and his mother in the kitchen amidst occasional hushed whispers. But he is drained of his spirit due to the incongruence between his youthful vigour and his stunted desires. After spending a lifetime together, listening with awkwardness to his father's voice, he wants to shout now, "Look at the man with the golden past" (54). Slowly he dies "a more gentle death" (55). But for the son who is longing for his death, it seems as though the years of airlessness becomes one big lie. He describes thus:

> I became a man, at long last, in the funeral atmosphere of shame and guilt that he lay dying. (55)

In the shadow of death, the young man feels he needs forefathers. In this story, the patriarchal ideology not only destroys the women, but the men too. The young boy defies the cloistered existence of his family under the headship of his father, who derides the expression of their individualities. Caught in the psychological-emotional web, he struggles to evolve but only after his father's death. Death comes as a psychic relief for the boy's tormented spirit to open up. Githa's vision of the male protagonist succumbing to the patriarchal system is a realistic portrayal of a strange tale of victimization.

The title story "The Art of Dying" is a pathetic tale of the mother and the daughter who were like "willing victims of a time machine". They spend their time together with past as the inevitable appendage. The daughter is a counsellor who glamorizes the idea of death during her consultation with the patients. She stays with her mother who is struggling alone with death. The mother is haunted by the memories of her son's death, the dregs of her past. The story abounds in meditative outbursts about death.

The narration moves to and fro with the haunting memories of the mother interspersed with the daughter's case studies in her clinic. The narrative strategy employed by Githa in the story abounds with sane and insane excesses:

> Death is like tomorrow, two lone combatants or lovers the rest of us forgotten.
>
> Death demands strength, not a final weakness. (66)

The mother feels that she has betrayed her husband's love as she did not stop breathing. The dual or ambiguous feeling of longing to live when death approaches her is evident in the story. The daughter also thinks about her father, the epitome of male supremacy.

> You could say he wrote his biography, in our child's mind for posterity, word for word. We remember him as he wanted us to, one dimensional firm fatherly hand, totally unbelievable. (71)

These incisive comments reveal the power structure of the normal Indian family and the women under duress. She concludes that "Most of the cases I have seen, spoke through their families" (75).

The mother's death throws light on the Art of Dying. The daughter reconceptualises her self by the revelation she gets through the diagnosis of patient's mental illness and her mother's approach to death. She says:

> There is life in death in spite of all its ancestral legacy of terrors. The true healer labours to ease this passing. (78)

"The Will" has the thematic preoccupation with death too. As a meticulous planner for the family, Raghu looks on the details of every aspect of his wife Sushila's and children's lives. He leaves a letter as his will to his wife through which she inherits moral nuggets of practical wisdom. He believes his ideas would keep her sane and happy with her children. She scans the letter at times of counselling the children in the practical ways of life. The loving husband never teaches her to make decisions nor allows her private decisions but takes a faltering step to teach her after his death. It reads as follows:

> You will be with them, not of them.
> You will stand apart like a friendly tranquil island. (148)

Thus instead of being a helpless mindless burden, she steps forward to counsel the children when needed. Her efforts reflect Raghu's words and ideas. But one fine day she loses the letter that has guided her and becomes disastrously sick. The grandchild approaches her when the whole house is empty and starts reading the morals from his textbook. It awakens her psyche suddenly, and leads to the exploration of herself.

The subtext implies that Sushila has reconceptualised herself and looks for practical wisdom which is dispersed around her. Raghu's companionship does not provide her the moral strength to learn her own lessons. She takes back life with a deeper perspective and with dauntless courage. Her self-awareness is thwarted by Raghu's domination, thereby not allowing her to mellow down naturally. As Pam Morris remarks:

> To be heroic, plots tell us men must embrace action seeking to shape circumstances to their will, whereas for women, heroism consists of accepting restrictions and disappointments with stoicism. (32)

Further the idea of self-reflecting on their self is important for a woman. It seems that it is a natural part of one's cultural psyche to accept subordination without rebellion by these characters. Here the patriarchal perspective does not count woman's experience.

Men display power of dominance and undermine the other men and women. The fragmented self of both men and women is anatomized not only to display the parts of the self but make the readers feel the pain of realization. One can observe that there is absolutely no fictional representation of the characters in these stories. Subtle satire, sarcasm and the realistic details often jolt the reader.

The story, "The Closed Room" shows the woman being the "Angel of the house" and the man, the writer. The woman is described thus: "Her voice lends itself as a medium like a wife, a faithful helper to complete his act of creation. The man faithfully records her support in the interview. She is a recording machine. It helps of course, that she comes from a family of scholars, that she too wanted to be a writer" (161). Thus his wife is denied the role of a writer but helps him to be one. In this closed room the protagonist has no room of her own.

Though her keen observation of the characters and analysis of their thoughts and their feelings are enough impetus for her to emerge as a writer, she does not make an autonomous choice about her professional growth. The woman, the real self is struggling inside echoing Woolf's statement, "The world did not say to her as it said to them, write if you choose; it makes no difference to me". (59) In short, she reflects on Lady Winchelsia of the sixteenth century as mentioned by Woolf:

> To write or read or think or to enquire
> Would cloud our beauty and exhaust our time
> And interrupt the conquests of our prime
> Whilst the dull manage of a servile house
> Is held by some our utmost art and use. (66)

The woman senses his impending death after spending "the years of tunnelling in the purgatorial limbo"; he frames sentences through the hands of the woman to describe his dying. Githa Hariharan attempts sharp sarcasm through an image that the writer has "maintained his journals and somewhere opened now and then, like mistresses you remember only because of guilt" (163). The masquerade of the Angel of the House is unveiled with his death and the woman was revealed. Like the virus infecting the air, she wields the pen out of sheer habit. The fragmentation of her self is revealed in her disjointed sentences and paragraphs. The woman feels that "He trusted only his fictional shifts of perspective; his own fallible eyesight" (163). The writer who had no intention of understanding the new bearded young writers, gets the judgment in the closed room, in the woman's words: "I rewrote your manuscript; the one that was lost from memory" (166). The cultural entitlement of the power and privilege of man over woman is evident in this story.

"Voices in the Twilight" examines the psychodynamics of the family beginning with the event of the mother's death. The children, the three of them—Arjun, Shaku and Vidhya who were not always orphans, "who know too much about the other"—meet as strangers and share the nostalgic memories of their childhood and adulthood in the flat.

Githa Hariharan has set the story to flow without interruptions in the form of stream of consciousness technique as multiple narratives. She makes all the three characters analyze the past through their monologues during their brief stay for sharing the common grief over their mother's death. The whole story is an enigma where every paragraph lends the texts and subtexts to explore the identity of the narrator.

Arjun introduces himself as a "the sole male of the surviving family". He also explains about the gender construct of the family as a matter of fact.

> I am surrounded by women, the object of their day to day womanly cares. They sweep my floors, cook my rice, sew my buttons and wash the dirtiest of underwear without murmur. In return they dont make outrageous demands. Merely duty, responsibility, sacrifices the rest. (129)

Arjun makes no introduction about the male-female antagonism, as domesticity and subordination is seen as a part of the cultural psyche. Shaku with her two children and a miscarriage makes a reluctant entry into the flat. She raises questions about her existential self in the flat and exclaims thus: "There is no time in this flat that I want back. I always hated it. it reads on my back like an ugly monkey" (132). She continues her life daydreaming about a man who will heal and comfort her.

Vidya, the hostel inmate, explores the life of the lonely widow, her mother in the cupboard with "piles and piles of romantic novelletes and magazines-syrupy, just slightly sexy stories in the family" ... (133). The widow's helpless state and passive submission to the family is disturbing and is understood as the internalisation of the mores of her cultural community. She never comments or has any complaints about anything. She answers thus: "I am not educated like you so no talk, no discussion, just a string of platitudes linked with sighs punctuated with half smothered exclamations (135)". Vidya too feels the family to be a trap:

> The net lies waiting: It can trip me up the instant the door is opened.
> I can breathe only if I cut myself off ruthlessly (134).

For all the efforts taken by the mother, every one feels embittered about their existence. Vidya raises the question, "Is pain the inescapable price for an unstinting mother's love?" She surmises that her mother's self sacrificing martyrdom with her widowhood did not give anyone the satisfaction. The outsiders never appreciated her assumption and obedience to her cultural barriers which only made her as the victim.

Shaku who loves her sweet-smelling flesh turns helpless when the burden of life weighs her down with mocking wrinkles. The emptiness of her life devoid of care, the boredom of monotonous existence, fades away the freshness of her life. She wakes up every day to the alarm rings set for Ravi, her husband.

The loneliness of her life is expressed in the hermeneutics of suspicion that extends through out the story. The hypothetical question is raised with her gloomy feeling about women's lives:

> You can play sensibly, you can be wily or obedient at the right times, play the rules and even then you lie in bed and worry. Will the whole fragile mansion come crashing down? (139)

Arjun's life is also spent wearing the mask. The man, the present crown prince in the house, has been the willing victim along with his mother. But he stealthily settles scores against the stifling conditions of the middle class values with his illicit relationship with Rita. Thus the endless need for the masks and disguises results in fragmentation. But the power relations and gender equations were not thrust on anyone but are deeply seated due to internalization. Claramma Jose in *Feminisms: An Introduction* quotes Anna Anastasi:

> From all that has been said, it is apparent that we cannot speak of inferiority and superiority, but only of specific differences in aptitude and personality between the sexes. These differences are largely the result of cultural and the experiential factors. . . . The overlapping in all psychological characteristics is such that we need to consider men and women as individuals rather in terms of group stereotypes. (25)

This story not only reveals the mental disorder of a character but also gives a vivid picture of the disorder of the family. We find them breathing the air of freedom away from the stifling thoughts of their mother's death and the haunting past.

Thus Githa Hariharan draws our attention to and prompts critical reflection on patriarchal setup and analyzes the characters as individuals, rather than as stereotypes. The reader exercises the faculties of connoting, associating and inferring the pragmatics of life through these realistic portrayals. Githa Hariharan's fictional landscape is no contradiction to the reality of our existence. Further, the stream of consciousness technique adopted by the author displays the varying moods and the inner flux of the characters.

Githa Hariharan's seven stories are structured on the notion of female and male subjectivity. To be more precise, human values and factual realities are the thematics of the text. Death is treated as "the inevitable reminders of the life lost". The hackneyed life is desperately clutched at by these characters and the tormented selves fight to live. The angst of their lost lives is the lifeline of these stories. They express their escalating resentment against the imbalanced social order and their anxiety to live well. Their lives had been deficient in so many aspects and their realization of the bitter truisms of life maddens them. But they resurface with more vehement assertion. They create their own identities ungrounded in the sense of patriarchy. The devious acts for the sake of community or the age old ideologies are erased from their century old memories.

Githa Hariharan succeeds as a great literary artist in her realistic portrayal of the male-dominated ideologies and the sufferings of women. In her own inimitable style, she encourages the humans to sense 'the taboos to be tasted'. The characters make a spiritual odyssey to understand life in the shadow of death. The structural unity and the narrative strategy of the stories glide smoothly with the thematics of the text. These stories with open endings and multiple narratives, offer several planes of approach. The author attacks the very notion of conventionality and patriarchy, and demands more complex levels of response from the readers. This Art of Dying is the subtle expression of the Art of Living.

Works Cited

Chesler, Phylis. *Contemporary Women Fiction and the Fantastic*. Ed. Armitt, Louis. United Kingdom: McMillan Ltd, 2000.

Felman, Shoshana. "Women and Madness: The Critical Phallacy" (1975) in *Feminisms: An Anthology of Literary Criticism.* Ed.Robin.R.Warner and Diane Prince Herndl. 2nd edition, New Jersey: Rutgers University Press, 1997.

Friedan, Betty. *The Feminine Mystique*. New York: WW Norton and Co Inc, 1997

Hariharan, Githa. *The Art of Dying*. India: Penguin Books India Ltd, 1993.

Jose, Claramma. *Feminisms, An Introduction*, Chennai:Aresseril House Publications, 2005.

Millet, Kate. *Sexual Politics*. Illinois: University of Illinois Press, 1990.

Wheeler, Katherine. *Modernist Women Writers and Narrative Art*. Basingstoke: Mcmillan Publishing Company, 1994.

13

Power of Relationship: A Study of Anita Nair's *The Better Man*

— R. Revathi

Anita Nair has carved a niche for herself as an Indian writer writing in English, especially in the field of regional fiction. Her works include novels, short stories, cookbooks etc. and her books have been published in several languages. Her first novel *The Better Man* (*BM*) has been translated into 21 languages. Born at Mundakotta Kurissi in Kerala, she had her education in Chennai. Her career as a writer began, when she was working in an advertising agency as a creative director in Bangalore. In the novel, she reveals her remarkable understanding of the psychological tensions which can arise in the father-son relationship as well as her ability to delve deep into the minds of her characters.

In *The Better Man* Anita Nair narrates the story of Mukundan, a retired government employee, settling in his native place Kaikurussi. He is the son of Achuthan Nair, who remains a nightmare for his wife and son throughout his life. In order to escape from his father Mukundan finds employment in Trichy and after retirement, he finds he has absolutely no other option than settling in Kaikurussi. This kind of obsession to escape his father is evidently the result of his upbringing. Achuthan Nair brought up Mukundan like a bonsai tree. The bonsai tree, which is grown in a small pot needs pruning very often, in a special manner. Achuthan Nair does the same with his son, Mukundan, by pruning his emotions, self-esteem and confidence at every opportunity. The rivalry between the father and the son and its impact on the latter are beautifully portrayed by Anita Nair with a special emphasis on highlighting every subtle nuance of emotion.

There is something unique here, as everyone is aware that Kerala is a matriarchal society even though some anthropologists prefer to use terms such as matrilineal or matrifocal. The reason is to erase the wrong connotation associated with matriarchy. Matriarchal society, it is believed, offers ultimate power to the women in the political, cultural and social spheres. Matrilineal or matrifocal refers to the power given to the women or the mother within the family. There was good reason for this, as the menfolk in those days were warriors who were likely to lose their lives in the battlefield and hence the women were trained to wield control over their family. Anita Nair, having hailed from Kerala, has opted to deal with the men instead of the women characters in the novel, offering fresh insights to the readers, relating to the operations of power within the family.

Gender discrimination has been one of the vices of Indian society, since time immemorial. A father always prefers a son. Quoting the Laws of Manu, Prabhu says that "a man conquers the world by the birth of a son, he enjoys eternity by that of a grand son; and the great grand father enjoys eternal happiness by the birth of a grand son's son (242). Achuthan Nair is an exception. He has not conquered any world or experienced happiness over his son. The question of grandson or great grandson does not arise as he has failed in his father's duty of getting a suitable bride for his son. Mukundan's reaction to such a father is surprising. He longs for the love, affection and recognition of his father, even though his father has evoked only negative feelings in him. The Law of Manu also insists that a father in addition to giving birth has to perform several other duties also such as feeding, teaching, enlightening and protecting his son. Likewise, a son also has to follow some rules as always going according to the wishes of his father or parents as the pain and difficulty they have undergone for his birth and upbringing cannot be compensated easily. Implicit obedience is expected out of the son and he is never to quarrel with his father. These laws, people may argue are not pragmatic but they are relevant to the modern world also.

The theme of rivalry between father and son is nothing new in the literary scenario. It was often dealt with in the Greek stories. The theme which often recurs is the sons killing their own fathers. Uranus is murdered by his son, Cronos, the Titan, who in turn, is murdered by his son Zeus, the Olympian. The kingdom and power were not handed over to their sons willingly and the sons have to usurp the throne from their fathers. The fathers never nurture a healthy and good opinion about the sons. It is always suspicion. Sometimes, the fathers go to such an extent of abandoning their sons at birth itself and the sons take revenge without knowing that they are avenging their own fathers. This happens in the case of Oedipus who is rejected by his father Laius as he happens to listen to an Oracle that his son will kill him and marry his wife that is his mother. It is this, which motivates him to kill Oedipus. As predicted by the Oracle, Oedipus unknowingly kills Laius and marries his mother Jocasta. It is this story which was interpreted by the great psychologist Sigmund Freud. He called it Oedipus Complex. According to Freud, children develop a sexual longing for the opposite sex parent and this naturally leads to the rivalry with the same sex parent.

While the son triumphs in Greek mythology, it is the father who wins in the Hindu mythology. If it is Oedipus Complex which dominates the Western world, it is Yayati Complex which is celebrated in India. Yayati, as a consequence of his sins, is cursed to become old and impotent. Unable to bear the thought, he begs his sons to take on his curse. While the eldest is reluctant, the youngest accepts and sacrifices his youth while his father happily enjoys his youth without any guilt. The story of Hiranyakashipu is yet another example of how the fathers torture their sons. Hiranyakashipu, by his rigorous penance cleverly extracts a strange boon from Brahma that he cannot be killed in the normal manner. The very next moment, he starts acting in an atrocious manner, torturing everyone and leaving none including his own son Prahlada who has been worshipping Lord Vishnu constantly. Hiranyakashipu's attempts to kill his son become null and void and one day Lord Vishnu himself in the form of a Narasimha, which is half-lion and half-man, kills him, which naturally Hiranyakashipu never expected.

Initially Freud's Oedipus Complex rocked the entire world. However, gradually it started to lose its attraction. According to evolutionary investigators, it is the Natural Selection which plays a vital role in the conflict between parent and child. While some of them feel that natural selection contributes a lot to the typical forms of parent-child conflict, others are of the opinion that the Natural Selection is responsible for avoiding inbreeding on the part of humans and animals so as to prevent genetic factors from harming their children.

Apart from the contribution of Natural Selection, there are other factors too which lead to the conflict between the father and the son. In the relationship between the father and the son, at one stage or other, disagreements and differences of opinion are bound to happen. Several factors are responsible for this such as generation gap, educational background etc. It may also be due to the craving for power, the obsession to control and insecurity on the part of the father. In some cases, the rivalry is nipped in the bud with the timely intervention of people, who are interested in the welfare of the family. In some cases, it is a love – hate relationship. Both the father and the son are at loggerheads. Yet when a situation arises, they go out of the way to protect the other. There lies an undercurrent of love and affection which comes to the fore when they confront problems. In some instances, the gap between the father and the son becomes the gulf and both of them nurture anger towards each other and it is a pity that some of them take it to their grave.

In most cases, it can be seen, the rivalry starts between the father and the son, when the son attains his adolescence. However, in *The Better Man* problem starts for Mukundan and Achuthan Nair even from Mukundan's early childhood. Four-year-old Mukundan, who has seen his father only in the photograph, is scared, when his father turns up all of a sudden from Burma. Dressed in black, he appears tall and when he starts talking to him Mukundan is all the more afraid and starts calling his mother. When she comes to the boy's rescue and tries to pacify him, Achuthan Nair becomes wild and blames her for bringing up his son like a 'pathetic creature'. So the very first meeting between the father and the son starts on the wrong foot.

When Mukundan is eight years old, the relationship between them has not improved. On the other hand, it has become worse, for Achuthan Nair chooses to settle in Kaikurussi after resigning his job. Home becomes hell for Mukundan. According to Sajal Kumar Bhattacharya, a home should be "an imagined space which would reaffirm and consolidate the bonds of personal love, security, selfless feeling,. . . ." (129). While this is one dimension there is another too. "Home is often a space that one strives to dominate, not necessarily through violence but rather by playing the role of caring guardian or any other central figure" (129). Achuthan Nair does not pretend to be a caring father and he resorts to violence to show his power. Hence for Mukundan, the concept of home has changed from the first to the second when his father has returned from Burma. It starts early in the morning when he wakes up a little bit late. His father will start preaching on discipline and this will go on and on and finally end up in a curse that Mukundan is fit only for "ploughing the fields". Achuthan Nair always ends his talk invariably with a question and Mukundan is expected to answer not on his own but merely to repeat his father's last words. While it boosts the confidence of Achuthan Nair, it gradually kills something vital in Mukundan. Yet he gives the answer which is expected of him with all reverence and obedience.

Mukundan is also expected by his father to arrive home immediately after school hours. When he is unable to do so, as he has to attend the compulsory games, he becomes a victim of the wrath of his father. Mukundan does not know whether to convince his father or the drill master. If he obeys the words of his father by missing the games, he would be caned the next day by the drill master. If he attends the class, it would be caning by his father. While the drill master stops with three sharp blows, Mukundan's father will stop only when the cane is broken.

When he is 13 years old, he is introduced to David Copperfield by his English teacher. Dickens's choice of words appeals to Mukundan to a great extent that he decides to become a writer for he feels that with words he can wield the magic wand and rule the entire world. He is so elated that he starts writing, rather pouring out his emotions which give him an immense joy till it is found out one day by his father who considers the profession of a writer to be a waste of time. His father instead gives him plenty to write, like official letters, complaint letters etc. and Mukundan becomes adept in writing formal letters. While Mukundan's mother, Paru Kutty, can sense the sorrow of her son, she asks him to write when his father is away, but Mukundan refuses. Actually, Mukundan's mother is mortally afraid of her husband. It is not only his mother, but a host of people in the house like Balammaven, Ammuma, and his three Cheriyammas do not dare to speak against Achuthan Nair. So Mukundan, a small boy, is not an exception. He does not dare go against his father even behind his back. However, it is not a happy acceptance and it has produced scars in his mind. It is one of the stages of his life which is ruined by his father. When he is living away from his father, he is given the charge of a library belonging to a club. While the previous librarians have neglected, Mukundan has contributed a lot, such as buying books once in two months for the library. He has carried out changes in the library and cared for the welfare of the youngsters by keeping them away from the trashy books. It is almost like a family with Mukundan as its head. He likes it a great deal because "unlike human beings it demanded little from him and claimed no rights" (*BM* 14). Nevertheless, he is not interested in reading books and never touches a book. He browses only through the magazines. Such is the influence of his father and as far Mukundan is concerned, that particular chapter is over and he is not interested in raking up the past to revive it.

When Mukundan gets an opportunity to work in an explosives factory, he grabs it, so as to escape from his father. The relationship between Mukundan and his father gradually declines as he becomes an adult. Achuthan Nair has earned the hatred of his son by having an illicit affair, deserting his wife.

After Mukundan's departure, he dares to express his desire of bringing her to the home where his wife lives. For the first time, Paru Kutty, Mukundan's mother, stands up to him despite her fear. Her rebellion is ineffectual as Achuthan Nair brings his concubine and she settles comfortably in a house, which is just opposite to the main house. One cannot expect Mukundan to question this injustice done to his mother by his father, but at least he could have protected her from his father's insults and ill treatment. Mukundan's mother literally begs him to take her with him to his place. However, he convinces her with lame excuses that he is himself sharing a house with another friend. It is actually the fear of his father which makes him refuse her. He feels guilty about it especially after her death from falling down the stairs. His mother's death remains a mystery to him and he wonders whether it is an accident or a murder. But he does not have the courage to ask his father. So he is assailed by fear, hatred and anger towards his father.

Achuthan Nair, as a father, has not fulfilled his duty of getting a bride for his son. Instead he blames Mukundan saying that every man must find his own woman and according to him, Mukundan is not man enough to do it. Hence, the obsession to escape from his father remains just the same even at the time of his retirement. A few months before his retirement, he has made plans with his close friend Narendran. Narendran is willing to accommodate Mukundan near his house in his native place and they have started planning their life after retirement. The opportunity provided by Narendran seems to be ideal for Mukundan, but to his great shock, Narendran, who has frequently complained of headaches, dies of brain tumour a few months prior to retirement. Mukundan is devastated more for his future than over his only friend's death. Now Mukundan, miserable because of his dependence, Mukundan has absolutely no options except to return to Kaikurussi, his native place.

It is not that Mukundan has completely deserted his native place. He had gone for the funeral of his mother and afterwards made a few visits to Kaikurussi, but has stayed only for a short time. During his visits he never forgets to bring a few gifts for his father such as fine cotton undershirts, a woollen shirt with long sleeves, a blanket, a torch and a tin of tobacco. Apart from these, he sends money orders every month. Even though he says that he is doing the duty of a son, in his heart of hearts, he knows that it is a lie. The truth is he wants to gain his father's affection at least through these gifts. It is true that he feels angry with his father and hates him for destroying his life, yet he still remains a child who longs for the love, affection and recognition of his father. But, there does not seem to be any change in Achuthan Nair. He remains the same old Achuthan Nair in whose eyes Mukundan, now a 59 year-old man, can never be a man but a "weak creature" (*BM* 82). Every now and then he proceeds to prove this. Staying in the opposite house, he calls Mukundan and asks him to assist him in crossing the road to come to the main house where Mukundan is staying. When Nair raises his walking stick, immediately Mukundan's fear comes to the fore. It is a reflex action, for whenever his father raises a cane it will land on Mukundan's back. Mukundan regrets his reaction and tries to behave in a casual manner, but Achuthan Nair is subtle enough to find that he has still got power over his 58 year-old son, which ultimately gives him happiness. Such is the state of affairs for Mukundan, when he settles in Kaikurussi after his retirement.

The first few days in his house are a nightmare for Mukundan, for he is sure that he has seen the ghost of his mother, which is furious with him. He thinks that he has fallen from the stairs and he is unable to decide whether it is a dream or reality. However, with the arrival of Krishnan Nair, who has been the caretaker of his house since his childhood, Mukundan feels a kind of normalcy. It is exactly after one month that he ventures to go out to make friends with the villagers. He wants to go to Shankar's Tea Club which is the meeting place of the villagers. He takes great care in his appearance and proceeds to wear a shirt and mundu. Looking at the mirror, he admires himself that he appears like a "mature dignified man. A natural leader. . . Rather like his father had been when he returned from Burma" (*BM* 109). It is surprising to note that even though he hates his father, his role model is invariably his father. However, to his utter dismay, the villagers refuse to give him the recognition which he yearns for. What is all the more irritating to him is that the villagers pay their respect to the man, who has become filthy rich overnight by winning in the lottery, namely, Powerhouse Ramakrishnan. Mukundan is disappointed to the core, when he does not become the centre of attraction, for he wants to expose his knowledge of what is going on around the world to everyone. He is actually motivated to do so because of his fancy that he can take his father's place. Nevertheless, he is not discouraged by the initial disappointment. He proceeds to offer his advice and suggestions, but unfortunately they invariably meet with the disapproval of the villagers.

While Mukundan feels that he does not belong to the village, one thing irks him. It is the painter Bhasi, who has been given the nick name One Screw Loose Bhasi by the villagers. There is something in the expression of Bhasi, which disturbs Mukundan and hence he tries to avoid him but, Bhasi is not willing to give up. Bhasi does not belong to this village. He was a lecturer, who taught undergraduate students. He had put his heart and soul into his teaching, but it came to nothing. While Bhasi faced disappointment professionally, there was yet another disappointment which happened in his personal life. He happened to fall in love with one of his students, who rejected his love. He was actually attracted to her by her beautiful presentation of an essay. When she had not only rejected his love, but also informed him that she has plagiarized this essay, Bhasi felt "Hurt. Betrayal. Anger. Humiliation" (*BM* 101). That was the last day for Bhasi, the lecturer. He left the place and became a painter's apprentice. The change is not only in his profession but in his mind as well. Without any plans about his future, he settles in Kaikurisi. Here, where he knows none and where nobody knows about his past, he feels safe, secure and happy. He does the work of a painter and with his knowledge of herbs, he cures the physical problems of the villagers. He is also adept at recognizing psychological problems and he is the first one to recognize Mukundan's problem and restlessness. He has decided to save him and wants him to come out of his shell.

Nevertheless, Mukundan is not an easy person to be coaxed or cajoled. Even though he was a close friend of Narendran, he had never opened up about his past. He confesses to no one and it is deeply buried in him. Hence, Bhasi has to wait for a long time. Mukundan, not discouraged by the attitude of the villagers, attempts to continue in his own way. Instead of going with the flow, he tries to rectify the prevailing value system in the village. When his telephone is not working, he is expected by everyone to pay a bribe. However, he is not willing to do that and he writes a letter of complaint, since he is well versed in that. He is under the impression that the mentioning of his name and designation as a retired government servant (a Class I Gazetted officer) will carry some weight but, unfortunately it fails. Thus his attempts to bring about some changes in the village are not acknowledged by the villagers. However, he is reluctant to give up.

It is the guilt that he is responsible for the death of his mother which makes him commit many blunders. It so happens that the telephone calls for Mukundan go to Valsala's house by mistake. When he goes to Valsala's house to find out the reason, he is much affected by her appearance. She has married an old man Prabhakaran Nair, a school teacher. And after sometime, when Prabhakaran Nair disappears all of a sudden, Mukundan feels sure that he has deserted his wife like his father and has gone after another woman. So he has planned to act this time, which he had failed to do in his mother's case. He informs the police through a typewritten letter and the police arrive to investigate. Ironically, the outcome of this investigation is not as he expects. Valsala is having a clandestine affair with a young man by name Sridharan and both of them have planned and killed Prabhakaran Nair. Hence, in order to absolve his past Mukundan commits further mistakes, which depresses him all the more.

However, he is not to be deterred from making further misjudgements. He invites Kamban, the postmaster, a harijan, to tea at his house. When the caretaker Krishnan Nair enquires about it, Mukundan realizes his mistake, but does not want to exhibit his foolishness. The next day onwards he avoids going to the post office to escape from Kamban, and for Kamban, this is nothing new. Finally, it is Mukundan's fear of the ghost of his mother, which makes him seek Bhasi to confide in. From the day of his arrival to Kaikurussi, he has been haunted by the wild thoughts and he finds it difficult to make Krishnan Nair, the caretaker, his confidant. Mukundan firmly believes that his mother was murdered by the Odions of the village as per the plan of his father and now she is haunting him.

Bhasi's reaction to Mukundan's confession is shocking to him. He feels pity, which gradually develops into affection and this development is alarming to Bhasi for he wants to become a part of Mukundan's life. He is also afraid that once Mukundan is cured, he will desert Bhasi and this is quite frightening to him. He is unable to analyze his reaction to Mukundan's confession. It is he, who is the first person to observe the good features of Mukundan which are concealed behind glasses and a thin moustache. Bhasi can also visualize Mukundan being caned by his father, when he sees the white scars. Nevertheless, Bhasi helps Mukundan to overcome his fear and to look back into his past without the feelings of guilt and hurt.

The transformation is so great that Mukundan himself is unable to believe it. For the first time, he indulges in an argument with his father. Achuthan Nair, who is very shrewd, naturally blames Bhasi. Gradually Mukundan becomes so dependent on Bhasi that he is afraid of losing his new-found strength. It becomes a daily routine for him with his drink and Bhasi with his ice water to sit and talk to each other. Mukundan feels at home and is quite comfortable.

It is while Mukundan goes to meet his old boss, that he meets Anjana whose beauty and serenity bowl him over. Anjana, a school teacher, is married but her husband has deserted her. He used to come infrequently to torture her. For the first time in his life, Mukundan feels that he has fallen in love with a woman. When his love is reciprocated by Anjana, he is elated. Both of them decide that she should move in with him and that they would get married after her divorce. It is Meenakshi, his cousin, who has actually sown the seeds of doubt whether their marriage will be successful because of the 22-year age gap between them. Mukundan, so far haunted by his past, now starts worrying about his future with Anjana as his wife. However, this does not last long. He becomes confident and decides to proceed with his plan. He is positive that he will lead a contented life with Anjana as his wife and Bhasi as his friend, philosopher and guide.

Problems arise in the form of Achuthan Nair. The relationship between Achuthan Nair and his daughter, through his concubine, becomes worse and hence he decides to settle in his own house along with Mukundan. He has given Mukundan his mother's jewels. In return, he asks him to take care of him till he dies and to arrange a grand funeral feast after his death. Though Mukundan responds that it is his duty to look after him in his old age, he is immediately worried about informing Anjana about the change in plans. He is also unable to feel any kind of joy that his prodigal father has returned because it is not love, which has brought him to his son. It is merely that he does not have anyone other than Mukundan. Yet his caretaker Krishnan Nair takes great pains to make him feel comfortable. It remains a wonder to Mukundan when Achuthan Nair gets from everyone "adulation and deference, respect and reverence" (*BM* 263). Mukundan is naturally frustrated.

Mukundan misconstrues the respect Achuthan Nair commands, and this forces him to make a wrong move, thereby damaging his friendship with Bhasi. Powerhouse Ramakrishnan, who is already in the good stead of the villagers, wants people to talk about his benevolent attitude. Hence, he wants to build a community hall where people can perform a wedding or conduct political meetings. While he is in search of a suitable place, it is highly disappointing for him to find none. While he is contemplating, he happens to see Mukundan's house with vacant lands and immediately he decides to talk to him. Hence his visit to Mukundan's house, but he is unable to proceed with it, as he is afraid of broaching the subject in the presence of Achuthan Nair and Krishnan Nair. There is yet another interference, namely, from Bhasi. Though Powerhouse Ramakrishnan is least bothered about Bhasi, something happens which makes him beware of Bhasi. Bhasi has seen Powerhouse Ramakrishnan in Thrissur along with his mistress in a restaurant. While Powerhouse Ramakrishnan is not at ease with Bhasi, innocently, Bhasi asks him about his next visit to Thrissur. Immediately Powerhouse Ramakrishnan decides that it is not safe to ignore Bhasi. He should be sent out of the village. So his target shifts from Mukundan to Bhasi and his land. While Bhasi seems to sense that Powerhouse Ramakrishnan is going to do him some harm, Mukundan, on the other hand, is elated because the most respected and revered person of the village has visited him. It is evident that Bhasi has cured Mukundan of fear and guilt but nobody can save him with reference to his wrong notions of becoming of more powerful than Powerhouse Ramakrishnan, thereby achieving the respect that his father commands.

Very soon the situation arises for Mukundan to save his saviour Bhasi. In the meantime, Achuthan Nair's physical condition starts deteriorating. When Mukundan is caring for him for the first time, the physical intimacy moves him so much. He has got several questions for which there are no answers from Achuthan Nair:

> What is it that you expected of me, father? What deeds of valour did you require me to perform? What lines of duty did you expect me to toe? What battles did you demand I fight? What hopes did you expect me to fulfill? What kind of man did you want me to be? (*BM* 292)

Mukundan is unable to accept the fact that his father is dying. He still wants the recognition and approval of a 90-year-old father for his marriage with Anjana. He is confident that once Achuthan Nair accepts his marriage, then it will be accepted by everyone in the village: "For what Achuthan Nair had permitted, no one had yet condemned" (*BM* 293). Mukundan's dream of getting permission from his father remains a dream when Achuthan Nair attains the stage of senility. Mukundan childishly believes that Bhasi can find a cure for old age. Bhasi comes to meet Mukundan and confesses to him about the threat of Powerhouse Ramakrishnan, and asks him openly to help him. Mukundan assures him but Bhasi is unable to trust Mukundan.

The next day Mukundan enters the lion's den with the intention of saving Bhasi. However, when he is informed that he is one of the community hall committee members, he is dumbfounded. He is torn between his desire to speak on behalf of Bhasi and his long cherished dream of getting recognition. The battle in his mind lasts only for a short time. Soon, he feels at ease. He is happy that these people having power and importance are going to become his friends. He feels like saying to his father, "I am as much a personage in this village as you are. Father, you might not think so, but they value my presence like they did yours" (*BM* 308). Nevertheless, he does not forget his intention of speaking for Bhasi. He makes a feeble attempt of speaking, which is overruled in a convincing manner by the committee members. What is ironical here is Mukundan is asked to mediate between the committee members and Bhasi to convince him. Mukundan should have been frustrated. Instead, when they all pressurises him to convince Bhasi, he feels as though a crown has been kept on his head. He never understands that it is a crown of thorns. Thus he has ditched Bhasi for the sake of his friendship with these vain people, who have assumed power and authority overnight.

What is more vexing is that Mukundan is ready to sacrifice Anjana as well, as a measure of safeguarding his reputation as a committee member of the community hall. When he informs her that they have to wait till the divorce, Anjana puts an end to their relationship. Earlier, when he was waiting for his father to become well, it seemed to be reasonable for her. Now she is able to see him in a different perspective. Mukundan should have been hurt but he is not. The friendship of both Bhasi and Anjana which had transformed his life is sacrificed because of his selfishness. When he tries to keep in touch with both of them, they do not encourage it.

In the meantime, Achuthan Nair's condition becomes worse when he has a fall. It is now complete bed-rest for him with a nurse taking care of him. For Mukundan, this Achuthan Nair, helpless like a child, is a stranger to him. When he happens to see bedsores, he is horrified and realizes with a shock that death is not very far. Still this does not prevent him asking his father when he is almost in a coma, about the death of his mother. When Achuthan Nair dies, Mukundan does not know how to react to the death of a man, who has crippled his mind and spirit. He also wonders when many people turned out to pay their homage to his father. It is frustrating and dejecting that his father till his death remained a man, who was not satisfied with his son.

When Krishnan Nair also takes leave of Mukundan, the loneliness paves way for the rumination of his behaviour leading to this state without a relative or a friend in the world. His regret becomes worse when he happens to see Bhasi's land, which once upon a time attracted the onlookers with the lushness of trees and plants, now accommodating a building, which is being built with great speed. Mukundan does not want to wallow in remorse but decides to rectify his mistakes. He has decided to give a quarter of an acre of his land to Bhasi. Bhasi finds it difficult to understand the transformation but when he sees his eyes, he happens to see the determination. It is the same with Anjana also. She had been assailed by doubts initially, but is now convinced.

Thus rebirth occurs in Mukundan's life twice. Earlier, it was due to the assistance of Bhasi but the second transformation after the death of his father is the result of turning inward and self-analysis. It is a universal truth that change should come from within. However, one cannot altogether ignore the attempts of Bhasi as futile. They were helpful to Mukundan to a certain extent. It is the second transformation which takes place in Mukundan's life that is more effective. It is a kind of solace, when he tries to amend his mistakes. However, it is shocking to the core as he tries to assuage his guilt by choosing a wrong path. He considers the community hall as a symbol of his "weakness, his cowardice, and his lack of integrity" (*BM* 356). It is Mukundan's decision to destroy the building with gunpowder during the celebration of Pooram festival, which makes one realize the shallowness of his character, though post-retirement he is still mentally immature. He has chosen this path in order to become a better man but once again it is the wrong choice, a choice that will leave him racked with guilt for the rest of his life.

In the conflict between Achuthan Nair and Mukundan, it is a pity that nobody is allowed to interfere. One expects Paru Kutty to interfere and smoothen the relationship between them, but she remains a victim of her husband till her death. It is not only Paru Kutty but all the women characters in this novel who live circumscribed lives. Such a depiction of a matrilineal society is very nuanced, as it interrogates the vey notion of matrilyny. Anjana's fate is reminiscent of Paru Kutty but Anjana is not a victim. She emerges from her problems stronger, and she has a good influence on Mukundan. Yet Mukundan is tempted to ignore her initially for the sake of temporary fame in the village. In short, the novel presents a man's world which seems to imply that women should be seen and not heard. In the end, Achuthan Nair has taken his grievances to his grave and there is absolutely no transformation in Mukundan's character. Critical opinions on the novel seem to suggest that Mukundan becomes a better man, but his stasis and lack of judgement at every critical juncture of his life would seem to belie such a conclusion. In the final analysis it appears to be his destiny to suffer from guilt all through his life.

Works Cited

Sarbojit Biswas, ed. *Indian English Fiction A Reader.* Calcutta : Books Way, 2009.

Gupta, Monica, ed. *Women Writers in the Twentieth Century Literature.* NewDelhi: Atlantic, 2008.

Nair, Anita. *The Better Man.* New Delhi:Penguin India, 1999.

Prabhu, P.H. *Hindu Social Organization.* 3rd ed. Bombay: Popular Prakashan, 1958.

14

Transformation of Regional Identities: A Comparative Study of Anita Nair's *Ladies Coupe* and Malathi Rao's *Disorderly Women*

— M. Parimala

> Can a woman stay single and be happy, or does a woman need a man to feel complete?
>
> (Nair)

> Must a woman always belong to another? Could she not belong to herself as a man could!
>
> (Malathi Rao)

In India, the twenty-first century has brought in its wake various transformations in cultural, political, religious, economic and social domains as the impact of modernity and globalization is manifested. Modernity and globalization impact all other nations as well, in the process of "diffusion, homogenization and integration" (Sivaramakrishnan and Agarwal 8) via the merging of regional and national boundaries. Hence, each and every individual in India today, has become 'the subject' of development and modernization in danger of reaching the destination of erasing the cultural and regional boundaries, at the micro level. Indian literature plays a prominent role in creating an awareness of the necessity of transformations and emphasizes the causes and consequences, in different contexts, of these transitions. As a part of such an endeavour, this paper attempts to discuss the transformation of religious and regional identities of the orthodox brahmin communities in India, with the focus on two select novels for the study – Anita Nair's *Ladies*

Coupe and Malathi Rao's *Disorderly Women.* This paper analyses the two important women characters, Akhila from *Ladies Coupe* and Kamala from *Disorderly Women*, the former a spinster and the latter a deserted wife respectively; to evince the extrication of women from their entanglement in conventional roles. The narrative of these novels depicts how these two women characters from traditional orthodox brahmin families dismantle and subvert the firmly established conservative brahminical values, ethics and customs to converge with the changing egalitarian modern society of India.

Indian women during colonization have undergone 'Double Colonization' (Spivak) – colonized women have been simultaneously exploited by the patriarchal system and the dominance of the colonizers. This is more so in the case of brahmin women, when compared to women from all other marginalized castes. The brahmins give religious connotations for the subjugation/delineation of women and have placed greater emphasis on the social or cultural reasons for such subjugation unlike other castes. Due to this societal sanction, throughout the ages, brahmin women's suppression has been invisible to the society. In a manner similar to Dalit women, brahmin women have also played a 'voiceless' role in their communities. It has been considered by many, that brahmin women are "cowardly, frightened, superstitious and want to keep away from all change" (Rao 177). But now the time has come to change such fixed personalities with the greater awareness of education and the impact and influence of modernization and globalization. Now those women expect to live an independent life, by moving away from the regional and religious identities to approach a wider space and identity. So far, down the ages, the orthodox women lived a tortured life in the name of the institution called marriage and family. Today, they know that they are capable of surviving even without the crutch of marriage and family.

In Hindu religious mythology, women are presented as mere symbols of 'victim-bodies' (Bacchetta 2). This has been practised down the ages not only in India but throughout the world. Today, in India, due to the resurgence and the impact of Women's Reform Movement; Women's Liberation Movement and the Feminist Movement from the West have revealed the fact that women can excel on par with their opponent sex, if provided an opportunity. These movements have been gradually extricating women from their traditional repressive stereotypes and lead them in a progressive manner to establish their identity. The novels selected for the study shift between the traditional brahmin society and the modern/transformed brahmin society of India and are set in the time frame of 1930s to the 1990s. Anita Nair depicts the conservative brahmin family in Chennai and Malathi Rao portrays the conventional family from the brahmin community of Chandragiri and Chamrajpet in Bangalore.

Both the protagonists Akhila and Kamala are born, nurtured and instilled in certain ways of life to play their dutiful roles in their life in future. But certain unexpected twists and turns in their life bring transitions in their characters. Both have nurtured carefully in order to endure and sustain their rest of the life as a wife of so and so. They have been raised with all the good qualities required to become a dedicated and chaste wife of a stranger. "May you live for a hundred years. May you be a good wife too your husband. May you bear twelve children. May your wisdom and your good fortune increase day by day like a growing moon" (Rao 7) is the common lullaby sung by the elderly women of the brahmin family. Moreover, the girls are taught at their tender age, of how to serve and survive in their in-laws' house. They are given intensive training in household chores like cooking, serving meals, washing clothes, scouring vessels and such like. Most of the Brahmin girls are skilled at these things at their childhood and will be ready for marriage before they are 12 or 13. If they failed to do any such chores then "she would be condemned as unworthy and lazy, arrogant and slovenly" (Rao 14). They were not allowed to go outside other than to the temple, so as to avoid the casting of male eyes, and are always accompanied by their mothers alone and not even their brothers, "But even to go in the company of a brother was forbidden. A girl's best friend until she was married was her mother and once she was married it was her husband" (Rao 27). According to the older generation women characters, Chandra from *Ladies Coupe*, Subbi and Venku Bai from *Disorderly Women,* marriage is the only way of life, endurance is their only principle and husband is their God, "Hindu wife would rather die than leave her husband even if he is a monster or a madman. Marriage is her salvation and the husband her God" (Rao 176). All these three women have lost their identity in the presence of their husband and are proud to be so. Akhila's mother Chandra and Kamala's mother Venku Bai, who are traditionally submissive and dependent did not realize their suppression nor did they question their slavery. They lived in complete loss of their identity and accepted their dominance and endured the pains throughout their life. They are contented with their husband and home as their only world:

> Everything ended in this, in this loss of identity, in this utter submission. She simply lost herself in him. She was a part of him and so was not separate from him. How could she then feel angry with him, or condemn him ...?
>
> (Rao 35)

Fortunately or unfortunately the younger generation characters, Akhila and Kamala have challenged the aforementioned traditional manner of living life. With these two characters in particular, one could see the gradual change as the traditional ways and customs and beliefs lose their significance and sacredness to the upcoming generation. They begin to mingle with other people dispensing with their caste and are open-minded about the degrading practices that the Brahmin dare not perform, "But this is Kaliyuga, when Brahmins will degenerate to the level of Sudras, and a day will come when there is going to be no difference between a Brahmin and a Sudra" (Rao140). Changes in them takes place "as much as cultural, social, economic, which inevitably reflects modern western experience" (Mendelsohn 806). Education plays a prominent role in instilling moral values in the minds of the people and so has replaced religion in contemporary society. Neglecting one's religion or caste does not mean deprivation of humankind rather education and economic freedom ameliorate and unite people globally. Therefore, women will no more "suffer as a result of the deterioration of tradition and ancient values at the hands of our men" (Rao 114). Akhila, the eldest daughter of Pattabi Iyer and Chandra, is an educated woman and has also been employed as a clerk. Since her father has died (when she was 19 years) willingly or unwillingly, she is forced into the role of a breadwinner and the head of her family, "Akhila became the man of the family" (Nair 75). At this moment all her dreams of becoming a wife and a homemaker have been shattered and in the meanwhile, she has forgotten that she is a woman. Since then, till the age of 36, she has been burdened with all the responsibilities of the well being of her family and none of her siblings nor her mother reminded her of marriage, nor made her realize the existence of a woman in her or empathized with her:

> In their minds Akhila had ceased to be a woman and had already metamorphosed into a spinster. She longed for a life before she was 30 years. But she was 34, still remained the same. (Nair 77)

Consequently, she has been made into a spinster by her own family members by suppressing her emotions and feelings. They have adapted the social norms to their selfish ends, in forcing her to earn for the family, which is against the brahmin ethics. As per the Tamil brahmin culture, women are not allowed to work outside and they are married off at a tender age. But in the case of Akhila, everything worked to the contrary. Moreover, spinster women in their community are treated on par with a widow. They are seen as the outcasts, who undergo death-in-life sentence. They are isolated from the rest of the world and considered as 'inauspicious' beings. It is only at the age of 36, Akhila that realized that she has lost her self-identity as a woman. She didn't exist as a woman in that house but existed as a 'sister', 'Ammadi', 'Akka', 'Madam', etc., "The name Akhila no more existed" (Nair 85).

> So who was Akhilandeswari? Did she exist at all? If she did, what was her identity? Did her heart skip a beat when it saw a mango tree studded with blossoms. (Nair 84)

She is seen always as an extension of someone else's identity like "Chandra's daughter, Narayan's Akka, Priya's aunt, Murthy's Sister-in-law. Akhila wished for once someone would see her as a whole being" (Nair 200-201).

Once she realizes that she has lost her self-identity, Akhila decides to step out of the shell that has confined her so far. She begins to venture into the outer world in search of her identity. Her customs, religion and culture stand as an obstacle on her way to discover her 'self'. So to prove her individuality she has stripped away her "traditional India Structures like caste" (Mendelson 808). And, she very tactically, bravely and gradually dissipates the blind customs and culture to continue her journey, "She would go. She had to, or she would go mad confined within the walls of the house and the life she was expected to live" (Nair 4). Thereafter, her attitude and behavior begin to change. She is determined not to continue the same hypocritical life to satisfy others but to live a life of her own by shunning her regional identity, craving to wear a new identity of a woman of a common society. She has moved away from the 'aghrahar'-brahmin community after the death of her mother. Even before that she had asked her mother not to bare her widowhood, expects her to be the same with 'bottu' and 'pretty madisars':

> Didn't we as young girls wear colorful clothes and jewelry and a bottu? It isn't a privilege that marriage sanctions ... who made these laws anyway? Some man who couldn't bear the thought that in spite of his death his wife continued to be attractive to other man. (Nair 202)

In addition, Akhila converses with people of other communities, shares her food with other caste colleagues, tastes egg, which is considered as a non-vegetarian food, spends weekends with her boyfriend, keeps away from the rituals and does everything that a Brahmin women dare not do.

Padma, her younger sister, who is enmeshed with her religious ethics like her mother, has raised objections against Akhila's strange behaviour. She expects to see Akhila as a brahmin woman, with all coyness and humility. The change takes place not only in her mind but is also visible in the way of her dressing. She clad herself in a brightly coloured sari, which she had long ago ceased to wear. The transition in Akhila, surprises, rather agitates, everyone. Padma, too hates to see a 'new' Akhila, a completely transformed character. Padma's vision asks:

> Yet, this morning Akhila was a butterfly with magical hues and gay abandon where is the moth? Why aren't your wings folded? Why aren't you trying to pretend that you and the wood are one? Why aren't you hiding yourself among the curtains (Nair 4).

Padma also blames Akhila as a "misfit" (Nair 162) to live amidst the brahmin community. The women of that community cannot endure the activities of Akhila. They all blame her for not participating in 'bhajans' being a brahmin woman:

> Anyway, she doesn't like all this. She is a different kind of person (163-164).
>
> She is not like us. She is not interested in any of the things that give us or any normal person pleasure. Sometimes I think she isn't even a practicing Hindu. She won't light the lamp in the puja room or go the temple or observe any of the rituals we Brahmins do. When she has her periods, she continues to water the plants and if I object, she bites my head off. (164).

Thus, Padma criticizes and mock her for committing sacrilege. Akhila has everything, authority, power to control her family, economic independence but she feels that she lacks something. Still, she cannot realize the woman in her - so is in search of the woman within her. Once it happens that she encounters male fingers exploring her body. Where she does no react angrily but endures and welcomes the new feeling, there she realizes the woman in her. From then onwards, she begins to search for man, who can stimulate her feelings, meanwhile she is also bit afraid of society. It is Hari, younger than Akhila and a north Indian, who comes to rescue her with his touch and makes her feel like a woman. With his touch the emotions, feelings and passion gush out of her heart, for which she has been longing for years. Revelation and realization take place at the age of 45, "Akhila most desired in this world was to be her own person? In a place that was her own. To do as she pleased. To live as she chose with neither restraint nor fear of censure. Akhila didn't want to be a mere extension again" (Nair 201). But Akhila hesitates to take a step towards autonomy wondering whether it is possible for a woman like her to lead a life on her own without the support of a male.

She often undergoes introspection to relieve herself from her vacillation. At this moment, she seeks the advice of five women who have shared the Coupe with her. Except Janaki, no woman in that Coupe advises her to live with a male partner. For instance, Margaret said, "the truth is I know it and as I live it is that a woman needs a man but not to make her feel whole" (Nair 95) and Prabha Devi is also convinced out of her experience that a woman can live alone. She has performed many things against her cultural values and why not try this. As she travells from Bangalore to Kanyakumari, her thoughts too travel from innocence to experience, timid to self-confident, object to subject. In Kanyakumari, she begins to invite males, like a prostitute, use them for her sexual pleasure, not to make her whole but to satisfy her bodily pleasures. At the same time she is clear that sex alone does not make a woman whole. It is one of the factors that makes a woman complete. It also applies to men because a man cannot feel complete without a woman and vice versa. It is not that she needs a man throughout her life, otherwise she would have married a man even at the age of 45, but she wants a companion, "As far as I am concerned, marriage is unimportant. Companionship, yes, I would like that. The problem is I wish to live by myself but everyone tells me that a woman can't live alone" (Nair 21).

When she returns from Kanyakumari, she is a completely transformed personality, who could no more identify her with the traditional, brahmin culture. She has discovered her self-identity. There she "discovers that she liked being alone…And perhaps that is all she needs to ask of life now. That she be allowed to try and experience it…" (Nair 271). In a strange society she experiences living alone. "I don't want a man trying to broaden his horizon with my body. I don't want to be another experience." (272). Therefore, she wins her game in seducing a man. "A need satiated" (275). She does't care anymore for gazes. Now she is Akilandeswari. "Nobody's daughter. Nobody's sister. Nobody's wife. Nobody's mother" (206-207). She becomes all powerful now, very broad-minded, has no more fears. "Why then should she walk with a downcast head? She throws her head back and voices her triumph" (Nair 275).

Unlike *Ladies Coupe*, in *Disorderly Women* one can find conversions in the minor characters too. Krishna, brother of Kamala; Seshagiri Rao, father of Kamala, Rukmini, Vasudeva are the characters who so explicitly accept the changes and induce Kamala in one way another. When her husband deceives Kamala, her brother Krishna, who knows the importance of education and the dissemination of women's emancipation in the 50s in India, induces her to apply for her graduation, and also explicates the need of education for a woman. His father is more convinced at Krishna's lecture of independence:

> The nationalistic dream of freedom have abolished slavery of all kind and have brought enlightenment about Indian women's education and economic and social independence, of coming out of their homes to participate in the public and professional capacity. (Rao 123)

As a consequence, Kamala is allowed to enter the college so that she would be equipped for a job in a school, "India after a long struggle was on the brink of Independence, and in the hour of this new dawn for her country, Kamala too saw visions of a new life free from the shackles of life" (Rao 123). Thus, one can see the transformation in Seshagiri Rao, the traditional man of the family home, 'Himalaya', whereas his sister Subbi, the child widow, has raised an objection to educating Kamala, the victim of patriarchy, and to send her out of the home. She thinks that the outer world would ruin her life forever. Subbi who has remained as an outcast, expects Kamala to undergo the same empty life till her death. According to her, if a woman goes out like a man then she is disqualified as a woman losing her modesty, virtue, chastity and all other traditional womanly characteristics. Unlike Seshagiri Rao and Krishna, she is adamant to deny the changes that are taking place around her.

Kamala, on the other hand, pulls her chains off from her mind and body, crosses the threshold to gain knowledge and freedom. Moreover, she wishes to express her hopes and desires like men and to erase the stigma of being another outcast of 'Himalaya', "behind the doors and in corners, crossing the path of no one" (Rao 132). Thereafter there are many transitions that occur in 'Himalaya' – like Kamala, her younger sister Janaki has also entered college for graduation, Seshagiri Rao accepts Govinda, who has fled to Germany without the permission of his father, regrets Kamala's desperate life for rejecting Vasudeva when he proposes to her, permits Kamala to stay with her friend Marakatha and family in Bombay for almost a month and at last agrees to marry her youngest daughter to Subramanian, from a sub-caste. Secondly, Krishna who has been questioning the villainous act of his father towards his mother Venku Bai, since his childhood, lets his wife Rukmini carry out things on her own, "Krishna did not want his wife to shut herself up in the house and become a drudge like his mother" (Rao 108). He treats her with love, care and respect. He expects her to be more outward, extrovert and a fun-loving character to participate along with him in parties and so. He is frustrated when she cannot speak English, and he always sees to it that she walks abreast of him on the road and becomes irritated when she lags behind a few steps. Thus, Rukmini, behaves unlike the other married women of her village.

Kamala leaves her husband when she is seventeen years old. She is afraid of death and so returns to her home. She might have failed in her married life but not in her life as such, as she is courageous enough to step out of her husband's home that any other brahmin woman dared not do. Unlike her mother, Kamala does not endure her suffering; as a result, she walks out of the marriage. Getting divorced and remarried is not permitted in the orthodox brahmin family. In that community, widows, spinsters and deserted wives should undergo death-in-life sentence or are castigated as 'evils' or 'outcast'. Thus all the brahmin women are made to live in such an 'invisible' life like slaves with the loss of their self-identity. This vision has been challenged by both Akhila and Kamala throughout the novel.

After Kamala's re-entry to 'Himalaya', she is a completely changed person. She receives her education, spends time with her friends, has physical relationship with her childhood friend Vasu, even after knowing that he is married and also decides to get a job and live a life of her own.

Committing adultery is a serious crime according to the Hindu religion. Women are not permitted even to talk to a stranger in public, they are taught to control their emotions and feelings. Flouting such restrictive codes, Kamala and also Akhila, commit adultery and never feel guilty of their unconventional actions. They cannot control their passions and feelings; their bodies crave for a male body and long for a male touch. They find themselves comfortable in the embrace of their boyfriends. Kamala does not feel life whole without the male, after experiencing almost a month of her loneliness in Bombay. She tries hard to forget Vasu and deliberately avoid him and wills herself to stop thinking of him. She suffers from her loneliness but she has a room of her own, a private place in her home 'Himalaya'. The private space also denotes a change in the brahmin household, because women are not given a separate room in their house, "A progress from mother to daughter, you might say. Kamala's room signaled a new change in 'Himalaya', a female space in the male bastion" (Rao 242). She has succeeded to the extent of living a life of loneliness. Thereafter, she does not belong either to Gundanna or to Vasudeva. She is now herself.

While comparing Akhila and Kamala, Akhila has been portrayed as more revolutionary than Kamala with all her constraints. This is also perhaps a reflection of the more contemporary timeframe of Nair's novel. Both the women are educated, courageous enough to dismantle the conventional ideals of firmly established brahmin culture and have created a unique space, identity and freedom among their community people because they have done things which another woman of their cultural background would not dare to do. In this way they become trendsetters in their community respectively. Both the characters thought that they are old enough to do anything they wanted and they do not allow anyone to question their independence. They have also ventured into an outer world to experience the life of independence.

Akhila travels from Bangalore to Kanyakumari and Kamala travels from Bangalore to Bombay. Akhila, the 45 year-old spinster does not prefer to live like an outcast in her community with the loss of identity and so she breaks the shell and explores the outer world in search of her freedom and a life of her own and succeeds. In contrast, Kamala, who has been blamed and tortured for her barrenness, chooses to confine herself in a desolated room of her house 'Himalaya', a "self-created tomb" (Rao 176), even after experiencing the limitations of transformation. Unlike Akhila, Kamala cannot bear her loneliness and comes to the conclusion that a woman cannot live or exist without a man, "She felt such a longing for him that it seemed that as long as she lived she would seek his encircling arms as the only home where her spirit and body could find rest" (Rao 193). Therefore, she fails to gain her self-identity.

Thus in the rebellious battle, to extricate themselves from falling prey to Hindu brahminical ideals and to discover their 'self', Akhila succeeds and Kamala accept her failure, "All said and done I felt a woman cannot hold her own in a man's world, Ila. So I retreated into my shell. I've failed in life. I malingered in my goal to be independent and I took the easy way out. I fell back on the family in Himalaya as my last refuge" (Rao 189).

At the end of the novel, *Disorderly Women,* the narrative reveals the letters written by Kamala to Ila, they reveal her inner thoughts, her modern and broad-minded view of life, where she sees nothing wrong in her relationship with Vasudeva and it is only her traditional upbringing that condemns her friendship. Kamala does not worry about her niece's marriage though she is 26; rather she is quite happy to see her with a Master's degree and a job, which Kamala could not get in the 1950s. When Ila is working, Kamala finds her as a mere extension of herself and realizes "the transition period of history" (Malathi Rao190). Ila has achieved what Kamala could not do because Ila belongs to the transitional fourth generation of 'Himalaya'. She too wants to follow the footsteps of her aunt to become an independent individual, "wanted to be like her ... stand alone, be strong and courageous, be an individual, family or no family" (Rao 189).

To conclude, as the saying goes, "Success comes to those who dare" (Rao 194), both the protagonists dares to step out of their regional and religious identities and succeed to an extent. The analysis of these two novels has explicated how the contemporary Indian writers Anita Nair and Malathi Rao, question the superstitions, traditional values, customs and the entanglement of brahmin women. Both the writers propagate the necessity of change and emancipation of women through their characters Akhila and Kamala respectively. They question the fundamental social construction of women, which applies not only to the brahmin women but to women universally, "Can a woman stay single and be happy, or does a woman need a man to feel complete?" (Nair) and "Must a woman always belong to another? Could she not belong to herself as a man could!" (Rao 172).

Through the novels, it is also evident that all people in the older generation are traditionally portrayed and those in the younger generation are on the verge of transformation by violating the age old customs, beliefs and mores. Initially the names of these characters itself show the change. For instance, in both the novels, the older generation characters are named after 'Iyer' or 'Rao' as in 'Doraiswamy Iyer', 'Vishwanatha Iyer', 'Pattabi Iyer', 'Seshagiri Rao', with which one can identify their caste and community, whereas the following generation characters do not carry the name of their caste after their names. This might be a deliberate narrative encoding by the author for the readers to understand. These two novels depict how the characters that are analyzed in this paper move away from their regional identity, to experience an autonomous life. The authors seem to suggest that confining oneself to the region and the religion would always bring frustration, hopelessness, emptiness and dissatisfaction as seen in the case of Kamala. When we isolate ourselves from the world, we are invisible to the outer world. One should keep venturing out or exploring the world like Akhila, Kamala, Govinda and Vasudeva to experience a life beyond social and cultural boundaries.

Works Cited

Bacchetta, Paola. *Gender in the Hindu Nation: RSS Women as Ideologues*. New Delhi: Pauls Press, 2004.

Kamat, A.R., 'Women's Education and Social Change in India'. *Social Scientist*, Vol. 5, No. 1, 1976, 3–27.

Mendelson, Oliver, 'The transformation of Authority in Rural India'. *Modern Asian Studies*. Vol. 27, No. 4, 1993, 805–842.

Nair, Anita. *Ladies Coupe*. India: Penguin Books, 2001.

Rao, Malathi. *Disorderly Women*. Bangalore: Dronequill Publishers Pvt. Ltd., 2005.

Spivak, Gayatri Chakravorty. *A Critique of PostColonial Reason: Toward a History of the Vanishing Present*. Cambridge: Haward Universisty Press, 1999.

Sivaramakrishnan, K. and Arun Agarwal (Eds.), *Regional Minorities: The Cultural Politics of Development in India*. New Delhi: Oxford University Press, New Delhi.

15

Creativity, Motherhood and the Negotiation of Identity in Tulsi Badrinath's *Meeting Lives*

— R. Priya

> Greater than ten teachers is the Preceptor, greater than ten Preceptor is the father; and greater than ten fathers is the mother – the mother is greater than even the earth. There is no guru greater than the mother.
>
> Because she bears, she is called *dharti;* for giving birth, she is called *janani; amba* because she nourishes the limbs; and *virasu* because she carried a child with courage. In rearing with love and care, she is *sushru,* the mother is one's own intimate body. (Badrinath, 212)

A Hindu woman approaches motherhood from her culture, tradition, philosophy and ethics that teach her the truth about being a mother. She is the benevolent mother goddess, the food-giver; she depends on *desha* - the culture in which she is born, on *kala* — the period of historical time in which she lives; on *shrama* – the efforts required of her at different stages of life; and on *gunas* – the innate psychological traits which are the heritage of an individual's previous life.

Manu declares:

> The women who always does good,
> Who is efficient in work, sweet in speech,
> Devoted to her duty and service of mankind,
> Is really no human being but a goddess...
>
> — (qtd in Kakar 35)

The female is the form of the Divine. Woman represents the Divine embodied. In ancient India women occupied a very important position, superior to men. In the predominant Western religion, the Divine is worshipped as father but not as mother. The Heavenly Father is often portrayed as a stern, angry man who awards punishment to his children who violate his seemingly arbitrary laws. Protestant Christianity and Islam have banished the Divine as mother from their religions. But Hindu religion traditionally has always recognized the Divine as a mother. According to Hinduism, the deepest relationship that one can have with God is that of the mother. No human relationship is closer then that of the mother and child. It best mirrors in the relationship with God. India itself is looked upon as the mother – *Deshmata*.

Listed for the Man Asian Literary Prize 2007, Tulsi Badrinath's *Meeting Lives* is the story of Aditi, a young woman trying to mesh the philosophy of motherhood with the reality of bringing up a child. It focuses on questions such as What does it mean to be a mother? Does rejection of the maternal role create identity crises? The novel also raises intriguing questions regarding the status of the mother in the family, in society and in cultural representation.

An Indian woman defines herself in relation and connection to the dominant social realities of her life. They are treated in three stages.

1. First, she is a daughter to her parents.
2. Second, she is a wife to her husband and daughter-in-law to his parents.
3. Third, she is a mother to her son and daughter.

Tulsi Badrinath's *Meeting Lives* unfolds through the involved consciousness of Aditi, the narrator. The novel delineates a symbolic cannibalism of women, how it takes a long time for a well-trained passive women to overthrow her frailty and susceptibility. Being an educated, self-reflective, sensible young woman, Aditi's mind is filled with liberal ideas. But the world, which she inhabits, is a patriarchal society, where there is no place for a woman to establish her 'self'. In this society Aditi faces the problem of individuality both in her personal and professional life. The paper is an attempt to study her quest for individuality in the novel which operates within the framework of tradition and the mythological ideology of motherhood. Aditi, a well–informed, well-educated, Vedanta-inspired, independent woman, reflects periodically on her various roles as a daughter, friend, wife and mother and an empathizer of an abandoned women, Thayee. The novel engages with the protagonist Aditi's concerns about her married life and motherhood which discloses a sequence of disappointments and frustrations.

The plot traces the journey of a protagonist who questions her decisions at some points and revels in them at others. Who is Aditi? Her life is an amalgamation of so many parts that of a daughter, student, a friend and a mother. This journey of hers is a process of self-discovery. The inner urge and passion to follow her heart makes her go back to her dance. But in doing so, she is plagued with unending questions that make her wonder whether she has made the right decision in choosing to follow her desire of becoming a dancer. The conflict between pursuing her dreams and whether or not she is becoming selfish is presented through the story.

At one point she asks:

> In placing one's child at the center of
> One's life does one displace oneself?
> Does the Progression from being
> self – center to bring selfless as a
> mother, necessarily involve a loss of self.
>
> (Badrinath, 233)

Aditi, traditional wife and mother in an orthodox brahmin family, struggles through the period of motherhood in trying to raise her son, Sanju, an energetic, restless and accident-prone child, who asks some of the wisest question like "does Ravana has one pillow or ten pillows under his heads?" (Badrinath 140). Living in her parental home, she regrets giving up a creative career as a classical dancer to bring up her son.

She says, "love and weight of motherhood descend on me" (Badrinath 21). When Sanju is three months old, Aditi leaves him alone for the first time under the care of her mother to attend the dance class.

The place seems to be new to her, but the joy of dancing again is boundless.

She says:

> I am back. I am back. I dance! (Badrinath 22)

The thrill of rehearsals, live music, rhythm, excites her. Yet the motherly instinct within her over powers her and she says:

> How can I leave him?... Once he grew inside me. Now he does so lying along side, his hand spread like a flower.
>
> (Badrinath 83)

By portraying the reality of the role of mother in the Indian context, Tulsi Badrinath focuses on what it means to be a mother. This is presented through the beautiful verses from the spiritual treatises interwoven with the narrative. She attempts to juxtapose instances drawn from Hindu mythology to link the theme of motherhood and Vedanta. This is seen in the relationship Adi Shankara and Swami Vivekananda had with their mothers, a link they had to forgo in order to attain sanyasa. The story moves from Shankara to that of Vivekananda to that of Aditi's son, Sanju. There is a mystical moment in the writings of Badrinath, when she interweaves the narratives with myths of Shiva and Punyavathi, of Krishna, the most beloved of all the Hindu gods. For his worshippers he embodies divine beauty, joy and love. As a child Krishna was playful and mischievous, innocent and obedient in his mother's presence. He missed no opportunity for mischief when her back was turned. Whether, it is Swami Vivekananda's mother, who had to forego her claims as mother, so her son could attain sainthood or Adi Shankara who returns to his mother to fulfil her last wish. Swami Vivekananda one of the most fascinating figures in the history of modern India, practising yogi on the one hand and religious teacher in the ancient Indian tradition, but before becoming so exalted he was just Narendranath Dutta, a dutiful son to his mother. According to him,

> ...the ideal women in India is the mother, the mother first and the mother last. The word woman calls up to the mind
> of the Hindu, motherhood; and god is called mother...
> to the ordinary concentrated man in India the whole force of womanhood is motherhood.
>
> (Vivekananda 57)

Aditi, the protagonist of the book, is also surrounded by verses from the Sanskrit hymn, from the Krishna Karanamitram, extolling the mystic child Krishna, the divine mother to the Devi myth.

> *Ya devi sarvabhuteshu, Vishnu mayeti shabdita,*
> *Namastastyai Namastastyai Namastastyai namo namaha.*
>
> (We bow to the divine Goddess in all existence who is addressed as the perceivable form of the consciousness which pervades all. We bow to her, we bow to her, we continually bow to her).
>
> *Visrishtau srishtirupa tvam stithirupa cha palane tatha,*
> *Samhrti rupante jagato's sya jaganmaye...*
> *(O Devi of a form pervading the whole world, at the same time the creation Your form is one of creative force; when sustaining it Your form is that of a protective energy; and at the time of dissolution Your form is one with the destructive force.)*
>
> (Badrinath 120)

Aditi herself has been brought up by a doting mother to be an independent young lady. Her mother says:

> Even if you get into the worst of trouble; come
> to me, we will sort it out together some how.
>
> (Badrinath 120)

These reassuring words ensure that Aditi had the most wonderful childhood atmosphere. Aditi was blessed with, "A mother and father who dotes on me, gifts me the wealth of a happy childhood, make me secure in their love" (Badrinath 130). This emotional security is what Aditi is trying to create for her child. Being married to an emotionally cold husband, for whom career is all, who relocates to France after depositing Aditi with a son at her parental home. Her desire to have her separate identity makes her choose the path of creative freedom through writing. Marriage is bliss if there is trust and understanding in the relationship otherwise it is not less than a curse. Aditi's marriage did not give her the emotional security which she needed. As a wife and mother she tries to articulate her emotion in a cultural ethos that sanctifies matrimony and deifies motherhood. She ponders on the irony of her situation,

> It is a strange paradox, I who treasure solitude
> have found myself alone in a marriage and very
> alone in bring up my child. It wrings from me
> the kind of strength that I do not want to possess.
>
> (Badrinath 174)

Fragmented by various claims on her selfhood, she realizes that she is not the only one who struggles to find her space. At a re-union of her old classmates, she discovers that motherhood is not always a blissful experience; it can leave you feeling very tired. She says:

> We share the same predicament, of once have
> been independent, earning an income, of wanting
> to make something of our lives but finding it
> more difficult than we have imagined.
>
> (Badrinath 72)

Aditi's identity as a Hindu woman has evolved out of the particulars of her lifecycle and childhood: out of the dreariness of her relationships as a daughter to her parents, as a wife to her husband and a mother to her son. For her maternal identity seems to be splitting of the self, a bondage from which she wants to become individuated and free. But she realizes the word, a *maa* has its own indescribable intoxication.

Tulsi Badrinath presents through this novel the lacunae of women's freedom. The theme which has engaged her imagination is the place and predicament of women especially as a mother in the modern society and the quest for her individuality even as a child occupies immense space in its mother's life. A sense of helplessness underlines Aditi's struggles to find her individuality. The aspects of nurturing, tenderness and protectiveness are the fundamental quality of a good mother. For the young Indian wife, imminent motherhood extends to her a respect, emotional well-being not only at the level of personal fulfilment but also reinforces her identity formation. The predominant element in this identity, the core element around which it is established is what Helene Deutsch has called "motherliness" (Deutsch 57). Aditi, who is preoccupied with her dance and achievements, asks how she would find the connectedness with her son?

Aditi as a nurturant realizes that:

> One knows oneself but partially. Two steps behind reality, I am still trying to understand the changes that Sanju's presence have brought in my life, a life that is still to be lived, still an unfinished story.
>
> (Badrinath 233)

Mother, in the Indian tradition, is the embodiment of Shakti – the Prowess. She saves her children and acts as their custodian. In any construction of an ideal mother, she has to have many-sided virtues apart from ensuring that her children are glorified and also protected. She gets defined and glorified by her capacity to protect, provide, endure and sacrifice for her child. Through her struggle to find the connectedness, Aditi discovers her creative freedom. She expresses her feeling this time not through *bhavam and lyam* but through her writings. This discovery describes her consummate control over herself and a complete confidence and harmony with her role as a nurturer – a mother.

Works Cited

Badrinath, Tulsi. *Meeting Lives*. New Delhi: Niyogi Books, 2008.

Deutsch, Helene. *The Psychology of Women. Volume 1: Girlhood*. Allyn & Bacon, 1943.

Hirsch, Marianne. *The Mother / Daughter Plot: Narrative, Psychoanalysis, Feminism*. Bloomington and Indianapolis: Indiana University Press, 1989.

Kakar, Sudhir. *The Inner World*. New Delhi: Oxford University Press, 1989.

Myles, Anita. *Feminism and the post-modern Indian women novelists in English*. New Delhi: Sarup & Sons, 2006.

Prasad, Amar Nath, ed. *New light on Indian women novelists in English*. Volume 2. New Delhi: Sarup & Sons, 2004.

Tandon, R.K. *Women – Customs and Traditions*. New Delhi: Indian Publishers Distributors, 1998.

Vivekananda, Swami. *Complete Works*. Volume 8. Calcutta: Advaita Ashram, 1964.

16

Crossing Cultural Borders: A Study of Bharati Mukherjee's *Desirable Daughters*, Salma's *The Hour Past Midnight* and Shashi Deshpande's *In the Country of Deceit*

— **N. Chandra**

Culture has imposed many restrictions on women, and one among them is liberty in sexuality. Sexuality is common for every animal yet some restrictions over women exist in most sections of society. In Gloves's words, it is just pleasure of the human, "Sexuality is here much more than a facet of human nature, the seat of pleasure and desire" (xii). Sexuality has a link with gender and even then usually it is referred to heterosexuality, "Gender and sexuality are, of course, empirically interrelated: sexuality is gendered in fundamental ways and gender divisions sustain, and are sustained by, normative heterosexuality" (Jackson and Scott 20). Normally sexuality is encouraged in the society through the bondage of marriage, a social institution (Chandiramani 227). It is also claimed that, "Sexual pleasure is a human right" and everyone has the right to have it amidst the difference whether they are homosexual, heterosexual, young or old, without any variations of one's physical appearance or due to one's societal status (228).

Even though it is mentioned that it is common for both men and women, sexuality is often treated to be men's ground to claim their power and authority over women. According to Butler, sexuality is an "organization of power, discourse, bodies and affectively" and through Foucault, Butler understands the concept that sex as "an artificial concept which effectively extends and disguises the power relations responsible for its genesis" (125). Usually, men show themselves as aggressive personalities and thus imply that they are more in need of sexual pleasure than women are and thus men are given more priority than women in this regard. Men are thought to be perfect in sexuality, "Man is the yardstick of perfection, against which the female sex is measured" (Peterson 60). Thus, the penis is seen as the representation of activity and thus as a symbol of power (Kibby and Costello 356). This notion has made one to believe that pleasure is only for men and women are supposed to fulfil the need of men, by giving pleasure. Likewise, women are trained to please the men as they could, "In patriarchal cultures it is normative for the pleasure of men to be placed above the pleasure of women. In fact, women are given the message that their pleasure lies in pleasing men, sexually and otherwise" (Chandiramani 228). It is thought that men are violent in attaining sexual pleasure and is claimed that they have no control over their bodies. On the contrary, it is also expected from men to be gentle while pleasure seeking and to control their bodies to attain healthy sexuality. Thus the idea of controlling men's body in sexuality remains contrastive,

> For men especially having control over the body is an important component in the achievement of healthy sexuality. Paradoxically, male sexuality is simultaneously constructed as being always potentially uncontrollable; this version appeals to the inherent aggressive and passionate urges of unfettered male sexual expression as represented in sociobiological and evolutionary discourses.
>
> (Potts 91-92)

Moving away from these ideas, Mackinnon points out that men are aggressive only because women are more resistant to sex, and this resistance is due to the imposed cultural stereotype (163). That is true, but who has imposed this cultural stereotype is the point to be noted. It is also to be noted that women are not resisting all the men, but only the ones with whom they do not want to have physical relations. Women, too, want to seek pleasure but their tastes differ; they do not resist sex, but the way it is presented. Apart from the restriction, women satisfy their sexual needs through secret extra-marital affairs, so that they would live in the society with the branded *pativrata* stereotype and at the same time, they could meet their sexual needs. Otherwise, the society would blame them as whores. Therefore, women, who are not satisfied with their husbands, or those who want to venture sexuality, have to live covert lives by constructing themselves as 'homely' women to satisfy their sexual thirst. Some women, by decorating themselves, attract men and attain their needs. Skeggs points out that, women are comfortable in glamour because it gives way to perform sexuality in a respectable manner:

> They felt most comfortable with glamour because it enabled them to hold femininity and sexuality together in respectable performances and generate value in local circuits of exchange.... However, glamorous performances could be compromised by the desire to be seen and legitimated as desirable. (323)

Feminist writers have initiated research to bring out the hushed up facts/obscenity that are kept in the minds of women, "Such an appreciation of the uncontainable fluidity of sexuality and desire, and of the complexity of representational practices, is what lies behind recent feminist arguments against censorship of 'obscenity' and pornography" (Menon xxviii). Indian women's writing, since the beginning, has been attempting to bring drastic changes in women's lives either through silent protest or by a provocative outburst. Especially in the last two decades, Indian women's writing has entrusted women to lead rebellious lives and their rebellion sounds very open. Mahashweta Devi, Kamala Das, Shoba De, Jaishree Misra, Malathi Rao, Arundhati Roy, Anita Nair and other such writers have represented the women's inner minds unabashedly. Women writers have been yearning for economic and societal equality to that of men and now they have brought the issue of sexuality and likewise equality in attaining sexual pleasure too. Contrary to the patriarchal imposition, women writers are now open to explicit women's sexuality and their pleasure-seeking adventure. The writers depict that when society gives any restriction to women in the name of culture, women satisfy themselves by blinding or fooling the society which means women would attempt their adventures in secret.

The paper utilises the women protagonists of Bharati Mukherjee's *Desirable Daughters*, Salma's *The Hour Past Midnight* and Shashi Deshpande's *In the Country of Deceit* for analysis. The aim of the paper is to analyse critically the select novels, the way the women protagonists cross the borders of cultural codes, and the way they overcome the troubles from society when they cross the borders. The paper also brings into light the courageous nature of those women characters, who outwardly engage in sexual fervour, amidst societal restrictions. In *Desirable Daughters*, the three daughters, namely, Padma, Parvati and Tara, are brought up in an orthodox brahmin family and it is believed that the sisters are disciplined based on their cultural norms. Padma initially settles in London, and she lives with her husband as well as enjoys life with her admirer. Parvati has fallen in love with a man and this shocks her family. Tara divorces her husband and sleeps with another man, which is unacceptable to her orthodox family. Thus, it is the story of three sisters who have walked away from the orthodoxy of their community.

In *The Hour Past Midnight*, the Muslim community in a particular area is represented. The Muslim women are expected to be more 'loyal' to their husbands, especially by not having any extra-marital affairs. Throughout the novel, it is repeatedly shown that the women in the community cross their cultural barriers to satisfy their sex-hunger.

Deshpande's *In the Country of Deceit*, is a story of Devayani, a 26-year old 'spinster', who lives alone in a house deliberately avoiding her relatives and others presence. She is attracted towards Ashok, a police officer, and she suffices her body needs through him. The relationship has no hope for future since Ashok is old and married and Devayani too has no interest in marriage. All these three novels, in a way, are a blow to the male-biased society, which rules women and gives guidelines to women favouring men.

According to psychoanalytic theory, a child too could experience the pleasure of its body and so in the age of adolescence one tries to learn the language of one's body. Due to this, a girl or boy has flirtation or affection towards her or his opposite sex. The girls in the select novels attempt the same in their adolescent ages and they are careful to indulge in sexuality without the knowledge of the elders. In *Desirable Daughters*, Padma has fallen in love with Ronald Dey, the brother of Poppey Dey, her classmate. Whatever the restrictions are set out, attraction in the teenage could not be prevented and most of the girls are ready to flirt with Ronald Dey. Tara imagines, even after many years, those girls would blush if they are reminded of him, "Say the name 'Ron Dey' to a Bengali woman of my class and generation anywhere in the world today (and by now we are everywhere), and there'll be that flush of embarrassment as though awakened from a titillating daydream and a flurry of questions" (Mukherjee 30). Tara later comes to know that Padma has begotten an illegitimate child through Dey in her adolescence and has hidden the fact from her parents.

Rabia, in *The Hour Past Midnight*, has been learning the art of sexuality through her companions and she listens to the elders' private chats to get an extra coverage on the unexplored area. Madina, her intimate friend and neighbour, accompanies Rabia in the adventure and they together learn the secrets which are with held from them. Rabia's debut attempt starts when she goes to cinema with Madina, without the knowledge of her family, that too in the sacred month. More than the beatings they get from their mothers, they are more shocked to see the obscene scenes in the picture for the first time in their lives. In the beginning, Rabia plans to go to the movies, because she is tempted by Ahamad, who often watches movies. Only later, she realizes that the movie is for the male audience and thus the movie has induced Rabia's sexual fervour and she starts learning things through her companions.

Another incident shows Rabia's adventure of learning sexual passion through Ahamad. When Ahamad touches her for the first time, she realises that the male touch is different. They plan to play the game of 'mother and father' and Rabia pretends to do domestic chores when Ahamad pretends to go shopping as part of the game. Towards the end of the game, Ahamad asks Rabia to feed the 'naked-male' baby doll, assuming it is crying for milk. She too pretends as if she is feeding the baby, by inserting the doll into her blouse. Ahamad is curious to see how she feeds and then he himself becomes the child by sucking her breasts. This initiates Rabia's arousal of sexual zeal. She later keeps the doll under her pillow and sleeps by hugging it tightly and she does the same even towards the end of the novel, when Ahamad leaves to town for his studies. She enjoys the touch of Ahamad, "His hand brushed against hers lightly, sending a thrill through her. She realized at once what he was looking for and was filed with an unnameable joy" (476-7).

Madina and Rabia's intimacy help them to learn that certain changes occur in their bodies due to maturation. When Madina starts getting her periods, she is eager to share her feelings with Rabia. When Madina is asked to pass some pornographic books to Wahida, Madina hides one of the books to share it with Rabia. Both watch the picture and read stories in the book, in the absence of elders, and they start learning the hidden secrets. Rabia and Madina have started learning things on their own, "Gradually they understood the riddle of sex just a little, and found it of absorbing interest. The notion of nakedness, which had frightened her all this while, changed somewhat, and began to excite Rabia" (Salma 360). These show the girls cooperate among themselves to learn the unexplored facts of life.

The woman characters in the novels are quite open to exhibit their sexual needs. The women could be divided into three types. The first one is, married women, who are not satisfied with their husbands and search for other men. Tara and Padma in *Desirable Daughters* and Nafiza and Firdaus in *The Hour Past Midnight* come under this category. The second one is, married women, who do not want to indulge extramarital relationship, yet suffer and suppress their body needs. Sherifa in *The Hour Past Midnight* is that type of woman. The third one is, unmarried women, who want to satisfy their needs of the bodies by approaching men. Devayani in *In the Country of Deceit* is one such woman.

Padma, in *Desirable Daughters*, works in theatre, is married to Harish Mehta, and is settled in New Jersey now. Tara is shocked when she realises that Harish is Padma's husband for the sake of appearances, and she has a beloved companion, in her office, who shares everything with her. Nafiza, in *The Hour Past Midnight*, is married to Bashir, has an affair with Aziz and she passionately loves him so that she could not even think of getting separated from him. She remains in servitude to her husband, yet she could not satisfy herself with her husband's body and so she could not take Aziz's marriage very easily.

Tara, in *Desirable Daughters*, is portrayed in-between two lovers; one is Bish, her ex-husband, for him, love is "the residue of providing for parents and family, contributing to good causes and community charities, earning professional respect, and being recognized for hard work and honesty" (Mukherjee 27) and her other lover is Andy, for him, love is "having fun with someone, more fun with that person than with anyone else, over a long haul" and this "fun" part has attracted Tara more and so she readily goes with Andy, by leaving her husband Bish. Though Tara has shifted to Andy from her husband, it does not mean that she has no other options meanwhile. She admits this as, "He was not my first American lover" (77) which implies she has a lot more on the list. Once Andy leaves her loft, Tara has felt a longing for Bish and wants to join him.

Mumtaz and Nafiza, in *The Hour Past Midnight*, show interest in sexual matters and they watch cassettes and read books related to sexuality, like men do. Other than that they indulge in such talks, whereas other elderly women feel their talk as obscene. When Wahida is reluctant to have sex with her husband, Mumtaz is ready to elude away her fear, "I'll rid her of her shyness in a single day" (Salma 343). When Mumtaz comes to know that her husband sleeps with her just to beget a child and not for deriving pleasure, she becomes very upset, "he was so unaware of her feelings" (350). This has led her to become a frenzied woman and people have decided that Mumtaz is haunted with an evil spirit. The fact is she could not attain the bliss of love with her husband and she becomes helpless since she cannot go with another man. When woman could not attain the needs of her body then she becomes helpless in this closed society which might lead her to madness.

Firdaus, in *The Hour Past Midnight*, leaves her husband since she dislikes him but she likes Siva, her neighbour. Firdaus has a policy, to live and enjoy the life to the ultimate and she thinks there is no wrong in such living, "She was determined to enjoy all the happiness that was destined for her. She would not give up this world for anyone or anything. But she wanted Siva too. She could not contemplate a life without him" (Salma 259). The community restrains Firdaus from living with Siva and thus she needs to keep the relationship secret.

Sherifa's case, in *The Hour Past Midnight*, is different. She has lost her husband, yet she has no place for another man. She has said that she would not remarry. It does not mean that she has no sexual fervour, but she suppresses her feelings:

> All the same, the question rose urgently in Sherifa's mind, whether it was going to be possible for her to live alone all her life, controlling her desires and feelings. She thought again how painful every night proved to be, how hard she had to try, to overcome her frustration. Would the memory of her husband and her love for her child be sufficient support for her, for the rest of her days? She lay still on her bed, overcome with confusion, not knowing what she should do (Salma 466).

She also regrets that she has been saying the prayers regularly yet Allah has not showered his blessings.

Devayani, in *In the Country of Deceit*, is shown the goose bumps on her body by Ashok, and she too could understand that her bodily desires a man, "I know that too, I know the desire for a man, the longing to be held by a man, to feel his body against mine" (Deshpande 115). She has not shown it to him, or to her sister because she herself is confused about her body's needs as an unmarried woman, "I cannot tell her that this time I am frightened, not of the man, but of myself, of my desire to run, not away from him, but into his arms" (94). Before their first love making, she is scared, "This is terrible, it's a terrible mistake, what have I done, what am I doing?" (129). She thinks over that after having tea she would leave the place immediately. But she has not taken any step to get away from that place, even when he asks her whether she wants to go, she boldly replies, "I haven't come here to go back" (132). Devayani explores the pleasure within her body which is aroused by strong desire, during her first experiment with him, "He began to trace my features with his fingers–my eyebrows, my nose, my chin, my lips. I could have never imagined that such a gentle touch, a touch so light that I could scarcely feel it, could evoke such a strong response from my body" (132). Later on she has learnt how to get more pleasure out of him and she has become skilled in it, "I was part of it too, my lips were seeking him, my hands began roving over his body, my body made room for him and finally, painfully, joyfully, accepted him..." (132) and she accepts that she gets more pleasure in the next attempts of love making. When he asks her about her experience, she happily says that, "It was beautiful" (136).

Devayani does not require any details about his family and she does not care anything about him, she wants only him and wants to know about his body, "I know his body well, I knew its feel, its contours, its odours, its strength, its gentleness" (Deshpande 174). When they meet they do not converse anything, and they need not converse, they want at first to communicate with their bodies. Devayani too is always in an urge to quench her thirst and even his murmurs of loving words disturbs her, "Only his murmurs in my ears. And as always when he did this, the line running through my head, 'For godsake hold your tongue and let me love' " (164). Devayani realises that only this man could give the joy of the world by love making, "it was this man, not the sex. This man's love, not the sex. And yet, the sex too..." (Deshpande 193). Thus she admits that it is for sex she continues the relationship yet it does not mean she would have the same relationship with everyone. When he meets her at home after she has met with an accident, she lies down and forces him to make love her. Devayani is reluctant to give up the relationship, "But how can I give up what I want most in the world, how can I give up the only thing I want in life?" (226). Devayani finds out the reason that it is the problem of sleeping with him, otherwise, Savi or Sindhu has no problem with it:

> But how can you love a man and not sleep with him? How can you not long for the physical union? It's not just sex, it's showing your love through your body, it's seeing and feeling his love through his body. It's the desire for union, the most complete union two human beings can achieve. (226)

Society becomes the villain to women, since it has many impositions, expectations and restrictions over them. The upbringing of a girl in an Indian family is different from a boy, since the family honour is placed on the shoulders of the girl of the family. Thus, an extra care is taken to shape the character of the girl by suppressing her wishes. Certain codes of conduct are given to the girls to be followed. A girl would be taught the way she has to perform in her in-laws' house too. In such a situation, the woman cannot be open to utter her likes and desires. In case, if the woman is away from her society or family she could enjoy freedom and could live as she likes. Tara and Padma in *Desirable Daughters* enjoy such freedom, since they are away from their country. Devayani, in *In the Country of Deceit*, as an unmarried woman living alone enjoys freedom at times. This also shows that the society plays a major role in deciding one's personal affairs.

Tara, in *Desirable Daughters*, comes from a Brahmin-Bengali family, which is strict in following custom and tradition. Especially, when it comes to the matter of women, little freedom is given. Tara describes how she and her other sisters are protected and safeguarded by their father before marriage, "Our father couldn't let either of my sisters out on the street. Our car was equipped with window shades. We had a driver and the driver had a guard" (Mukherjee 29). Tara and her sisters, anyhow, come away from the bond and as Balakrishnan reads this, "The three sisters – Padma, Parvati and Tara– survive by flouting these codes of conduct" (258).

Tara explains that it is part of tradition that a woman is expected not to tell the name of her husband. However, when she moves to America, she has learnt to adopt the new culture, and thus is ready to call her husband by his name. Though Tara has been brought up through Indian way of living, that of one man for one woman; when she has crossed the border of her country, she too, has learnt to change her way of living. She has opted for another man, Andy, after she is divorced from her husband. She asks for new things and expects to make new adventures in Andy's company, "I don't live exclusively with my son. There's Andy, my balding, red-bearded, former biker, former bad-boy, Hungarian Buddhist contractor/yoga instructor, the man Bish calls "Tara's mistri," "my carpenter" (25), which shows her intimacy with Andy. This is possible only because she is out of her native country. Divorce is a ridiculous thing in India, so Tara's family has not revealed the news of her divorce and in that case; it is impossible to reveal her lover. In Parvati's letter, "Have you become so American that you don't realize how absurd your request is? We don't even mention your divorce to friends and relatives here. I don't mean that we lie, or that we are ashamed of anything, but we don't let the wrong questions come up" (Mukherjee 97). Newman points out this as, "in India Tara's identity was fixed by family identity" (251).

Tara could not even believe it when a boy, claims that he is an illegitimate son of Padma. She is hurt by the news that her elder sister has ditched her baby and has married another person. Later Tara thinks about it, and convinces herself that whatever Padma has done is not wrong, "Didi's not a monster. She really is a romantic… Didi's the only one of us who followed her heart. Her mistake made everything possible" (Mukherjee 135). Tara feels bad for her sister and thinks that her father has become an obstacle for her elder sister's future. When Padma does not want to recognize the child, Tara could understand that Padma has wanted to save her family reputation by abandoning her illegitimate child. Yet Tara wants to protect her family reputation, by proving her sister's innocence even when she complains to the agency, about the stranger's interruption claiming he was Padma's illegitimate child.

Codes of conduct have been preached by the relatives to the girls, and once Rabia's uncle, in *The Hour Past Midnight*, gets annoyed when he comes to know that she has not learnt table manners. He is angry with Rabia's mother, Zohra, for not bringing her up in a proper way, "Teach her to respect what is good conduct and proper behaviour. Let her learn which things we are commanded to do and which things we may aspire to do" (Salma 35). Rabia, as a girl of protest, readily breaks all those codes whenever she gets chances, but she has to do it every time secretly. Rabia begins to tell lies to Madina and her own mother and avoids Madina when she wants to spend time alone with Ahamad. Ahamad comes to get his transfer certificate, since his uncle plans to shift him to a better school in another town. Rabia goes with Ahamad to school, by telling lies to her mother.

Wahida and Firdaus's mother, in *The Hour Past Midnight*, happened to see the love making scene of Firdaus and Siva. In the same night, Firdaus's mother has forced her to consume poison and has reported the public that Firdaus has died of an electric shock. Firdaus does not want to die, she has so many dreams to live, and her mother's emotional blackmail has made her to consume the rat poison. Though her mother has made her to drink the poison in the name of family honour, she herself regrets her loving daughter's death, "How much she had loved this world. In spite of so many difficulties that beset her, how clearly she had demonstrated that she would never willingly die" (Salma 394).

Fatima, in *The Hour Past Midnight*, has eloped with a Hindu boy, leaving her son as an orphan. The whole community is against it and has punished her mother Nuramma by excluding her from the community. Nuramma has pleaded for kindness to include her in the community. She has explained as a mother, she need not be punished for her daughter's action. The community men have not agreed with Nuramma and thus she is provoked and vents her anger:

> Ayya, all you elders and big men, so you are going to ban me from the community! Very well, let it be so. You say it was a sin for my daughter to elope with a Kafir. Is there a single man who hasn't slept with one of our Hindu worker women? Speak out, let me hear. Let just one of you stand up; I'll agree my daughter did wrong. (Salma 254)

She is furious when she is driven to a helpless situation and she is fearless to point out the mistakes of men in public, whereas nobody has raised a voice in response to it, instead, they have tried to hush her. This shows men's partiality in the community to nourish the flavour of sex with different community women yet restrict their women.

Devayani, in *In the Conceit of Deceit*, regrets what she has done, she is not thinking it is a mistake but regrets that she could not admit the relationship openly to her dear relatives, "I had entered the country of deceit. I could no longer be open and honest with people I loved; I had to deceive them" (Deshpande 147). She wants the relationship to be a secret thing and she is scared that people would find out and gossip around. When people say that her face looks bright nowadays, she is frightened whether her face gives any clue to adultery, "I turned my face from side to side and wondered, do I look like an adultress?" (148). Yet, she does not like the term adultress and she feels it is an ugly word. Thus, she refuses the birthday gift from him saying that she feels cheap that she is being paid. She realises when a married woman is caught with her secret lover, they have abused that women for adultery. Even when she thinks of Anna Karenina and some other people whom she knows and concludes to herself that adultery remains adultery, it cannot become an open relationship since the couple always want to meet secretly and "it is always riddled with guilt and fear, constantly swinging between euphoria and despair. I knew this too, that the main preoccupation of all adulterous couples is: how do we meet? And where?" (149).

Savi, in *In the Country of Deceit*, finds it is her own fault that she has left her sister, Devayani unmarried and alone, which has tempted Devayani to commit adultery. Savi is shocked and she shouts at Ashok, then, tells Devayani, "You could have avoided this – this disgusting thing you're doing. I never thought you would do such a dirty thing, just for sex..." (Deshpande 184). Shree, Devayani's brother-in-law advises Devayani to give up the relationship saying it is wrong. Sindhu, Devayani's aunt, writes to her that she could not believe what she has done.

Socialization has frightened certain women of crossing over the restrictions and that is why Farida in *The Hour Past Midnight* could not cross the boundary. She has a liking towards a Hindu boy, yet she is scared to develop her relationship with him and silently marries a man, whom she dislikes very much. All these show that the society has certain expectations and imposes conformity over women and the same is not followed in the case of men. It can be noted that one's privacy is decided by society in certain circumstances and Firdaus' death in *The Hour Past Midnight* and Padma's abandonment of her illegitimate child in *Desirable Daughters* are such instances.

When there is no such restriction or vigilance by the society over women, they feel free to do things on their own. In *Desirable Daughters*, the way Padma shows interest in making-up her face and dressing herself to get the attention of men. Padma's nature is shown when she advises her younger sister Tara, to get a nice companion, "You can't seem to do very well for yourself up and resurrected your flirting skills, there are dozens of catches out there. There are scads of divorced men just waiting, even for girls like you" (Mukherjee 186). Danny Jogtiani, who is called as DJ, is the intimate companion of Padma. Their intimacy shocks Tara, since it exists in the presence of Padma's husband, "The whole transaction, everything about Didi's job and her relationship with Danny was odd and confusing" (217).

Tara, in *Desirable Daughters*, gets courage to select her companion, once she crosses the national border. Likewise, her sister Parvati becomes courageous to select her mate when she is away from her family for higher studies. Her love marriage itself is considered as a rebellious one (Balakrishnan 260). From the beginning both Tara and Padma have been made to believe by the society that they are adopting Indian way of living, by marrying the bridegroom selected by their father, yet to the contrary they have changed a lot by shifting themselves from one person to another person. Comparatively Padma and Tara, who stay in abroad, have crossed the cultural boundaries by sleeping with many men, whereas Parvati is stuck with her husband.

Devayani, in *In the Country of Deceit*, realises that it is not possible to continue her relationship with Ashok, by cheating her sister and other close relatives. She gets more freedom and feels more comfortable when she spends time with Ashok in Bombay and Delhi because those places are full of strangers. This cannot be done in her native place since people would keep an eye on everyone. Every time, the lovemaking between Devayani and Ashok happens in an hurry because they do not want to be caught by anybody. She longs to have an undisturbed-open relationship, "Not enough, it's not enough" (Deshpande 164). Therefore, in extramarital relationships, one needs to be secretive and careful not to be caught by society and they enjoy the relationship when they are away from their usual place of living.

Marriage system in India is one of the major reasons for extramarital relationship. Most of the time, the willingness of the bride is not even considered when marriage is arranged. Apart from that, marriages are arranged between two strangers and one does not have any idea of one's partner before marriage. After marriage, when one gets disappointed with one's sexual partner, it also leads one to search for a change. In *Desirable Daughters*, the people admire Tara that she is brave to marry and love a stranger, "I married a man I had never met, whose picture and biography and bloodlines I approved of, because my father told me it was time to get married and this was the best husband on the market" (Mukherjee 26).

Firdaus, in *The Hour Past Midnight*, dislikes her husband on her first look itself, boldly says to his face on the same day of their marriage that she does not want him, "I'm not going to live with you. Don't touch me" (Salma 17). This is a rebellion by a woman in the community, who has refused her husband. Wahida, in *The Hour Past Midnight*, is scared of her husband Sikander and the way he has sex with her aches her physically and mentally. Thus, she is given books to make her more comfortable and to get her involved in that. Wahida is furious with Mumtaz, Nafiza and with her mother, who have made her to watch a pornography cassette. In the beginning, she has not understood the charisma of lovemaking and has insulted Firdaus, when she has an extramarital affair. When Wahida herself undergoes the trauma of sexuality, she understands Firdaus's position and feels guilty for Firdaus's death. Wahida, finally, decides to leave her husband as Firdaus has done and asks herself why she needs to bear his child, when she does not even like him (469). Not only Wahida, but also most of the women, who have bitter experiences with their husbands walk away from them boldly. Firdaus, Maimoon and Amina are such women who are unhappy in their married life and refuse to live with their husbands. Thus, unhappy married life becomes one of the reasons for women longing for other men to satisfy their sexual needs.

The society has restrictions over women and at times, when women are not satisfied in their beds; somehow, they try to extinguish their sexual lust. Sexuality is a hormonal instinct that happens in almost all animals. Women are not excluded from that, they too have to satisfy their needs. When society restricts them in the name of culture and other patriarchal norms, women who cross such borders, have their own justifications for their actions.

Firdaus, in *The Hour Past Midnight*, is bold enough to face Wahida, after she has seen Firdaus and Siva's lovemaking. When Wahida insults Firdaus, Firdaus replies not feeling a bit of shame or remorse for her act and does not bother Wahida's warning, "What did you say? Did you question my behaviour? Before you go and tell everyone, you'd better check out with your Chaccha how your mother behaved with him" (Salma 384). She neither has lost her boldness nor has felt guilt of her action until her death. She feels everyone commits the restricted things behind the screen, so she is ready to face the public with her own justification.

Likewise, in *The Hour Past Midnight*, Fatima, a widow, falls in love with a Hindu boy and she has no fear or shame even when Sherifa questions her. She replies to Sherifa that whatever she is doing is of her own will and nobody has any right to intervene into that. She counter questions Sherifa, if men could enjoy the pleasures, why not women do the same, and she says that she is least bothered to save the honour of the community:

> Why do I have to safeguard their honour? The elders of this worthless town, what have they ever done for me so far? Nothing whatsoever. So why should I bother about all that unnecessarily? If something gives me pleasure, I'll go for it. Besides, I'm not a wealthy woman like you, amma, to renounce everything and sit in a corner for the sake of the family's honour (Salma 250).

Devayani, in *In the Country of Deceit*, counter questions Shree, who has asked to give up her relationship with Ashok, "Wrong? Why is it wrong? Why is that you can have your beloved and I can't have mine?" (Deshpande 199). These questions are not to get any answer from Shree, but Devayani tries to justify her action by asking them. Sometimes, Devayani regrets the relationship and she questions herself why has she entered into the world of deceit. She agrees that it is not because of love but because of 'atonement', she has indulged in that relationship (257). Sindhu has advised her to forget the past, but she is in a dilemma that she wants to forget the memories of Ashok and at the same time, she wants to remember those memorable moments (259). Devayani feels guilt at her action and at times, she gives justification to her action.

Socialization and conditioning have restricted women to pour out their whims and fancies. Sexuality is both for pleasure and eroticism in this century and that is commonly seen in both men and women, "sex was valued for its sensually pleasurable and expressive qualities. It became legitimate to pursue sex for carnal pleasure to the extent that eroticism acquired a higher meaning as a symbol or vehicle of love" (Seidman 227). Cultural codes, which are constructed as the consequence of socializing women, have prevented them being truthful to their desires. Apart from their wishes, women need to think what is right or wrong attempts in their culture. By keeping such cultural codes to women, the society to safeguard the honour and once when women attempt to cross those cultural codes, the honour of man is lost.

Usually Muslim women experience male domination more than the other communities. In *The Hour Past Midnight*, the writer has pointed out, the way those Muslim women overcome those male dominated rules and their survival by fooling their men. Generally, in Muslim families, the women are strictly insisted to follow the bounds of their community. In a recent survey, it is found that the community women have opened their minds to express their sexual urges, "In the current global scenario... Muslim women's struggles to gain control over their bodies and exercise gender and sexual will against male domination are precariously placed and inadequately understood" (*Muslim Women* 323).

Women in the select fiction belong to orthodox society, i.e. Brahmins and Muslims, who are strict in protecting the honour of their respective communities. Apparently, all the women protagonists, who are expected to up hold their family honour, readily cross the cultural borders and they do it in secret. They are not so provocative to do it outwardly, yet their border-crossing shows the courage within them and thus question the male-biased cultural construction. Though many men are unaware of it, the act of crossing such cultural codes itself represents their severe protest against their communal codes. Though the attempts of border crossing are made secretively, they are yet successful attempts, mocking at the male-biased cultural codes.

WORKS CITED

Balakrishnan, Anita. "Tracing Tara-Lata's Footsteps: Negotiating Authenticity and Alienation in *Desirable Daughters*." Mandal 254-269.

Butler, Judith. *Gender Trouble: Feminism and the Subversion of Identity*. (1990) New York and London: Routledge, 2006.

Chandiramani, Radhika. "Pleasure Me Safely, Can You?." Menon 227-232.

Deshpande, Shashi. *In the Country of Deceit*. (2008) India: Penguin Books, 2009.

Gloves, David. "Introduction: Gendered Histories, Gendered Contexts." *Genders*. Eds. David Gloves and Cora Kaplan. London and New York: Routledge, 2000. ix-xxxiv. The New Critical Indian Series.

Jackson, Stevi, and Sue Scott, (eds.) "Introduction: The Gendering of Sociology." Jackson and Scott 1-26.

_______, (eds.) "The Sexualisation of Love." *Gender: A Sociological Reader*. New York: Routledge, 2002. Print. Routledge Students Reader Series.

Kibby, Marjorie, and Brigid Costello. "Displaying the Phallus: Masculinity and the Performance of Sexuality on the Internet." *Men and Masculinities* 1.4 (Apr. 1999): 352-364. *Sage*. Web. 11.10.2008.

Mandal, Somdatta, (ed.) *Bharati Mukherjee: Critical Perspectives*. New Delhi: Pencraft Books, 2010.

Mackinnon, Catherine A. "Sexuality." *Second Wave: A Reader in Feminist Theory*. New York: Routledge, 1996. Print.

Menon, Nivedita, (ed.) Introduction. Menon xiii-lx.

_______, (ed.) *Sexualities*. New Delhi: Women Unlimited, 2007. Issue in Contemporary Indian Feminism.

Mukherjee, Bharati. *Desirable Daughters*. (2002). New Delhi: Rupa & Co, 2008. Print.

Newman, Judie. *Priority Narratives: Bharati Mukherjee's Desirable Daughters*. Mandal 245-253.

Petersen, Alan. "Research on men and Masculinities: Some Implications of Recent Theory for Future Work". *Men and Masculinities* 6.1 (July 2003): 85-103. Sage. Web. 11.10.2008.

Potts, Annie. ""The Essence of the Hard On": Hegemonic Masculinity and the Cultural Construction of "Erectile Dysfunction"." *Men and Masculinities* 3.1 (July 2000): 85-103. *Sage*. Web. 11.10.2008.

Salma [Rokaiah Maliq]. *The Hour Past Midnight*. (2004) Trans. Lakshmi Holmstrom. New Delhi: Zubaan, 2009. Print.

Seidman, Steven. "The Sexualisation of Love." Jackson and Scott 225-229.

Skeggs, Beverley. "Ambivalent Femininities." Jackson and Scott 311-325.

The Muslim Women's Rights Networks et.al., 2004. *Muslim Women and Sexuality*. Menon 320-324.

17

"Queering the Pitch": Gender Trouble in Manju Kapur's *A Married Woman*

— Debalina Banerjee

Judith Butler in her seminal book *Gender Trouble* observes that Gender is a contested category complicated by issues like class, ethnicity and sexuality. Gender for her is largely 'performative'. Indian English women novelists have largely concerned themselves with representations which are overtly heterosexual in nature. They have maintained a "massive silence" on issues of same sex relationships almost reminiscent of Oscar Wilde's famous speech at the trial. "the love that dare not speak its name..." Otto Weininger in *Sex and Character* talks about "all sorts of intermediate conditions between male and female-sexual transitional forms" (Bristow 39). He further asserts that "the 'ideal' types of men and women 'not only can be constructed, but must be constructed'... for society, he believes, must be guided towards producing an 'ideal' sexual antithesis out of a potentially chaotic 'bisexual' order" (qtd in Bristow 39). Manju Kapur's *A Married Woman* has a lesbian relationship at the heart of its narrative. But instead of gendering a defiant sexual model, she seems to endorse the kind of social order that Weininger talks about. By maintaining the heterosexual balance she keeps all trouble out of her gender politics.

One of the main agendas of second wave feminist activism was focusing on women as a social group and the need for the sexual autonomy of the female body. Writers like Robin Morgan began to talk about the powerful agency of sisterhood. In *The Woman Identified Woman* (1970), the Radical lesbians argued that while "feminism is the theory, lesbianism the practice" (qtd in *Routledge* 28).

> A lesbian is the rage of all women condensed to the point of explosion. She is the woman who, often beginning at an extremely early age, acts in accordance with her inner compulsion to be a more complete and free human being than her society...cares to allow her" (*Routledge* 28).

Just as the beginnings of feminism were grounded in politics so too lesbianism acquires a political colour as asserted by Charlotte Bunch in writing on behalf of the *Furies Collective*:

> Lesbianism is a political choice. . . . Whether consciously or not, by her actions, the Lesbian has recognized that giving support and love to men over women perpetuates the system that oppresses her. If women do not make a commitment to each other, which includes sexual love, we deny ourselves the love and value traditionally given to men (8).

The assumed heterosexuality of women was seen as instrumental in perpetuating patriarchal oppression. Hence Adrienne Rich observes in *Compulsory Heterosexuality and Lesbian Existence:*

> The assumption that 'most women are innately heterosexual' stands as a theoretical and political stumbling block for many women. It remains a tenable assumption, partly because lesbian existence has been written out of history or catalogued under disease; partly because it has been treated as exceptional rather than intrinsic; partly because to acknowledge that for women heterosexuality may not be a 'preference' at all but something that has had to be imposed, managed, organized, propagandized and maintained by force is an immense step to take if you consider yourself freely and 'innately' heterosexual.... To take the step of questioning heterosexuality as a 'preference' or 'choice' for women—and to do the intellectual and emotional work that follows—will call for a special quality of courage in heterosexually identified feminists but I think the rewards will be great: a freeing-up of thinking, the exploring of new paths, the

> shattering of another great silence, new clarity in personal relationships.

The ancient Vedic culture attached great importance to female power or 'stree shakti'. During the Vedic age, Indian women reached a very high standard of learning, culture and all-round progress. We find examples of brahmavadinis who combined scholarship with domesticity. In the age of Panini (5th cen.B.C) we find references to women teachers; reverentially called *upadhaya* or *upadhyayi* and *acharya*. Far more numerous however were the instances of women who led dedicated lives at home. The position of women in India gradually deteriorated as the Vedic ideals of unity and equality began to fade away. Women were bracketed with the shudras and denied the right to study the *Vedas*, to utter Vedic mantras and to perform Vedic rites. On the other hand, marriage or domestic life became compulsory for women, and unquestioning devotion and self-effacing service to husbands their only duty. To quote the well-known dictum of Manu: a woman is protected by her father during childhood, by her husband during youth and by her sons during old age. A woman is not fit for freedom. The *Manu Smriti* refers to the home and the family as the bedrock of society, and woman is the person on whom the stability and sanctity of the home and household rests. However the wife is the home, not the structure: As for divorce, he emphasizes that there is no kind of separation and marriage is indissoluble for life. The *Manu Smriti* also talks about punishments for aberrant sexual behaviors, punishable by the law.

> Interestingly, a man, in Manu's opinion, indulging in homosexuality has to bear the punishment of bathing with all his clothes on, while a woman found guilty of the same act, has a much higher price to pay (not to mention social shame). If it is between two virgins, the 'Seducer' virgin has to pay a monetary fine as well as bride price for the girl she seduced, and receive a lashing. A mature woman caught seducing a virgin shall have her head shaved; fingers (two) cut off and is made to ride through the town on a donkey. (Surely the most interesting part in this judgment will be the process of determination as to who seduced

> whom!!!!) The laws of Manu gives many variations on punishment to aberrant sexual behavior, which can be safely classified under non-procreative sexual behavior... as against sexual contact for begetting children (Goswami).

Most of the first generation Indian English novelists focused on the problem of East-West culture clash. A major agenda of these novelists would be to establish the superiority of Indian culture to the west by glorifying Indian women. Denying her a human dimension and negating her sexuality would valorize her to a point of saintliness. She would be drawn in sharp contrast to all that is modern as modernity was considered to be associated with Westernization. Since lesbianism as a concept was largely western hence representation of lesbian relationships was completely uncalled for.

A new consciousness is evident in the works of contemporary novelists who seek to reevaluate the position of women in society. Arun Joshi rightly observes in *The Foreigner:* "'It is very bright outside' I said, turning to Sheila. She was getting my shoes from under the divan and I was filled with a sense of sympathy for all Indian women who always had their backs arched, stooping to someone's services." But contrary to expectations a close study of some of the contemporary novelists reveal that though there is an apparent change in degree, the representations of women largely suffer from a tendency to recline into passive acceptance. The note of emancipation that is promised is sometimes lost inspite of the feminist zeal of the narrative.

A Married Woman, the second novel by Manju Kapur, begins on an ironic note of subversive challenge, almost caustic in its humour:

> Astha was brought up properly, as befits a woman, with large supplements of fear. One slip might find her alone, vulnerable and unprotected. The infinite ways in which she could be harmed were not specified, but Astha absorbed them through her skin, and ever after was drawn to the safe and secure. (1)

Kapur almost at once addresses the fundamental premise of feminist opposition, the cultural conditioning of gender, effectively echoing the famous dictum of Simone de Beauvoir's *The Second Sex*, "One is not born a woman but one becomes one".

Astha 's heterosexuality is enforced right from the start with her mother saving and hoarding or her marriage, her secret dreams of a romantic suitor, her failed relation with Bunty, her desperation for "love in her barren life" and her responses to her fling with Rohan:

> Astha began to be included in groups that included him, at cinemas, restaurants, appointed meetings at the Coffee House, instead of casual ones. *A boy was interested in her. With every visit he made to the college back gate, her stock grew in college* [emphasis added]. (22)

Kapur is at her ironic best when she effectively portrays Astha's feelings after their first evening of physical intimacy, "Her neck, her ears, her throat, eyes, chin, lips, all had been explored, and at this time her strongest feeling was gratitude"(24). It is the masculine principle alone that brings to her consciousness, her awareness of her female sexuality and with it the associated notions of pleasure and pain.

In *A Married Woman*, Manju Kapur traces the life of Astha from her young adulthood through her early middle years. The narrative concerns itself with Astha's initial marital bliss, her gradual drifting apart from her husband, her attempts at painting and social activism and her falling in love with a woman. The initial impression of the book leads one to believe that its central focus is the lesbian relationship between the two women. Astha has to move between marital pressure and the pressure exerted by her attachment to Pipee, a woman she meets in the course of events. Kapur's representation of the love affair between Astha and Pipee is unrealistic and almost a forced strategy to counter conjugal discontent. Even for Pipee, bonding with Astha comes only in the wake of the death of her theatre activist husband, Aijaz. That neither Kapur nor Astha is able to imagine the love between women as real becomes obvious through Astha's comment: "So far as her marriage was concerned, they were both women, nothing was seriously threatened" (232).

The lesbian narrative loses its spark with Kapur implicitly suggesting that women turn to women once they've reached the limits of their emotional and physical passions with men. Terry Castle in the early 1990s, defined the lesbian as a "woman whose primary emotional and erotic allegiance is to [her] ... own sex." This is not the case with the protagonist of *A Married Woman*. We find that Astha is married, has two children, and feels morally responsible and emotionally attached to them. "Astha often looked at her family, husband, daughter, son. She had them all. She was fulfilled" (69). Even when things turn sour with Hemant, her heterosexual leanings become apparent through her aroused sexual response to Aijaz's flirtatious comments, during their interactions at the theatre workshop. While she is with Pipee, she worries about the children and wonders how they would be managing without her. Her heterosexuality is reinforced by her determination in continuing with her family at all costs. She wishes to move between both the worlds:

> ...paradoxically the heterosexual world becomes one of choice and the lesbian world an incidental happening, which she enjoys but which she is not prepared to acknowledge to the world by 'coming out,' nor is she prepared to give up on her children and husband and home. She is not a woman whose sexual desire is focused on another woman. Astha's bonding with Pipee is not a choice exercised by a woman who would take the initiative to start and sustain a lesbian relationship. It could be interpreted, in a certain sense, as an act stemming from resentment of her particular situation (Chandra).

To quote Kapur, "When she was with Hemant she felt like a woman of straw, her inner life dead, with a man who noticed nothing" (287). Yet ironically it is Pipee who relentlessly badgers her into snatching time and space for being exclusively together on the pretext of going to an Ekta Yatra.

Communities of women or powerful sisterhoods were viewed as essential by feminists in order to focus on significant emotional, spiritual bonds outside marriage. In *A Married Woman* Astha and Pipee too share tender moments, yet their love making is described almost in a rush in contrast to the graphic detailing of the various heterosexual affairs interspersed throughout the novel, "...Astha felt strange, making love to a woman took getting used to. And it also felt strange, making love to a friend instead of an adversary"(231). The relationship is not allowed to travel the expected trajectory. "The author making Pipee abruptly leave for the U.S. to pursue her Ph.D., a narrative strategy which Patricia Juliana Smith calls 'lesbian panic'" (Chandra). Smith defines lesbian panic as: "In terms of narrative, lesbian panic is, quite simply, the disruptive action or reaction that occurs when a character—or conceivably an author—is either unable or unwilling to confront or reveal her own lesbianism or lesbian desire." It brings to mind the echoes of the abrupt and disjointed lesbian relationship between Ursula and her school mistress in D.H. Lawrence's *The Rainbow*, where Ursula ultimately bored with the relationship is instrumental in marrying the mistress off to her uncle, as she herself moves on in search of greener pastures.

The novel takes a sneak peek into one of the most disturbing chapters of Indian history, the Babri Masjid debacle. But Astha's political and social activism in the form of her associations with the Manch or going to Ayodhya to protest against religious fanaticism are treated rather cursorily. One of the main claims of feminist art is the exploration of female subjectivity. However in this case Astha's brilliance as a painter and her fight for a literal and metaphorical 'room of one's own' are lost into oblivion. The fight for women's liberation had centered around demands for political emancipation, individuality and sexual autonomy. Astha pursues education without interest, works without enthusiasm and remains tied to a wasted marriage because of her obsession with the fact that, "Now and forever she would be looked after" (63). Even when she actually has the spunk to observe to her colleagues, "If a marriage is terrible, it is good to be able to leave"(168), she immediately regrets making the statement as it would lead to speculations about her.

> In contemporary India, there are many surprising facts that owe their surprise to the efforts of various agencies to brush them under the carpet and firmly keep them there. While gay rights and homosexuality is of course an issue for those whom it matters, lesbianism is till not mentioned openly.... There are rights for a gay marriage, but scarcely any female couple has exchanged vows in India, openly that is. It would seem that centuries of brushing under the carpet has put the fact of lesbianism and female sexuality firmly in the dark recesses of Indian minds. Not even with the glorious revival of sexual rights in other fields, the right to dignity, the right to education, profession or financial freedom, can women ask for their most fundamental right – the right to be sexual beings...and if they prefer to love another woman...well, that much worse (Goswami).

Hence, though Hemant forces himself on her, curbs her attempts at self expression, misses no opportunity to display his male chauvinism (one of the examples being his shameless hankering for a male child), negates her individuality and even becomes a suspect of infidelity, yet in the end it is her relationship with Pipee that is easier to give up and the novel ends with Astha having to remind herself, "...if she wanted, she too had choices" (289).

Works Cited

Kapur, Manju. *A Married Woman.* New Delhi: India Ink, 2002. London: Faber and Faber, 2003.

Bristow, Joseph. *Sexuality.* London and New York: Routledge, 2007.

Bunch Charlotte, "Lesbians in Revolt: Male Supremacy Quakes and Quivers". *The Furies: Lesbian/Feminist Monthly* 1(January 1972): 8-9.

Castle, Terry. *The Apparitional Lesbian: Female Homosexuality and Modern Culture*, New York: Columbia University Press, 1993, p. 15.

Chandra, Subhash. Review. *A Married Woman.* Intersections: Gender, History and Culture in the Asian Context. Issue 14, November 2006. Goswami, Kanika. *Lesbianism and India.* httpwww.buzzle. comeditorials 12-4-2004-62492. asp.

Joshi, Arun. *The Foreigner.* Bombay: Asia Publishing House, 1968.

Mission, Ramakrishna. "The Manu Samhita", *The Cultural heritage of India. Vol. II: Itihasas, puranas, dharma and other sastras*. Kolkata: Institute of Culture, 1962. 335-363.

Narayan, R.K. "Some Reflections On the Ideals Of Indian Womanhood", *The Cultural heritage of India. Vol. II: Itihasas, puranas, dharma and other sastras*. Kolkata: Institute of Culture,1962. 601-609.

Rich, Adrienne. "When We Dead Awaken: Writing as Re-vision".*On Lies, Secrects and Silence*. New York, 1979. 35.

Routledge, Companion to Feminism and Post feminism. Ed. Sarah Gamble. London and New York: Routledge, 2006.

Smith, Patricia Juliana. '"And I wondered if she might kiss me": lesbian panic as narrative strategy in British women's fictions,' in *Modern Fiction Studies* 41(3-4) (Fall/Winter 1995): 567-607.

Index